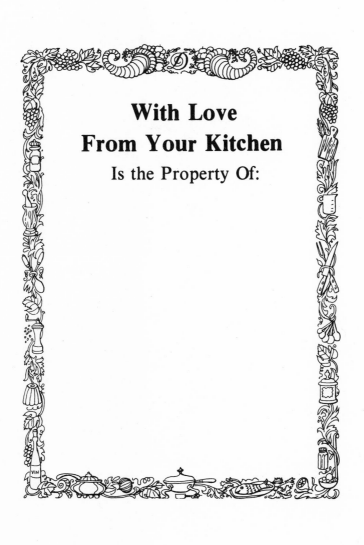

With Love
From Your Kitchen

Is the Property Of:

With Love from Your Kitchen

BY Diana and Paul von Welanetz
THE PLEASURE OF YOUR COMPANY (1976)

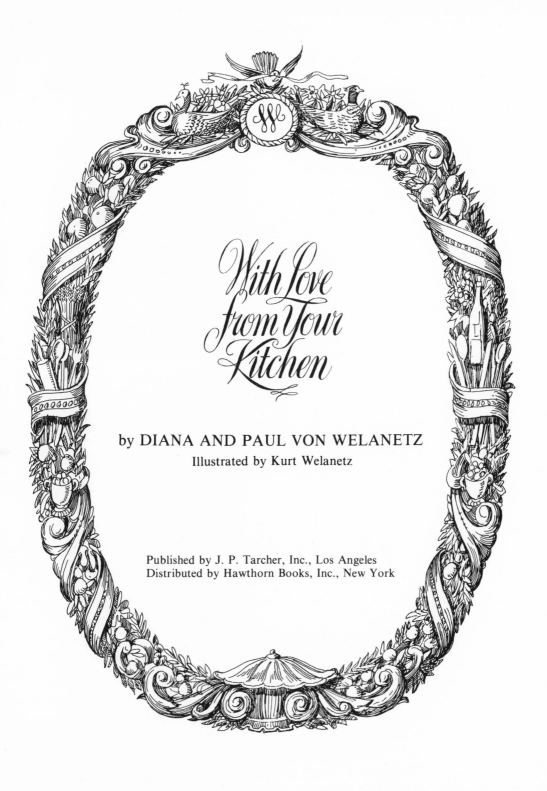

With Love from Your Kitchen

by DIANA AND PAUL VON WELANETZ

Illustrated by Kurt Welanetz

Published by J. P. Tarcher, Inc., Los Angeles
Distributed by Hawthorn Books, Inc., New York

Our thanks to these publishers who granted permission to include the following: "Butter-milk White Bread," from *Beard on Bread* by James A. Beard. Copyright © 1973 by James A. Beard. Reprinted by permission of Alfred A. Knopf, Inc. "Christmas Cranberries" from *Blueberry Hill Menu Cookbook* by Elsie Masterton. Copyright © 1963 by Elsie Masterton. Reprinted by permission of Thomas Y. Crowell. "Frozen Sliced Sweet Dill Pickles," from *The Pleasures of Preserving and Pickling* by Jeanne Lesem. Copyright © 1975 by Jeanne Lesem. Reprinted by permission of Alfred A. Knopf, Inc. "Sweet Cham-pagne Mustard," from *The Pleasure of your Company* by Diana and Paul von Welanetz. Copyright © 1976 by Diana and Paul von Welanetz. Reprinted by permission of Atheneum Publishers. "Stuffed Dates Baked," from *The Just Delicious Cookbook* by Ruth Mellin-koff. Copyright © 1974 by Ruth Mellinkoff. Reprinted by permission of Ward Ritchie Press.

For

Lisa

Contents

Acknowledgments

Our deepest gratitude goes to
Kurt Welanetz
Marge Welanetz
Alice Blair Simmons
Lucy Barajikian
Carol Schild
Barbara Swain
The friends who shared their recipes with us
Our students, who are some of the best cooks in the world
Lamont
and last, but hardly least,
Jeremy Tarcher,
who saw this book in his mind long before we did.

Introduction

The joy of making, the joy of giving

Most of us love to follow the pleasure of cooking with the joy of sharing the results. And most of us also find a handmade and homemade gift more delightful than a store-bought one. Put these two ideas together and you have *With Love from Your Kitchen*.

For several years, we have taught cooking classes in our home in Pacific Palisades, California. Invariably, our classes on making and packaging gifts have been the most popular, and we have seen our students leave with an almost evangelical excitement, eager to personalize their gifts and make a memorable moment for their friends. It is this enthusiasm that we wish to pass on to you.

The recipes here—which, of course, can also be used for feeding your family and for entertaining at home—can be made in advance and kept in your freezer, refrigerator, or pantry, ready for that perfect moment. We not only describe how to prepare and store, but we also suggest how you can attractively wrap and label them.

With Love from Your Kitchen has been an exciting book to write. Much of the material was acquired over the years from our families and friends, but we also did research that took us across the United States, filling notebooks with new-found recipes, food folklore, packaging concepts, and assorted whimsies. One of the pleasant things we discovered on our travels was that despite the availability of convenience foods and mass-produced gadgets in American life, do-it-yourself activities and handmade objects were wildly popular wherever we went. Even back home, our butcher is a weekend painter, our postman sculpts, and our banker bakes. Everywhere one looks there are county fairs, school and church bazaars, and arts and crafts exhibits. We welcome this happy turn of events and enter our book as one more joyful marcher in the parade.

Diana and Paul von Welanetz

Nuts & Nibbles

Nuts have a long tradition as gifts. In ancient Rome, children delighted in using them as toys, and when a Roman took a bride, he would scatter nuts to wedding guests, signifying that he had outgrown childish games.

Throughout history, nuts have been served before meals to whet the appetite, and at one time the presence of exotic nuts at banquets gave concrete evidence of the wealth of the host. Walnuts, for example, were not native to Italy or Greece and were imported at great expense by way of camel caravan from Persia. The Persians themselves used large quantities of powdered walnuts, pistachios, and almonds to thicken their dishes. This custom eventually made its way to Europe and Rome by caravan, passing down to fourteenth-century Europeans who grew fat on creamy almond sauces.

17

America's favorite nut by far is the peanut, or goober pea (goober is from the African word *nguba*). There are two views as to the origin of peanuts. One is that they were native to Peru and found their way to Africa. Another is that they were grown by Indians in America, and were adopted by the Virginia colonists. Possibly they are native to both hemispheres.

It is recorded that peanuts were used as food aboard nineteenth-century slave ships because, as a native African food, they were inexpensive, lightweight, and highly nutritious, and perhaps because of this the American slave loathed the peanut; for years it was grown in the South merely as a garden curiosity. In 1893, however, a St. Louis doctor promoted the world's first peanut butter, and today a jar of it can be found in nine out of ten American homes.

The second most popular nut in America is the pecan. While exploring the Mississippi River, De Soto noted some "Spanish walnuts," a variety of our present-day pecans. In 1799, Vice President Thomas Jefferson received a package of them from a D. Clark of New Orleans with the note: "These nuts are not, I understand, common to the Atlantic ports of the United States, though they grow everywhere on the banks of the Mississippi, from the Illinois River to the sea." Both Jefferson and Washington planted pecan trees on their estates, and Washington was known to carry them in his pocket as nibbles.

North America has always had a bountiful supply of other kinds of nuts as well: black walnuts, hazelnuts, butternuts, hickory nuts, beechnuts, chestnuts, and pine nuts. Since the days of the early colonists they have been valued for their high protein content, year-round availability, and long shelf life. Salted, toasted, sugared, mixed with cereals or other foods, they are unrivaled for their versatility and for the obvious pleasure they give.

Peking Pecans

There's a category of gifts from our kitchen that cries out for immediate consumption. Ranking first (is there anyone who would dispute it?) is bread, freshly baked, warm from the oven. Second, in our opinion, are these Peking Pecans, extraordinary tasteteasers with an undeniable Oriental flavor. They will easily find a permanent home on our Western coffee tables. We wouldn't care to speculate just how far friends on low-carbohydrate diets may indulge themselves but they need not fear restricting themselves to just a nibble or two.

This recipe makes 4 cups of seasoned pecans which will fill four 8-ounce or two 1-pint gift containers.

6 tablespoons (¾ stick) butter or margarine
4 cups (1 pound) pecan halves
2 tablespoons Kikkoman soy sauce
2 teaspoons salt
¼ to ½ teaspoon ground black pepper, to taste

Preheat the oven to 300°. Melt the butter or margarine in a large, shallow ovenproof pan, such as a jelly-roll sheet or roasting pan. Add the pecans and toss to coat thoroughly. Roast them in the oven for 30 minutes, stirring once or twice during the cooking to prevent burning. Allow to cool for a minute or two, then toss with the soy sauce, salt, and pepper to taste. Serve at room temperature or slightly warm.

TO PREPARE IN ADVANCE: These may be stored in an airtight container in the refrigerator for up to a month or frozen for up to three months. Bring to room temperature or reheat in a 300° oven for 10 minutes before serving.

SPECIAL PACKAGING: A glass or china ginger jar would make an imaginative container for these Oriental nuts.

THE LABEL: Serve as a snack at room temperature or after warming in a 300° oven for 10 minutes. *If you have not frozen the pecans, the label should read:* May be stored in an airtight container in the refrigerator for up to a month or frozen for up to three months. *If you have frozen the pecans, the label should read:* May be stored in an airtight container in the refrigerator for up to a month after they have been thawed.

Susie Gross's Sherried Walnuts

Her bursts of energy and high interest take our friend Susie Gross from one pursuit to another: from oil painting, to skin-diving, to raising chicks so her youngest might discover the source of the Gross breakfast eggs. Fortunately, speculative enterprises also engage Susie's attention. Like improving old recipes. For this nutty confection, she uses a few simple steps like boiling and beating. No problem. You can work solo. It's only at the final moment when turning it out of the pan, that you might benefit from another pair of hands, for if the nuts are not separated swiftly enough, everything hardens into a monolithic mass instead of the small and delightful nuggets they in fact were meant to be.

You will have about 4 cups of candy-coated nuts, enough to fill four 8-ounce gift containers. Do not double the recipe — it will be too difficult to handle.

> 3 cups (approximately 11 ounces) walnut halves or pieces
> ½ cup any kind of sherry (see Note)
> 1½ cups firmly packed dark brown sugar
> 2 tablespoons light corn syrup
> ¼ teaspoon salt

Note: Don't make the mistake of using a sherry in the preparation of your food which you wouldn't normally drink.

Place the walnuts in a strainer or colander. Shake to free them of any powdery fragments. Lay out a long strip of wax paper and two forks with which to separate the nuts when they have finished cooking. It will be necessary to work quickly at that point, so you might ask somebody to help if you are making these for the first time.

Combine the remaining ingredients in a heavy 3- or 4-quart saucepan. Bring the mixture to a boil, stirring often. After the mixture has reached a boil, insert a candy thermometer — you will have to tilt the pan to get a reading — and cook until the thermometer registers 240°. Remove the pan from the heat and stir in the walnuts, taking care not to burn yourself with the hot syrup. Stir constantly for about 4 minutes until the nuts are heavily coated and the syrup starts to turn cloudy. Turn out onto the wax paper and separate the nuts quickly, using the forks. Let cool, then break apart any nuts that have stuck together.

TO PREPARE IN ADVANCE: These may be stored in an airtight container at room temperature for up to a week or frozen between layers of wax paper for up to three months. Thaw and let dry before packing into gift containers; the condensation from thawing might cause the nuts to stick together.

SPECIAL PACKAGING: These look spectacular when packed into old-fashioned canning jars (see page 19). They may be frozen in candy tins between layers of wax paper, ready for last-minute giving right from the freezer.

THE LABEL: *If the walnuts have not been frozen, the label should read:* May be stored in an airtight container in a cool place for up to a week or frozen for up to three months. *If the walnuts have been frozen, the label should read:* Thaw and let dry before using. May be stored in an airtight container in a cool place for up to one week.

Great Gobs of Granola

Out of all the sudden crazes to hit this country, this one has some point to its madness. And we hope it lasts. It's a toasty, crunchy conglomeration that has supplanted pancake, coffee, and toast breakfasts, and is especially fine for those who like their first meal of the day to be wholesome and munchable. There are no hard and fast rules to what constitutes good granola, so be as free spirited as you dare. Cut loose. Use our quantities as a guide, but toss in any nuts or dried fruits that turn you on or that you happen to have handy. You'll end up with your own singular brand. Eat it as a cereal with fresh fruit and milk or as a quick-energy snack right out of hand. Put some in a jar, tie it with a perky ribbon, and hand it over to gladden somebody's day.

The recipe makes approximately 2½ quarts of cereal, enough for four 1-pint gifts with a bit left over for you to nibble on.

6 cups old-fashioned oats (not instant)
1 cup chopped walnuts
¾ cup toasted wheat germ (without honey)
½ cup flaked coconut
½ cup firmly packed dark brown sugar
½ cup chopped blanched almonds
1/3 cup sesame seeds
1/3 cup shelled sunflower seeds, plain or roasted
½ cup vegetable oil
1/3 cup honey
2 tablespoons vanilla

Preheat the oven to 325°. Place the oats in a large rectangular pan, such as a roasting pan or jelly-roll sheet, and bake at 325° for 10 minutes while measuring the other ingredients. Remove the pan from the oven and stir in the walnuts, wheat germ, coconut, brown sugar, almonds, sesame seeds, and sunflower seeds. In a small saucepan over low heat, melt together the oil, honey, and vanilla. Pour this over the other ingredients and mix thoroughly. Return the pan to the oven and bake for 25 minutes, stirring twice during the cooking time. Let cool and transfer to containers. Store in the refrigerator.

TO PREPARE IN ADVANCE: Granola will keep indefinitely in the refrigerator or freezer.

SPECIAL PACKAGING: Any kind of empty jars you have around are handy for storing and giving granola. Soak labels off the jars in warm water. Paint and decorate the lids, if desired, and apply your own label.

THE LABEL: Enjoy with fresh fruit and milk or use in any recipe calling for granola. May be stored in the refrigerator or freezer indefinitely.

Sugar and Spice Nuts

"Sugar and spice and everything nice, that's what little girls are made of." You can now add almonds, walnuts, cashews, and pecans to the old rhyme. This is such a quick and easy recipe that either little girls or little boys can handle it, even if they lack total kitchen coordination. It's an economical treat to make if you buy your nuts in bulk. And because the sugar and spice add a heavy coating, only a scattering of nuts is required to fill the gift containers. It's sinful and shameful, we know, but we don't always wait until these frost-covered nuts are set out on the coffee table. When the mood strikes, there are split-second freezer raids in which the whole family participates.

This recipe makes about 6 cups of sugared nuts, enough to fill three 1-pint or six ½-pint gift containers.

> 4½ cups mixed, unsalted nuts (walnut halves, pecan halves, blanched almonds, cashews)
> 2 cups sugar
> 1 cup water
> The grated rind (zest) of 1 or 2 oranges
> ½ teaspoon ground cinnamon
> ¼ teaspoon ground nutmeg or mace
> Pinch ground cloves

Mix all the ingredients in a large, heavy skillet. Simmer over medium-high heat, stirring constantly, until the water evaporates and the nuts look sugary — about 5 minutes. Remove from the heat and pour the nuts out onto a large, greased baking sheet. Using two forks, separate them quickly to prevent them from sticking together. Let cool, then store in an airtight container in the refrigerator or freezer.

TO PREPARE IN ADVANCE: These will keep for up to a month in the refrigerator or up to six months in the freezer.

SPECIAL PACKAGING: These nuts may be given in a small serving bowl. Wrap in clear cellophane and tie with a ribbon.

THE LABEL: A nibble to set out on the coffee table. Serve at room temperature. *If the nuts have not been frozen, the label should read:* May be stored in the refrigerator for up to one month or frozen for up to six months. *If the nuts are frozen, the label should read:* May be kept frozen or stored in the refrigerator for up to one month after they have been thawed.

Sesame Nut Butter

Nut butters are fantastic when they're homemade. The granddaddy of all nut butters is, of course, peanut butter, but cashews, almonds, and even filberts make nutritious creamy spreads.

In one of the tales of *The Arabian Nights,* Sinbad used the words, "Open Sesame," to remove the huge boulder from the entrance to the cave. The term was a popular one in those days because the hulls of this common seed popped open so easily. The addition of toasted sesame seeds to either peanut or cashew butter enhances the already rich, nutty flavor and makes it irresistible. Don't use the finished product only as a spread; use it for flavoring cookies, frostings, and sauces.

This recipe makes a little more than 1 cup of nut butter, enough for two 4-ounce gifts.

2 to 3 tablespoons vegetable oil
2 cups dry-roasted peanuts or cashew nuts
¼ cup toasted sesame seeds (see Note)

Note: Sesame seeds are available, hulled, in health food stores, where they are always much less expensive than those available in bottles in the spice section of the market. To toast the seeds, spread them in a baking pan and bake in a 325° oven for 5 to 10 minutes, stirring often, until golden. Watch them toward the end of the cooking time as they burn easily. Let cool. After toasting, the seeds may be stored in a jar at room temperature for months.

Place 1 tablespoon of the oil in the container of an electric blender with ½ cup of the peanuts or cashews. Blend on medium speed until smooth, stopping the motor often to scrape down the sides of the container with a rubber spatula. Add another tablespoon of oil and the remaining nuts and sesame seeds. Blend until smooth. If the mixture seems dry, add more oil, 1 teaspoon at a time, blending after each addition, until the nut butter has the consistency you desire.

Serve as a spread for crackers or sandwiches.

TO PREPARE IN ADVANCE: Store, covered, in the refrigerator for up to one month. Do not freeze.

SPECIAL PACKAGING: Tiny mustard pots, available at cookware shops, or baby food jars are a nice size for this. Cover with a lid or plastic wrap and tie a circle of printed fabric over the top and secure with a piece of yarn.

THE LABEL: Serve as a spread for crackers or sandwiches. May be stored in the refrigerator for up to one month. Do not freeze.

Hors d'oeuvres & Cheese Spreads

Every sophisticated culture that has learned to enjoy the pleasures of the table prefaces feasts with vast assortments of appetizers, for appetizers tease the palate, stimulate the gastric juices, please the eye, and prepare one for all that is to follow. People all over the world grace this first course with well-deserved and imaginative, exciting names: *antipasto* from Italy, *acepipes* from Portugal, *maza* from Syria, *mezeler* from Turkey, *zakuska* from Russia, and the beautiful French *hors d'oeuvre*.

These magnificent combinations of tasty tidbits have even produced poetical outbursts such as this one recited at a tenth-century Persian banquet by one Ibn al-Mu'tass:

Here capers grace a sauce vermilion
Whose fragrant odors to the soul are blown . . .
Here pungent garlic meets the eager sight
And whets with savor sharp the appetite,
While olives turn to shadowed night the day,
And salted fish in slices rims the tray . . .

It would take considerable bravado to compare our American chips and dips with the hors d'oeuvres and appetizers that were part of the glory of French *haute cuisine* during the mid-nineteenth century. Dozens and dozens of exquisite appetizers, each more lavish than the one before, rolled dramatically from elaborate kitchens as if the chef were composing an endless prelude to the latest masterpiece soon to be conducted into the banquet hall.

Ironically enough, *haute cuisine* rose to its heights through the hands of Antonin Marie Careme, the son of an impoverished family of twenty-five children, who was released to a competitive and demanding world at the age of eleven because his father couldn't bear to see him starve. He found his way to a pastry shop and worked his way to greatness, achieving the exalted position of chef to Tsar Alexander of Russia and later the Prince Regent of England, who became King George IV.

Money among the notoriously rich was, of course, no object, and a chef of his position could command an army of kitchen helpers, including assistant pastry and roasting cooks, general assistants, plus apprentices, salad chefs, wine stewards, and numerous waiters. Careme matched an artist's eye to his culinary genius and evolved elaborate and monumental culinary edifices, such as an eight-sided Indian pavilion (complete with ornamentation and orange roof) and cakes sculptured in the form of broken Grecian arches and waterfalls. The French Revolution quickly put an end to all of that. The great homes were broken up and chefs found refuge in public restaurants.

Today, of course, most household budgets permit only occasional outside help. This levies the burden of entertaining on the hostess. There are several ways of easing the situation. If invited for dinner as honored guests, you might send flowers, as we like to do, preferably a day in advance, since this gives the hostess time to find a vase, arrange, and place the flowers, rather than ruin her composure the day of the party by bringing a bunch of flowers she must do something about at the last minute. However, if you are just one of a number of guests, you might like to take a gift from your kitchen. An extra hors d'oeuvre is always welcome, since most parties start with cocktails. This is one aspect of dining where you can get as spectacular as you wish. You may not match the splendor of the French past, but it's a fine place to try a dramatic hand.

To compete with cocktails, hors d'oeuvres must have an extremely pronounced flavor, such as a strong cheese like our Tipsy Cheese Log or a Boursin or a Roquefort or perhaps pungent Mushrooms a la Grecque — something that can be tasted over the martini. Equally important, hot hors d'oeuvres should be served hot (not lukewarm) and cold ones cold (not just chilled).

Whether it's something fresh or baked, pungent or bland, smooth or crunchy, hors d'oeuvres are just curtain-raisers to the joys and pleasures of the evening before you. Much more lies ahead. Make it a first act worth remembering.

Cream Cheese with Garlic and Herbs in the Manner of Boursin

We often loiter in the imported cheese sections of markets, somewhat like children at drugstore magazine racks. Someday we fully expect the management to put up a sign that says, "Von Welanetzes, please don't squeeze the cheese."

The simple truth is that cheese fascinates us. The one we've had a romance with for years is Boursin. When the commercial variety of this popular French import soared to over 35¢ an ounce, we decided it was time to put together our own version. Here is the recipe for half the price of the imported variety, but with all the flavor intact. It tickles the palate with its half rude, half exquisite freshness, seasoned as it is with herbs that recall the countryside of France in summer. Made our way, it's a bargain of a gift.

This recipe makes 1¼ cups of spread, enough for two 5-ounce gifts.

8 ounces cream cheese
½ stick (¼ cup) butter (not margarine), at room temperature
   (see Note)
½ teaspoon Spice Islands Beau Monde seasoning
1 medium to large clove garlic, pressed
¼ teaspoon Herbs of Provence (see page 146)
1 teaspoon minced fresh or dried parsley
1 teaspoon water
¼ teaspoon red wine vinegar
¼ teaspoon Worcestershire sauce

For Serving
Crackers

Note: We specify butter rather than margarine because we prefer the flaky consistency it lends to this particular recipe.

Place the cream cheese and the butter in a large bowl of an electric mixer. Beat at high speed until the mixture is smooth and fluffy, stopping the motor often to scrape down the sides of the bowl with a rubber spatula. Add the remaining ingredients and continue beating until well combined. Pack the mixture into containers and allow it to mellow for at least 12 hours in the refrigerator before serving. Serve the cheese cold with crackers.

TO PREPARE IN ADVANCE: If wrapped airtight, this will keep for at least a month in the refrigerator. Do not freeze.

SPECIAL PACKAGING: The mixture may be packed into crocks or molded. To mold, line containers of the desired size with plastic wrap, enough to enfold the cheese, and pack firmly. When chilled, the cheese will retain the molded shape. Tie a ribbon over the plastic wrap and present it as is or, just before giving, place it on a cheeseboard with a spreader and crackers and wrap entirely in cellophane.

THE LABEL: Serve chilled with crackers. May be stored if wrapped airtight in the refrigerator for up to one month. Do not freeze.

Tipsy Cheese Logs

The secret is out. Or rather *in!* Whenever we serve this tangy, orange-colored cheese log, tumbled in crunchy nuts, we start counting smiles. Then, as the inevitable question is asked, the eyebrows go up, and the jaws drop, as we reveal the secret ingredient to be...beer!

The recipe makes about 5 cups of cheese spread, enough for six ¾-cup logs with a bit left over for sampling.

> 12-ounce can of light beer
> 1½ pounds natural cheddar cheese, grated or cubed (see Note)
> 5 ounces blue cheese, crumbled
> 3 tablespoons butter or margarine
> 1 teaspoon dry mustard
> 1 teaspoon Worcestershire sauce
> ⅛ teaspoon onion powder
> Several dashes of Tabasco
> 1½ to 2 cups (6 to 8 ounces) chopped nuts of your choice to coat the logs
>
> *For Serving*
> Crackers

Note: We use our Cuisinart food processor when making cheese spreads, pates, etc. because it gives the mixture a velvety consistency that is more difficult to obtain in a blender. If you are using a blender, grate the cheddar cheese; if you have a Cuisinart, simply cut the cheese coarsely into cubes and process with the steel blade.

Place half the beer and the cheese in a blender or food processor and blend until smooth. Add half of each of the remaining ingredients and blend again until completely smooth. Transfer to a large mixing bowl lined with foil or plastic wrap. Repeat with the other half of the ingredients. Chill until firm, then roll in wax paper to form logs about two inches in diameter. Cut into 4-inch lengths. If you have some empty 6-ounce cans, such as those used for frozen orange juice or tomato paste, freeze the cheese spread in them to form the mixture into perfect 6-ounce (¾-cup) logs. When firm, push the cheese out one end of the can and coat with nuts. Wrap and keep chilled or frozen. Press chopped nuts into the entire surface of each log. Serve chilled with crackers.

TO PREPARE IN ADVANCE: These cheese logs keep perfectly for two weeks or even longer in the refrigerator. They freeze well, though the consistency of the spread will be flakier, and may be kept frozen for up to four months, or in the refrigerator for up to two weeks after being thawed. The logs make such a perfect snack to have on hand for last-minute entertaining that we recommend keeping some in the freezer at all times.

SPECIAL PACKAGING: Wrap the logs in clear plastic wrap, and then wrap again in clear cellophane, allowing four extra inches or so of cellophane at each end. Use narrow ribbon to tie each end, giving the package the appearance of a party popper.

THE LABEL: Serve chilled, with crackers. *If the log has not been frozen, the label should read:* May be stored in the refrigerator for up to two weeks or may be frozen for up to four months. *If the log is frozen, the label should read:* May be kept frozen for up to four months, or in the refrigerator for up to two weeks after it has been thawed.

Liptauer Cheese

We refer you to Funk & Wagnalls' *Cook's and Diner's Dictionary* (which is now regrettably out of print) and to the definition of a cheese (not so readily available), Liptauer, "a soft, sharp, fatty cheese made in Hungary (and named after a Hungarian province)." This long, rather discouraging introduction just serves to lead you to consider our version of this exquisite pink cheese. It is creamy with strength of character, a direct result of the pungent seasonings of dry mustard, capers, and anchovies. Serve with plain crackers to avoid confusion of flavors.

This recipe makes 1¾ cups of spread, enough to almost fill two 8-ounce crocks or four 4-ounce crocks. The recipe may be doubled.

> 2 teaspoons dry mustard
> 2 teaspoons warm water
> ¼ pound (1 stick) butter or margarine, at room temperature
> 1 (8-ounce) package cream cheese, at room temperature
> 1 tablespoon minced shallots or the white part of scallions (green onions)
> 2 anchovy fillets, drained and minced
> 1 teaspoon capers, drained and minced
> 1 teaspoon dry parsley flakes
> ½ teaspoon paprika
> Salt, to taste
> 1 teaspoon dry parsley flakes for decoration

> *For Serving*
> Crackers

In a small cup, combine the mustard with 2 teaspoons of warm water to make a paste. Let stand for 10 minutes.

Meanwhile, beat the butter and cream cheese in the large bowl of an electric mixer until the mixture is very creamy. Add all remaining ingredients, except for parsley flakes, along with the mustard paste. Taste and season with salt, if desired. Pack the mixture into containers. Smooth the top of the mixture, sprinkle with dried parsley, and cover with plastic wrap. Leave at room temperature for at least 12 hours for the flavors to mellow, then chill in the refrigerator.

This should be served as a spread with crackers. For ease of spreading, take out of the refrigerator several hours before serving.

TO PREPARE IN ADVANCE: May be stored for up to three weeks in the refrigerator. Do not freeze.

SPECIAL PACKAGING: Any small crocks, porcelain custard cups, or china flowerpots lined with plastic wrap make imaginative containers for serving spreads of this type.

THE LABEL: Serve as a spread at room temperature with crackers. May be stored in the refrigerator for up to three weeks. Do not freeze.

Madras Curried Cheese Spread

Whether it's cream cheese or sharp cheddar, cheese is cheese. This fluffy, saffron-hued spread contains them both. What transports it out of the ordinary is the addition of Madras Curry Powder. The practicality of the Eastern mind put together this blend of twelve or more spices, and we joined it with chutney (another bit of native ingenuity) to serve as an appetizer or as a spread for chicken or turkey sandwiches. As an appetizer, it will do what you hoped it would: draw your guests around a central point and help them mingle, mingle, mingle.

This recipe makes about 3 cups of spread, enough to fill three 8-ounce or six 4-ounce containers.

> ½ pound natural sharp cheddar cheese, at room temperature, grated or cubed (see Note)
> 1/3 cup pale dry sherry
> 12 ounces cream cheese, at room temperature
> 2 teaspoons curry powder, preferably Madras
> 1 teaspoon salt
> 1 tablespoon cut chives, thinly sliced scallions or minced parsley for garnish
>
> *For Serving*
> 8 ounces chutney (Major Grey's Mango or our recipe—see page 116)
> Crackers

Note: You will need a blender or food processor (Cuisinart) to make this spread completely smooth. If using a blender, grate the cheese; if using a food processor, cut it coarsely into cubes.

Place the cheddar in a blender or food processor, with the sherry. Blend until very smooth, stopping the motor often to clean the sides of the container with a rubber spatula.

Beat the cream cheese with the curry powder and salt in the large bowl of an electric mixer until it is light and fluffy. Add the cheddar-sherry mixture and beat until smooth and thoroughly blended.

Pack the mixture into containers, filling them almost to the brim. If the spread will be eaten within three days, garnish the top of the mixture at this time with chives, scallions or parsley. Cover tightly with plastic wrap and chill thoroughly.

Serve as an appetizer accompanied with crackers and a spreader. Provide chutney to top each serving.

TO PREPARE IN ADVANCE: The spread may be covered with plastic wrap and stored in the refrigerator for up to three weeks. It does not freeze well. To serve, bring to room temperature and decorate with chives, scallions, or parsley.

SPECIAL PACKAGING: This makes an exciting gift in a basket with crackers, a jar of chutney, and a tiny pot of chives that may be snipped to garnish the spread.

THE LABEL: Serve at room temperature as an appetizer spread for crackers. Top each serving with chutney. May be stored in the refrigerator up to three weeks. Do not freeze.

Silky Roquefort Spread

There are some who have mastered the art of instant hospitality. It seems that the only time they need to prepare is that split second between the moment their doorbell rings and their opening it to let in their guests. Such a hostess is Christa Zinner. After calling her only minutes before to say we were in town, we found ourselves one brilliant afternoon on the Zinner patio overlooking San Francisco Bay. Also spread out before us was a medley of marvelous tidbits: a whole German sausage ready for slicing, chilled cherry tomatoes, icy aquavit, and our two great discoveries of the day: this Silky Roquefort Spread and Norwegian flatbread. A guest couldn't hope for anything more.

This recipe makes almost 2 cups of spread, enough for three or four 4-ounce gifts.

> 6 ounces Roquefort cheese
> 2 (3-ounce) packages cream cheese
> ¼ pound (1 stick) butter or margarine
> Dash of Worcestershire sauce
>
> *For Serving*
> Norwegian flatbread (see page 175) or other plain crackers

Place the Roquefort, cream cheese, and butter or margarine in the bowl of an electric mixer and allow to come to room temperature. Add the Worcestershire sauce and beat until the mixture is very fluffy. Transfer to containers. Serve at room temperature as a spread with flatbread or other crackers of your choice.

TO PREPARE IN ADVANCE: May be stored tightly covered in the refrigerator for up to a month. Do not freeze. Store the flatbread, after opening, in an airtight container.

SPECIAL PACKAGING: Pottery crocks, custard cups, or miniature souffle dishes covered with plastic wrap are ideal. Include a packet of flatbread or a box of crackers as part of the gift.

THE LABEL: Serve at room temperature as a spread with flatbread or crackers. May be stored for up to one month in the refrigerator. Do not freeze.

Chicken Liver Pâté Maison

Celebrations demand appropriate gestures. We all know that. Those who choose to celebrate in style break open the champagne. We add one other touch to complete the moment for our special occasions. We also break open a container of this pate, the most elegant we know. It's our own adaptation of a recipe by the late great Michael Field, one of America's foremost food experts, which we've taught to our classes since they began in 1969. It even won an award for us in a *McCall's* magazine contest, no doubt because it has a certain smoothness and freezes with no change in texture, a notable achievement for patemakers. The edible clarified butter forms a perfect seal, enabling you to dispense with wrapping when refrigerating or freezing. Only when ready to give away need you envelope it with cellophane, tuck in the wine, and French bread, for the ideal dinner party or hostess gift.

This recipe makes five cups of pate, which will fill five 8-ounce or ten 4-ounce crocks or other gift containers.

> 1 pound (4 sticks) butter (not margarine)
> 1½ pounds chicken livers
> 1 large onion, minced
> 3 tablespoons shallots, minced (see Note)
> ½ cup peeled and chopped tart apple
> 3 ounces (⅜ cup) cognac, brandy, apple wine, or applejack
> 1 (3-ounce) package cream cheese, at room temperature
> 2½ teaspoons fresh lemon juice
> 2 teaspoons salt
> Scant ½ teaspoon freshly ground black pepper
> ⅛ teaspoon Parisian Spice (see page 144), optional
>
> *For Serving*
> Crackers, melba rounds, or French bread

Note: A shallot is a mild-flavored cousin of the onion-garlic-leek family. If not available you may, with slight sacrifice of flavor, substitute the white part of scallions.

Place 2¼ sticks of the butter in the large bowl of an electric mixer and let soften to room temperature. Wash the chicken livers and dry on paper towels. Cut each liver in half, and trim away any greenish bile spots.

Melt ½ stick butter in a large heavy skillet. Saute the chopped onion slowly over medium heat until it is soft and very lightly browned. Stir in the chopped apple and the shallots. Cook a few minutes longer, taking care that the shallots do not burn. Use a rubber spatula to scrape the mixture into the container of an electric blender (or Cuisinart food processor).

Add another ½ stick of butter to the same skillet and melt over medium-high heat. As soon as the foam from the butter begins to subside, add the chicken livers and stir them around for 3 or 4 minutes until they are brownish on the outside but still pink inside. Stir in the cognac, brandy, wine, or applejack and let simmer uncovered for 2 to 3 minutes longer. Add this mixture to the onions, apples, and shallots in the blender, let cool for 5 minutes or so, then add the cream cheese. Blend at the highest speed, stopping often to force the mixture down into the blades with a rubber spatula. When the mixture is as smooth as possible, transfer it to a small mixing bowl. Let the mixture cool thoroughly at room temperature before proceeding. It must not be even slightly warm or the finished pate will be oily.

When the mixture is cool, beat the 2¼ sticks of butter in the large bowl of an electric mixer until it is smooth and fluffy. Add the chicken-liver mixture to the butter gradually, beating well after each addition. Scrape the sides of the bowl often with a rubber spatula. Stir in the lemon juice, salt, pepper, and Parisian Spice. Taste and correct the seasoning, if necessary. Keep in mind that the flavor will be dulled somewhat when the pate is chilled.

Fill crocks or other containers, smoothing the tops as evenly as you can with a rubber spatula or the back of a spoon.

Melt the remaining ¾ stick of butter in a saucepan over low heat. Let it rest for a minute or two off the heat, then skim any milk solids off the top. Carefully pour the clear butter into a container with a spout for pouring, such as a glass measuring cup. This clear oil is called "clarified" butter, and has many uses. It will not spoil as quickly as plain butter, and it can stand a much higher temperature without burning, so it is better for frying. (Save the milk solids for seasoning vegetables, spreading on toast, etc.; most of the butter flavor is in these solids.) Pour the clarified butter carefully over the tops of the pates and chill thoroughly. As the butter hardens, it forms a lovely edible seal.

Serve the pate with plain crackers, melba rounds, or crusty French bread.

TO PREPARE IN ADVANCE: This pate keeps beautifully for up to five days in the refrigerator. It may be frozen perfectly for up to three months, but it does not keep as well after it has been frozen, so do not plan to keep it more than two days after thawing.

SPECIAL PACKAGING: Small crocks, souffle dishes, or custard cups, which come in many sizes, are ideal for giving. Watch your newspaper for special sales on this type of container.

THE LABEL: *If the pate is fresh and has not been frozen, the label should read:* May be stored in the refrigerator for up to five days or frozen for up to three months. After thawing, use within two days. *If the pate is frozen, the label should read:* May be kept frozen for up to three months. After thawing, use within two days. *If the pate has been thawed, the label should read:* Serve within 48 hours.

Easy Pâté en Gelée

If you ever see this impressive molded pate in aspic, you may feel intimidated enough to think it's a culinary feat impossible to match. You'll be pleasantly surprised to discover that it takes more time to read the recipe than to prepare the pate. Ingredients can be assembled and molded in just 10 minutes. Refrigerate for one or two hours to set the aspic and chill the pate. When ready to unmold, position on a plate and garnish with a ring of fresh parsley sprigs. It will evoke images of laurel wreaths ancient Greeks awarded to deserving victors. If the comparison fits, wear it.

This recipe makes two aspic-covered pates in 12-ounce molds or four pates in 6-ounce molds.

For the Pate
1 pound braunschweiger (smoked liverwurst)
3 to 4 tablespoons straight sherry
½ teaspoon Herbs of Provence (recipe on page 146) or other herb blend
½ teaspoon Lawry's seasoned salt or A Salt for All Seasons (page 142)
¼ teaspoon Worcestershire sauce

For the Aspic
1 envelope plain gelatin
2 tablespoons straight sherry
1 (10½-ounce) can Campbell's beef consomme

For Serving
Plain crackers or French bread

Note: This pate may be molded in any plain mixing bowls, dishes, or fancy tin molds of appropriate size.

To make this pate, place all ingredients in the container of an electric blender and blend until smooth, stopping the motor often to scrape down the sides of the container with a rubber spatula. Transfer to a mixing bowl and set aside while you make the aspic.

Sprinkle the gelatin over the top of the sherry in a small bowl. Set aside for 5 minutes to allow the gelatin to dissolve. Meanwhile, heat the consomme (do not dilute it) in a small saucepan just to boiling. Add the softened gelatin and stir until completely dissolved. Pour ¼ inch of the consomme into each mold and chill until set. Spoon the pate mixture carefully into the center of the molds, taking care not to let the mixture touch the sides. Smooth the pate evenly all around and flatten the top. Pour the liquid aspic around the sides of the pates in the molds and chill until set.

To serve, dip the bottom of the mold in warm water for a second or two and turn out the pate, slide into position and dry the plate. Serve chilled with plain crackers.

TO PREPARE IN ADVANCE: The pate mixture may be made three weeks in advance and stored, tightly covered, in the refrigerator. Mold it in aspic within two days of serving or giving. Do not freeze.

SPECIAL PACKAGING: A serving plate, or the mold itself, might be part of the present. Be sure to include the crackers or French bread; the recipient may not have any on hand.

THE LABEL: Keep chilled and serve within 48 hours with plain crackers. *If the pate is given in the mold, include these instructions for unmolding:* To serve, dip the bottom of the mold in warm water for a second or two and then turn out pate on a wet serving plate; slide into position and dry the plate.

Sherried Crab Fondue

We usually institute sessions of reciprocity toward the end of our cooking classes. Each student is encouraged to bring along to class on a chosen day a dish she enjoys serving. In other words, it's a trade, a swap, an exchange. It has resulted in a plethora of discoveries. Among one of our earliest samplings was this fondue brought by Sharon Rising. Since then, we have served it often as a chafing dish dip at large parties. It's not complicated to make. You can whip it up in a flash if you remember to keep a can of crab handy on your pantry shelf.

This recipe makes about six cups of fondue, enough for three 1-pint or six ½-pint gifts.

> ½ pound (2 sticks) butter or margarine
> 1 large onion, minced
> 1 pound natural sharp cheddar cheese, cubed
> ¾ cup catsup
> ¼ cup Worcestershire sauce
> ¼ cup medium dry sherry
> 4 cups shredded crab meat (fresh-cooked, canned, or frozen), with
>   all cartilage and tendons removed
>
> *For Serving*
> Melba rounds or other crackers

Melt the butter or margarine in a heavy skillet over medium-low heat. Saute the onion until transparent. Add all remaining ingredients except the crab, stirring constantly until the cheese is melted. When the sauce is smooth, stir in the crab meat and remove from the heat. Transfer to containers and let cool at room temperature.

If it is to be served immediately, transfer the mixture to a chafing dish with a water jacket or fondue pot. Serve with melba rounds or other crackers as dippers so that guests may help themselves.

TO PREPARE IN ADVANCE: May be kept refrigerated for up to three days or frozen for up to three months. If you have an appliance for sealing food in boilable bags, this is a good time to use it as the frozen mixture can be quickly thawed and heated that way. If not, simply thaw completely and heat in a double boiler.

SPECIAL PACKAGING: A cheese fondue set would be especially appropriate— they are available almost everywhere. Include melba rounds or crackers with the gift.

THE LABEL: Serve with melba rounds or crackers for dipping. *If the fondue is freshly made, the label should read:* Heat in a double boiler. May be stored in the refrigerator for up to three days or frozen for up to three months. *If the fondue is frozen, the label should read:* Heat in double boiler. May be kept frozen for up to three months or in the refrigerator for up to three days after it has been thawed. *If the fondue is frozen in a boilable bag, the label should read:* Drop into boiling water for 20 to 30 minutes until thoroughly hot. May be kept frozen for up to three months or in the refrigerator for up to three days after it has been thawed.

A Dilly of a Dip

This dip is a dilly to slip into a summertime gift. It makes a nice complement to the crisp crunch of raw vegetables and becomes a feast for the eyes if you tie a bundle of baby asparagus with lavender grosgrain ribbon and place it into a basket along with raw mushrooms, cauliflower, scallions, and cherry tomatoes. The transition from eye to palate appeal is as effortless and smooth as the dip itself.

This recipe makes a bit more than 2 cups of dip, enough for two 8-ounce containers or four 4-ounce containers.

1 cup mayonnaise
1 cup commercial sour cream
4 teaspoons dried dill weed
1 tablespoon minced parsley
2 teaspoons Lipton's onion soup mix
1 teaspoon Spice Islands Beau Monde seasoning or Aromatic
    Summer Salt (see page 142)
1 teaspoon garlic salt
½ teaspoon Worcestershire sauce
Sprinkling of dill to garnish

For Serving
Raw vegetables (crudites)

Combine all ingredients in a small mixing bowl and stir until well mixed. Cover and refrigerate for at least an hour to allow the flavor to mellow. Stir again to blend and transfer to containers. Sprinkle more dill over the top of the dip for decoration. Serve with freshly cut raw vegetables (crudites).

TO PREPARE IN ADVANCE: Cover tightly with plastic wrap. May be stored in the refrigerator for up to two weeks. Do not freeze.

SPECIAL PACKAGING: Fill a glass flower pot or basket with assorted fresh vegetables for dipping and accompany with a container of the dip.

THE LABEL: Serve as a dip with raw vegetables. May be stored in the refrigerator for up to two weeks. Do not freeze.

Celebration Caviar Dip

When friends deserve a celebration, drop off a crock of Celebration Caviar Dip, along with the champagne. This one goes well with almost anything—crackers or raw vegetables, and can even pass as a dynamic salad dressing. Our cooking friend, Joan Candy, invented this last-minute quickie, and covers herself with glory everytime she passes it around.

This recipe makes almost 2 cups of rich dip, enough for at least two small gifts with enough left over for your own mini-celebration.

1 (8-ounce) package cream cheese
½ to ¾ cup dairy sour cream
1/3 cup minced onion
1 (4-ounce) jar black lumpfish caviar

For Serving
Plain crackers, melba rounds, or an assortment of cut raw
    vegetables (crudites)

In the bowl of an electric mixer, beat the cream cheese until it is smooth and creamy. Thin the cream cheese to the desired dipping consistency by beating in ½ to ¾ cup sour cream. Beat in the onion. Finally, fold in the caviar and chill until serving time.

Serve with melba rounds, plain crackers, or raw vegetables.

TO PREPARE IN ADVANCE: The cream cheese, sour cream, and onion may be combined several days in advance and kept chilled in the refrigerator. Fold in the caviar just before serving or giving. Do not freeze.

SPECIAL PACKAGING: Place the dip in some kind of pretty gift container inside a basket surrounded by crackers or an assortment of cut vegetables for dipping. Include a bottle of chilled champagne and perhaps some champagne glasses.

THE LABEL: Hooray for you! Celebrate without delay!

Tapenade with Crudités

To induce a little speculation and mystery at the start of your dinner parties, consider Tapenade with Crudites. It's such a nippy dip that guests puzzle over its composition and also over another new thing: jicama, one of the assorted crudites (raw vegetables) we serve for dipping. Jicama is a deliciously crisp root vegetable that looks like a turnip but has a flavor reminiscent of fresh water chestnuts. Peel, thinly slice, and put in a basket along with squash, cauliflower, carrots, celery, or radish. Perhaps you prefer potato chips or fritos. No matter. Regardless of the kind of dippers you use, this dip with its elusive flavor is a hit with all.

This recipe makes about 2 cups of dip, enough for two 8-ounce gifts or four 4-ounce gifts.

> 1 (2-ounce) can anchovy fillets in oil
> 1/3 cup minced parsley
> 2 tablespoons red wine vinegar
> 1 tablespoon cut fresh or dried chives
> 1 medium shallot, peeled and cut coarsely
> 1 packet G. Washington's rich brown seasoning mix or 1 teaspoon Spice Islands Beef Stock Base
> 2 teaspoons capers, drained
> ½ teaspoon Poupon Dijon mustard
> 1½ cups mayonnaise
> 1 or more teaspoons fresh lemon juice, to taste
> Tabasco sauce, to taste
>
> *For Serving*
> Assorted raw vegetables (crudites)

Combine in an electric blender or food processor the anchovy fillets with their oil, parsley, vinegar, chives, shallot, seasoning, capers, and mustard. Blend for 2 to 3 minutes until completely smooth, stopping often to scrape down the sides of the container with a rubber spatula. Transfer to a small mixing bowl. Stir in the mayonnaise and season to taste with lemon juice and Tabasco.

Serve as a dip with assorted raw vegetables.

TO PREPARE IN ADVANCE: May be stored covered in the refrigerator for up to a week. The raw vegetables should be cut into serving pieces just before serving. Do not freeze.

SPECIAL PACKAGING: Place a container of tapenade in the center of a rustic basket and surround it with fresh raw vegetables for dipping.

THE LABEL: *If giving the dip only, the label should read:* Serve as a dip with cut raw vegetables. May be stored in the refrigerator for up to one week. Do not freeze. *If the dip and vegetables are to be eaten immediately and the vegetables are already cut, the label should read:* Serve immediately. *If giving the dip and uncut vegetables, the label should read:* Serve with cut-up vegetables for dipping. Dip may be stored in the refrigerator for up to one week. Do not freeze.

Cheesy Artichoke Squares

This dish can be ushered in at three different places on your next bill of fare. It all depends on the cut: small squares for hors d'oeuvres, rectangles for savory accompaniments to soup, big squares as a side dish of vegetable. Its beguiling flavor is the result of the union of cheddar cheese, marinated artichoke hearts, and a smattering of aromatic herbs and spices. It was introduced to us by our super-healthy friend, Margaret Skibitzke, who claims they put on a marvelous magic act. If you don't believe her, make them, and watch the squares disappear along with your skepticism.

This recipe makes seventy-two 1-inch squares, enough for up to six gifts of one dozen each.

> 2 teaspoons butter or margarine to grease the pan
> 2 (6-ounce) jars marinated artichoke hearts
> ½ medium onion, minced
> 1 medium clove garlic, minced or pressed
> 4 large eggs
> ¼ cup fine dry bread crumbs
> ¼ teaspoon salt
> ⅛ teaspoon dried oregano
> ⅛ teaspoon ground black pepper
> ⅛ teaspoon Tabasco sauce
> ½ pound natural sharp cheddar cheese, grated
> 2 tablespoons minced parsley

Preheat the oven to 325°. Grease a 7-by-11-inch glass baking dish with butter or margarine.

Drain the marinade from one jar of artichoke hearts into a small skillet. Saute the onion and garlic in the marinade for about 5 minutes over medium heat until the onion is transparent. Set aside.

Drain the other jar of artichokes, saving the marinade for future use as a salad dressing. Chop the artichokes finely. Beat the eggs lightly in a medium mixing bowl. Add the bread crumbs and seasonings and mix well. Stir in the cheese, parsley, artichokes, and onion mixture. Pour the mixture into the prepared baking pan. Bake at 325° for about 30 minutes, until the center feels firm to the touch. Remove from the oven and let stand 15 minutes before cutting.

Cut into 1-inch squares. The squares may be served warm or at room temperature, or may be reheated at 325° for 10 minutes.

TO PREPARE IN ADVANCE: When cool, wrap airtight in aluminum foil. May be stored in the refrigerator for up to four days or frozen for up to three months. To serve, thaw, if frozen, and heat in foil wrapping at 325° for 10 minutes.

SPECIAL PACKAGING: The squares should be wrapped in foil, one dozen to a package. Use a pen (available at stationery stores) that is made especially for writing on aluminum foil and other shiny surfaces to write directions for reheating the squares. Overwrap with cellophane and tie with a ribbon.

THE LABEL: Heat in foil wrap at 325° for 10 minutes. *If the squares are not frozen, the label should read:* May be stored for up to four days in the refrigerator or frozen for up to three months. *If the squares are frozen, the label should read:* May be kept frozen for up to three months or in the refrigerator for up to four days after they have been thawed.

Mushrooms à la Grecque

After a day at the typewriter—and the stove—we love having friends stop by to join us in a glass of wine and a nibble of whatever recipe we happen to be testing. And if, by chance, the test item emerges not quite the sensation we expected (oh, yes, the von Welanetzes have flops too), then to the rescue come Mushrooms a la Grecque. We always keep them on hand—and not just for cooking emergencies. Our daughter Lisa, in fact, likes them so well that they often find their way into her lunch box to the total astonishment of her schoolmates. The astonishment is matched by their pleasure when she brings enough to share. The simplified recipe for this classic dish was given to us by Diane Duplanty, one of our dearest friends. Although they are usually served as a first course in restaurants, we prefer to serve them drained, to be skewered on a frilled cocktail pick, along with other hors d'oeuvres. And to be absolutely sure that nothing of its marvelous flavor goes to waste, the leftover marinade may be tossed over a bowlful of crisp greens, creating instant herbal dressing, flavor unmatched.

This recipe makes 6 cups of whole mushrooms in marinade, enough to fill three 1-pint or six ½-pint gift containers.

2 pounds (50 to 60) medium fresh mushrooms (see Note)
2 medium cloves of garlic
1 cup red wine vinegar
1 cup water
½ cup olive oil
½ cup vegetable oil
2 whole bay leaves
½ teaspoon dried thyme
½ teaspoon onion powder
2 teaspoons salt
12 black peppercorns, whole (optional)
1 tablespoon minced parsley for garnish

For Serving
Ruffled hors d'oeuvre toothpicks

Note: When selecting fresh mushrooms, make sure they are closed under the caps and feel moist to the touch. If you are not going to use them right away, cover them with a damp paper towel and store in an open bag in the refrigerator. To clean mushrooms, hold them straight up like a tiny umbrella under cold running water and *quickly* run your fingers over the surface to remove any grit. Do this as fast as you can because mushrooms absorb water like a sponge. Immediately dry on paper towels and cut off the woody bottom part of the stems.

Clean mushrooms, set aside. Place the garlic on a chopping board and flatten each clove by whacking it with the flat side of a large knife. Remove the peel and place the garlic with all other ingredients except the mushrooms in a 4-quart saucepan. Bring the marinade to a boil, then lower the heat and simmer for 5 minutes. Add the mushrooms and simmer, uncovered, for 10 minutes; they will shrink considerably while simmering. Remove the pan from the heat and let stand until cool. Transfer the mushrooms to containers.

To serve, drain off and save the marinade, which may be used again for more mushrooms or as a salad dressing, and remove the garlic cloves. Arrange the mushrooms in a serving dish and sprinkle with chopped parsley. Provide frilled toothpicks for guests to help themselves.

TO PREPARE IN ADVANCE: May be stored in the refrigerator for up to three weeks. Do not freeze. To serve, drain and reserve the marinade.

SPECIAL PACKAGING: Any crock or clear-glass jar with a tight-fitting lid is ideal. You might include a package of fancy cocktail picks.

THE LABEL: Serve drained mushrooms (sans the garlic, of course) at room temperature sprinkled with chopped parsley. Save the marinade to use as a salad dressing. The mushrooms in their marinade may be stored in the refrigerator for up to three weeks. Do not freeze.

Tabooli in Pockets of Pita

Avoid first-course banalities by serving this unforgettable Middle Eastern dish. We list it here (it can double as a salad) because it's so appetizing that the appetizer designation somehow seems more appropriate. Tabooli escapes being conventional by the bulgur which grants a singularly nutty quality, and the parsley used in a quantity that may surprise you, some four or five cups. Serve it as a dramatic hors d'oeuvre by piling it high on a serving dish, surrounded by quarters of pita bread. Or mound it on lettuce leaves in a salad bowl, ringed with wedges of tomato. It is at its best when freshly made, but we have found it will keep up to a week in the refrigerator, losing nothing in the waiting. We make it in large quantities (we're hopelessly addicted), chopping parsley in an electric food chopper. Even if compelled to chop it all by hand, we would, gladly, for nothing could keep us from this naturally good palate pleaser.

This recipe makes 3 quarts of tabooli, enough for six 1-pint or twelve ½-pint gifts. The recipe may be halved or quartered.

> 1½ cups medium grind bulgur wheat (available in Middle Eastern and some Italian markets)
> 6 to 8 bunches of fresh parsley (enough to make 4 to 5 cups minced parsley leaves)
> 1¼ cups fresh lemon juice (from about 5 juicy lemons)
> 3 large tomatoes, peeled and diced
> 3 bunches scallions, sliced, including some of the green stems
> 3 tablespoons red wine vinegar
> ¼ cup olive oil
> ¼ cup vegetable oil
> 1 tablespoon [sic!] ground cinnamon
> 1 to 1½ teaspoons salt, to taste
> Pepper, to taste
>
> *For Serving*
> Armenian or Arab "pocket" bread (pita)

Place the bulgur wheat in a small mixing bowl with enough cold water to cover. Let stand at least 30 minutes while you prepare the other ingredients.

Wash the parsley and shake it dry. Cut off and discard the stems. Chop the leaves very finely, using a large sharp knife or the steel blade in a Cuisinart food processor. If chopping by hand or scissors, this is a time-consuming job, but well worth the effort.

Drain any water from the wheat and place it in a large mixing bowl (at least 4-quart capacity) with the lemon juice, parsley, tomatoes, and scallions. Toss to combine. Combine the vinegar, oils, and cinnamon and pour over the wheat mixture, tossing well. Season with salt and pepper to taste. Chill thoroughly.

To serve, cut pita bread into halves or quarters. Supply spoons for guests to fill the pockets in the bread with the chilled vegetable mixture.

TO PREPARE IN ADVANCE: The tabooli may be stored for up to five days in the refrigerator, though it loses a bit of its sparkle each day. Do not freeze. The pita bread may be frozen.

SPECIAL PACKAGING: Some kind of glass serving dish or salad bowl would be ideal. Cover tightly to prevent leaking. Include pita bread for serving in a separate package.

THE LABEL: Cut pita into halves or quarters and fill the pockets with chilled tabooli. It may be stored in the refrigerator for up to five days. Do not freeze.

Beverages & Liqueurs

It's true! It's neither against the law nor un-American to play around in your kitchen with distilled spirit recipes for your family's use or to give as gifts to friends. However, if you're nervous about revenooers, we suggest that you sample your work as it progresses. Then, at least, you'll have a smile on your face whenever you sneak a peek over your shoulder!

Brewing, in one form or another, has been going on for years. A recipe for beer was inscribed on a Mesopotamian tablet thousands of years before Christ, and the ancient Egyptians were very fond of *hydromel,* one of the world's oldest fermented drinks. It was made from honey and fermented easily. The Egyptians had the simplest of formulas whereby they'd mix one part honey to three parts warm water, set it aside to ferment, and happily watch nature take its course.

In Rome they sometimes let the same mixture sit for forty days and then stored it away in a smoke-filled room to add flavor. The English adopted this mildly intoxicating drink and it became a favorite aperitif of the Elizabethan court. They added malt to it, sealed it in a jar for a month, strained and drank it, and changed its name to *mead*.

Back in our own country, one evening outside of Stockbridge, Massachusetts, we were driving on an out-of-the-way old post road when we came across the Stagecoach Hill Inn and stopped for dinner. On an end table we discovered a small book entitled *All About Beer,* by John Porter, a light treatise on the pleasures, properties, and unusual uses of man's oldest friend. This is a marvelous book and we recommend it to you. It's published by Doubleday and gives a precise history of the brewing art along with information on where to buy a do-it-yourself beer-making kit and necessary supplies. There are some fascinating recipes as well, such as Elizabethan Smash-A-Roo, Red Cabbage with Beer, Ale Posset, and, for lovers of Americana, a photographic copy of George Washington's handwritten recipe for "small beer."

Another favorite beverage all over the world is tea. It was first grown as a crop in China before 4000 B.C. and only became popular as a drink in the eighth century when, legend has it, Budhidharma, the son of the king of India, traveled to China to spread his beliefs, vowing to stay awake for nine years so that he might spend all his time in the contemplation of the true Buddha. Unfortunately, he fell asleep after three years, and in punishment cut off his own eyelids, which dropped at his feet, blossoming into heavenly tea plants. The strong caffeine in the brew no doubt contributed toward keeping him awake for his remaining years.

Tea found its way to Japan, and by the twelfth century became popular in a ceremonial ritual called *cha-no-yu,* which went on for several hours. Its purpose, as defined by the tea master, was to cleanse the senses. Although this ceremony was invented and dominated by men for centuries, modern Japan has over two million female students enrolled in its current tea ceremony schools.

This section is not designed merely to supply you with recipes for brewing hard-stuff at home, but to offer a few pantry tricks where stored packaged spirits and a touch of imagination can be used. For those not of a bibulous nature, we include a delicious and nourishing instant spiced tea.

Spiced Tea

We were thinking of naming it "Antique Tea." We came upon the recipe one rainy afternoon while browsing for unusual kitchen items in an antique shop. The owner offered us a cup of this heady blend, and we savored it, not realizing that such recently developed ingredients could yield such good, old-time flavor. It takes just minutes to put together. Add boiling water, and you have a quick pick-me-up, packed with vitamin C.

This recipe makes 3¼ cups, enough to fill three 8-ounce gift containers with a bit left over to warm you on a blustery day.

2/3 cup instant tea
1 (9-ounce) jar Tang
1 (3-ounce) package Wyler's lemonade mix
1 cup sugar
1 teaspoon ground cinnamon
½ teaspoon ground cloves
¼ teaspoon nutmeg

Mix all ingredients and store in an airtight container. To serve, add 1 level tablespoon of the mix to a 6-ounce cup of boiling water.

TO PREPARE IN ADVANCE: May be kept unrefrigerated for up to three months in an airtight container.

SPECIAL PACKAGING: Moisture-proof containers are a must to keep the mixture from lumping.

THE LABEL: A bracing tea full of vitamin C. For one serving stir 1 level tablespoonful in a 6-ounce cup of hot water. May be kept unrefrigerated for up to three months in an airtight container.

Boerenmeisjes
(Scandinavian Apricot Liqueur)

The instant we thought of including this recipe in our book, we headed for our pantry where a large glass jar of this apricot liqueur has been aging for six months. As the late afternoon sun caught the translucent golden brew, it looked for all the world as if it belonged on the canvas of a seventeenth-century Flemish still-life painting. Ships are launched with Boerenmeisjes! Kings are coronated with it! Yet with incredible ease, you can put a gallon of it together in moments. There's just one hitch. Although you spend no time cooking, you do need to kill a little time before serving. At least one month must pass before this heavenly syrup passes your lips, either as a liqueur or spooned with the fruit over ice cream as a dessert topping.

This recipe makes almost 4 quarts, enough for sixteen 8-ounce gifts.

1 pound dried apricots
1 bottle (fifth) May wine
1 quart domestic brandy
1 quart water
1 small cinnamon stick

For Serving
Ice cream (optional)

Combine the ingredients in a 1-gallon jar or crock or divide evenly between several smaller containers. Allow to age at room temperature for at least a month before serving or giving.

Serve fruit and liqueur as is or over ice cream.

TO PREPARE IN ADVANCE: After aging for a month, this will keep at room temperature for up to six months. After six months it will last indefinitely if refrigerated.

SPECIAL PACKAGING: Any clear glass jar makes a wonderful gift container.

THE LABEL: An apricot liqueur to lift your spirits. Serve fruit and liqueur as is or over ice cream. May be stored in the refrigerator indefinitely.

 **Colorful Cordials**

When Paul was young, he used to pass drugstores that displayed apothecary jars filled with crystal-clear liquid of the most brilliant colors: amber, green, red, purple. He used to wonder at the liquid contents inside. He wonders no more. Now he prepares Colorful Cordials to match his childhood memory.

His recipe deals with the simple principle of evaporation. For instance, if you simmer four cups of syrup in a one-quart pan for thirty minutes and remove one cup after every ten minutes, you would have three cups of syrup, the fourth having evaporated. Each cup would have a different viscosity or density.

Add food coloring. Red in the first, none in the second, blue in the third. Add brandy or extract, pour carefully into a tilted liqueur glass, and you'll have a bangup firecracker of an after-dinner drink for the Fourth of July.

Now you're really on your way. Prepare another batch, add any colors you choose and any flavor (for example, strawberry or boysenberry syrup) or any extract (banana, lemon, almond). Combinations are limitless. Red and green for Christmas. Red, white, and green for a Mexican fiesta. Green and white for St. Patrick's Day.

As for the alcohol, we like to use a good brandy. However, one could also use a not-so-good vodka. You may, by the way, play this kitchen chemistry and manufacture your own joy juice, with one exception. You can give it away, throw it away or, as we intended you to do, serve it, but under no circumstances will Uncle Sam permit you to sell it. That seems fair enough. It would not make the choicest of donations to a church bazaar.

This recipe makes about 3-1/3 cups of colored liqueurs. Depending on the size of your containers, this amount is sufficient for one or two gifts.

> 3 cups water
> 2 cups sugar
> 3 teaspoons peppermint (or any other flavor) extract (see Note)
> ¾ cup brandy or Cognac
> 2 food colorings of your choice

Note: If you use anise flavoring, the mixture will become milky. If you wish to make liqueurs of *three* densities from the recipe, remove ¾ cup of syrup at 214°. Simmer remaining syrup about 5 minutes longer to 220° and remove another ¾ cup. Proceed as described in the recipe, except for adding only ¼ cup brandy or cognac and 1 teaspoon peppermint (or other flavoring) extract to each portion of syrup.

Bring the water to a hard boil in a heavy 3-quart saucepan. Stir in the sugar and bring the mixture back to a boil. Insert a candy thermometer and lower heat so the mixture remains at a hard simmer. When the thermometer registers 214° (in about 5 minutes), pour out a little less than half the mixture (about 1-1/3 cups) into a mixing bowl. This is the light liqueur. Return the pan to the heat and continue simmering about 10 minutes more, until the thermometer registers 226°. Let cool. This is the heavy liqueur. Stir 1½ teaspoons of the flavor extract and 3 ounces of brandy or Cognac into each batch of liqueur. Color them to your liking with different food colors, remembering which color you used for the light and which for the heavy liqueur.

Use a funnel to transfer the liqueurs to gift bottles. If desired, dip the corks in melted paraffin (directions for melting paraffin on page 231) to make a tight seal. Store in a cool dark place for at least a week to allow the flavor to mellow.

To serve, fill cordial glasses half full of the heavy liqueur. Then tip the glass to pour the light liqueur on top of the heavy one—it will float.

TO PREPARE IN ADVANCE: The liqueurs will keep indefinitely stored in a cool dark place. Refrigeration is not necessary.

SPECIAL PACKAGING: Matching cordial bottles make the best gift containers, though any attractive bottles will do.

THE LABEL: Cheers! Fill a cordial glass half full of the *(color of the heavy)* liqueur. Tip the glass and carefully pour the *(color of the light)* liqueur down the side of the glass. It will float on top. May be stored in a cool dark place indefinitely. Refrigeration is not necessary.

Hot Buttered Rum Batter

This bracing drink will put light in the eye and life in the soul. Dedicated winter sports enthusiasts will welcome it as they sit around a crackling fire after a day on the slopes. The drink has a number of components. To simplify its preparation, make up a gift basket that will leave the recipient little to do but add the half cup of hot water. It should include a container of batter, a bottle of light rum, a whole nutmeg, and an inexpensive nutmeg grater.

You will have 7 cups of batter to fill three 1-pint gift containers, leaving one cup extra for your own use.

For the Batter
1 pound butter or margarine, at room temperature
1 pound golden brown sugar
1 quart vanilla ice cream, softened
1½ teaspoons ground nutmeg (see Note)

For Each Serving
1½ ounces (3 tablespoons) light rum
1 heaping tablespoon batter (directions below)
½ cup boiling water
Sprinkling of ground or grated nutmeg

Note: Freshly ground spices have a stupendous flavor and aroma. We like to grind nutmeg in an electric coffee mill just before using it in a recipe.

To make the batter, beat the butter or margarine in the large bowl of an electric mixer at high speed until it is creamy. Gradually beat in the brown sugar until the mixture is smooth and fluffy, stopping often to scrape down the sides of the bowl with a rubber spatula. Add the softened ice cream and 1½ teaspoons ground nutmeg and continue beating until the batter is well combined. Transfer to containers. Store in the refrigerator or freezer.

To make a serving of Hot Buttered Rum, place the rum and a heaping tablespoon of batter in a mug or other serving cup. Add about ½ cup boiling water and stir to blend. Sprinkle lightly with ground or grated nutmeg.

TO PREPARE IN ADVANCE: The batter may be kept for weeks in the refrigerator and indefinitely in the freezer.

SPECIAL PACKAGING: One-pint canning jars, especially the French ones, with a rubber ring are attractive for this, though plastic refrigerator containers do the job just as well. A thoughtful gift basket for a skier might contain a jar of batter, a small bottle of light rum, and a whole nutmeg with an inexpensive grater.

THE LABEL: Into a mug put 1 heaping tablespoon batter, 1½ ounces (1 jigger) rum, and boiling water to fill. Stir until batter is melted, sprinkle top with nutmeg. May be stored in the refrigerator for weeks and in the freezer indefinitely.

Gazpacho Borracho

Gazpacho is marvelous! Think of all the ways you can either zig or zag with it. The makers of V-8 puree all the vegetables and get *juice*. Spaniards add red wine vinegar, Tabasco, puree some vegetables and dice others for gazpacho *soup*. Add a greater amount of chopped vegetables than liquid, and you get gazpacho *salad*. Finely chopped celery added to a Bloody Mary makes a gazpacho *drink*.

Which brings us to one New Year's Day when Paul, in his search for a quick pick-me-up (about noon), zagged with the ingredients and achieved a new kind of Bloody Mary which we call Gazpacho Borracho. Serve in mugs, garnished with a stalk of leafy celery, or present a large jar of it to your New Year's Eve hosts in a basket with a bottle of vodka and a head of celery for their morning after. One small caution: drink too many of these gazpachos and you'll become borracho (slightly tight). (If you serve it in a bowl, call it soup.)

This recipe makes a little more than three quarts, enough for three 1-quart gifts of four servings each with a bit left over for you to sample.

1 (1-pound, 14-ounce) can whole tomatoes, diced, and their liquid
1 (46-ounce) can tomato juice
1 cup red wine vinegar
3 tablespoons Worcestershire sauce
1 teaspoon dried oregano leaves, crushed
2 green bell peppers, seeded and finely chopped
4 stalks celery, finely chopped
1 medium cucumber, peeled and finely chopped
Salt, to taste
Tabasco sauce, to taste (8 dashes give a highly seasoned flavor)

For Serving
1 ounce vodka (see Note)
1 leafy celery stalk, if served in mugs (optional)

Note: If you wish to make a nonborracho gazpacho (party pooper!), omit the vodka and add ¼ cup olive oil to the mixture before chilling. We keep a bottle of vodka in the freezer at all times. It can't freeze because of its alcoholic content, but it is ice-cold and has a pleasant syrupy consistency—marvelous served in tiny glasses with caviar or just about anything else for that matter.

Combine all the ingredients, seasoning to taste with salt and Tabasco. Chilling dulls the seasoning, so add a bit more than you think it needs. Refrigerate for at least 4 hours.

To serve, pour 6 to 8 ounces of chilled gazpacho into a chilled bowl or mug and stir in 1 ounce of vodka. If desired, garnish each mug with a stalk of leafy celery to use as a swizzle stick.

TO PREPARE IN ADVANCE: May be stored in the refrigerator for up to five days. Do not freeze.

SPECIAL PACKAGING: Any quart container will do, though a glass one with a stopper or cork to prevent leakage is especially suitable. Accompany the gazpacho with a small bottle or container of vodka and, perhaps, some leafy celery stalks.

THE LABEL: To serve: Pour 6 to 8 ounces of chilled gazpacho into a chilled mug and add 1 ounce of vodka, if desired. Celery stalks make nice swizzle sticks. May be stored in the refrigerator for up to five days. Do not freeze.

Soups

Eons ago our ancestors filled small craters in limestone conglomerates with water and cast into them red-hot stones from a fire. Then into the bubbling, steaming liquid they would toss tubers, roots, nuts, fruits, seeds, pieces of meat, bones, berries, bark, creatures of the sea—whatever food their individual or communal efforts produced that day, that season, or in the place they called home.

And so soup became one of the most welcome benefits from the discovery of fire. Soup cries "home," "comfort," "nourishment." By the simple expediency of immersing solid foodstuff into boiling liquid, nutrients and vitamins are extracted as well as minerals from meat bones. It is all contained in liquid suspension, hot or cold, until consumed.

About the twelfth century, Europeans boiled meat in rain water, and dipped pieces of trencher bread, called *sop*, into the broth to soften it. This is the first written record we have of broth itself being used as a food. Eventually, the name *sop* became synonymous with the broth, and we know this *sop* today as soup. But soup, as it is today, did not mature as a singular dietary identity until spices from China were introduced, especially clove and cinnamon.

The romantic French are incapable, it seems, of using one word to describe a food. They insist upon a short story. To them *sop* became *pot au feu,* or pot on the fire.

We, too, constantly have a pot on the fire in our house. We'd like to tell you what we do. Into a 10-quart stainless steel pot on the back of our range we toss just about every nourishing scrap from our chopping block normally thrown away. Everything except for tin cans, bacon grease, and pineapple peelings. We even use parsley and carrot stems, the ends of celery, potato peelings, turnip scrapings, chicken carcasses—everything. Each morning we skim off the fat, strain out the solids, bring the liquid level up to three-quarters full (whenever possible using juices from boiled vegetables), and simmer just below the boiling point for 20 minutes. We turn the fire off and let it sit all day. (Boiling at a temperature of 200 degrees for 20 minutes every day allows us to keep our pot on the stove without having to refrigerate it.)

If we need a nibble, the soup pot's where we go. It makes a fantastic snack, especially when children come home from school. Each day it's a different flavor. There are times when it reaches a certain grandeur, but there's no way to remember what's in it. Finally, the day comes when we pour it into containers and freeze, starting all over again with a tablespoon of beef extract, some water or juices, and an inexpensive head of red cabbage. Our broth has a myriad of uses: as a thickener for sauce, as a base for stew, or as a soup guaranteed to give you all your minimum daily requirements.

And it makes a great gift, too! There's nothing superstitious, ethnic, or religious about giving a sick friend chicken soup. It's a powerhouse of condensed energy. It would also be appreciated by new neighbors just moving in, someone who's repainting a kitchen or home, or by a hostess who's asked you to bring the first course of a dinner party. Enjoy, enjoy!

Sherried Pumpkin Soup

After Cinderella got over her astonishment, we hope she went home and put her pumpkin coach into a soup pot, achieving a *tour de force* equal to our own Sherried

Pumpkin Soup. Our own version came when we drove all over the United States in search of recipes for this book. It was in Massachusetts that we found this one said to be served by the early settlers. On our return home, we embellished it with sherry and a touch of cayenne. It can be made any time of the year because canned pumpkin is used and it is equally superb hot or cold, garnished with cream and a sprinkling of chopped chives.

It makes 3 quarts of soup, enough for three 1-quart gifts of four servings each.

¼ pound (1 stick) butter or margarine
2 large onions, coarsely chopped
1/3 cup minced shallots (about 6 large shallots) or the white
    part of scallions
1 (2-pound) can solid-pack pumpkin
8 cups chicken broth, homemade or canned
2 tablespoons Spice Islands Chicken Stock Base
1 bay leaf
1 teaspoon sugar
6 sprigs of parsley
⅛ teaspoon ground nutmeg
1 quart (4 cups) milk
1 tablespoon pale dry sherry
Cayenne to taste

For Each Serving
1 tablespoon heavy cream (whipping cream) as garnish
1 teaspoon snipped chives, fresh or dried, as garnish

Melt the butter or margarine in a heavy 8-quart kettle or dutch oven. Saute the chopped onion over medium heat until transparent. Lower the heat, add the shallots, and continue cooking for 4 or 5 minutes longer, taking care not to scorch the mixture. Add the pumpkin and stir for a minute or two, then add the chicken broth, chicken stock base, bay leaf, sugar, and parsley sprigs. Bring the mixture to boil, then reduce the heat and simmer slowly for 20 minutes.

For the soup to have a smooth consistency, it is necessary to puree it in an electric blender or put it through a food mill. (A blender is easiest, so if you have one, puree the soup in four or five batches, filling the container only half full.) When smooth, pour the soup into a clean 4-quart pot. Place over medium heat, stir in the nutmeg, milk, and sherry and simmer for 10 minutes. Season the soup to taste with a few dashes cayenne and perhaps a bit more chicken stock base. (If the soup is to be served cold, it will require a bit more seasoning than if it is to be served hot.)

To serve, ladle hot or chilled soup into serving bowls. Drizzle 1 tablespoon cream over each serving—it will sink temporarily in hot soup, but will rise to the surface in a few seconds. Sprinkle each serving with 1 teaspoon chives.

TO PREPARE IN ADVANCE: This soup may be refrigerated for up to five days or frozen for up to three months. If it is to be served cold after being frozen, it should be reblended in an electric blender for a few seconds to regain its original smoothness.

SPECIAL PACKAGING: Most 1-quart containers are suitable. The gift package should include the cream and chives with which the soup is to be garnished. An elegant addition would be four abalone-shell soup bowls, our favorite serving bowls for cold soups. These inexpensive bowls are available at most shops that sell seashells. (There's a tongue-twister for you!)

THE LABEL: Serve hot or chilled. Garnish each serving with 1 tablespoon cream and 1 teaspoon chives. *If the soup is freshly made, the label should read:* May be stored in the refrigerator for up to five days or frozen for up to three months. If you serve the soup cold after it has been frozen, when it has been thawed put it in an electric blender at low speed for a few seconds to increase its smoothness. *If the soup is frozen, the label should read:* May be stored frozen for up to three months or in the refrigerator for up to five days after it has been thawed. If you serve the soup cold, after thawing it put it in an electric blender at low speed for a few seconds to increase its smoothness.

Crème Senegalese

This cold curried soup seems to be the easiest and most superior of all the versions circulating about. Garnished as it is with chunks of freshly cut apple, it is such a refreshingly cool summertime dish that it has become a popular first course at many fine French restaurants. (Senegal, as you may remember, was an overseas territory of the French republic in West Africa.) It is rich, so we usually serve it in small portions at lunch time before a main course of fish or seafood. When presented as a gift, no mention need be made of the fact that it was constituted with a minimum of effort. It will taste all the more delectable if the recipient is under the impression that the work was long and arduous.

This recipe makes about 6 cups of chilled soup, which—since it will be garnished with chopped apple and served in small amounts— should be sufficient for two 24-ounce gifts of four servings each.

1 medium leek (see Note 1)
4 teaspoons curry powder (preferably Madras)
4 cups well-seasoned chicken broth, either homemade or canned, undiluted (see Note 2)
3 egg yolks
2 cups heavy cream (whipping cream)
Salt to taste
Cayenne (ground red pepper) (optional)
2 apples, peeled and chopped, as garnish

Note 1: The leek is our favorite member of the onion family to use in soups. It looks like an immense scallion and must be carefully cleaned in the following manner: Cut away the root and most of the green stem. Cut the remaining leek in half lengthwise. Hold one half and riffle the layers, as you would a deck of cards, so that you can see any sand or grit that may be hiding between the layers. Hold it under cold water and riffle again to rinse it clean. Repeat with the other half.

Note 2: If you use canned clear broth, season it to taste with Spice Islands Chicken Stock Base, a product we find indispensable. Once you've tried it, we're sure you will use it often for seasoning soups and sauces.

Use a 3-quart or larger stainless steel or enamel saucepan; do not use aluminum, as it will discolor food containing egg yolks and cream.

After cleaning the leek, chop it finely. Place it in the saucepan with the curry powder and chicken broth. Bring to a boil, lower the heat, and simmer slowly for 15 minutes. Strain out the leek and return the broth to the pan. Do not return to the heat.

Use a whisk to beat 2 or 3 tablespoons of the hot broth quickly into the egg yolks in a mixing bowl. Stir in the cream, then whisk the mixture into the broth. Place the pan over very low heat and whisk constantly until slightly thickened and smooth, at which point it will thinly coat the back of a spoon. Do not let the soup come to a boil or it may curdle.

Pour the soup immediately into another container in which it may be chilled. Taste for seasoning, but wait a minute or two before adding more of anything, as the aftertaste of curry is delayed. Add salt if needed and a bit of cayenne if you like a hotter flavor. Keep in mind that the flavor of the soup will be dulled somewhat when it is chilled.

Press plastic wrap onto the surface to prevent a skin from forming on top of the soup. Let cool to room temperature, then chill thoroughly. Transfer to containers. Serve very cold. Garnish each serving with peeled, chopped apple.

TO PREPARE IN ADVANCE: May be stored, covered, in the refrigerator for up to five days. Do not freeze. The apples for the garnish should be peeled and chopped at the last minute to prevent discoloration.

SPECIAL PACKAGING: This soup has a rich yellow color, so any clear-glass containers would be great. Some suggestions are apothecary jars, glass souffle dishes, even bottles with corks. Accompany the gift with the apples for the garnish. If you wish to be even more generous, two-piece glass soup bowls that hold ice in the bottom would be perfect—they double as shrimp cocktail glasses.

THE LABEL: Stir well before serving very cold garnished with peeled, chopped apples. May be stored in the refrigerator for up to five days. Do not freeze.

Bookbinder's Soup with Melted Cheese

This luscious concoction, full of vitamins and vim, first appeared in a newspaper many years ago. We've changed it so much that the bookbinders would never recognize it, let alone the food editor, so perhaps we should christen it with a new name. Stringy Cheese Soup might do or Mozzarella Mystifier, or something equally picturesque. Call it what you will, the fact is that children love it, and so do we. As you ladle the soup into bowls in which the slivers of cheese melt, you'll end up with a good beginning for any meal.

This makes about 3 quarts of soup, enough to fill three 1-quart gift containers of two to three servings each.

1 tablespoon oil
1 tablespoon butter or margarine
1 medium red onion, finely chopped
1 medium clove garlic, minced or pressed
3 tablespoons diced green chiles
1 (1-pound) can tomatoes, diced, with their liquid
½ cup (about 2/3 of a 3⅛-ounce jar Spice Islands Beef Stock Base
10 cups water
3 medium-size white boiling potatoes, peeled and cut in ¼-inch cubes
¼ teaspoon ground black pepper
Salt to taste
12 ounces (three 4-ounce packages) Monterey Jack, mozzarella, or Armenian string cheese

For Serving
Sour dough French bread
Beer

Heat the oil and butter in a 5-quart pot. Add the onion and garlic and saute until the onion is transparent. Add the chiles, tomato, beef stock base, and water. Stir and bring to a boil over high heat. Reduce the heat and simmer, covered, for 30 minutes. Add the potatoes, pepper, and a dash of salt. Simmer, covered, about 20 minutes—until the potatoes are tender. Taste and correct the seasoning.

To serve, place a few strips of cheese in the bottom of each serving bowl and pour the hot soup over the cheese. Serve with sour dough French bread and ice-cold beer.

TO PREPARE IN ADVANCE: After cooling to room temperature, the soup may be covered and refrigerated for up to five days or frozen for up to six months. Do not freeze the cheese.

SPECIAL PACKAGING: A fun way to present this would be to fill a basket with a container of soup, a 4-ounce chunk of cheese, a six-pack of beer, and a loaf of sour dough French bread.

THE LABEL: Bring to a boil before serving. Place strips of Monterey Jack, mozzarella, or Armenian string cheese in the bottom of each serving bowl and pour in the hot soup. Serve with sour dough French bread and ice-cold beer. *If the soup is freshly made, the label should read:* May be stored in the refrigerator for up to five days or frozen for up to six months. *If the soup is frozen, the label should read:* May be kept frozen for up to six months, or in the refrigerator for up to five days after it has been thawed.

Peasant Cabbage Soup

This soup can serve as a dinner in itself for peasants, or family and friends. Surround with wine, Perino's Pumpernickel (see page 102), or crusty bread, but before giving it away, don't neglect the garlic! We did once when we were newlyweds. Garlic was not to Paul's liking, so we omitted it when preparing Diana's family recipe. What a mistake! We made the soup again. Garlic lent just enough histrionics to make the difference between the insipidness of the first batch and the visceral experience that became the second. And we learned a valuable cooking lesson: Garlic mellows in cooking, becoming almost undetectable, but definitely leaving its mark on gastronomy and morale.

This recipe makes about 4 quarts of soup, enough for four 1-quart gift containers of two servings each.

2 tablespoons butter or margarine
3 large baking potatoes, peeled and cut in ½-inch dice
4 medium carrots, peeled and cut in ½-inch slices
2 medium leeks, cleaned (see directions, page 57) and cut in ½-inch slices
2 quarts water
1 medium cabbage, finely chopped
2 medium cloves garlic, minced or pressed
Salt and pepper to taste

For Serving
Our version of Perino's Pumpernickel

Melt the butter or margarine over medium heat in a heavy 6-quart pot. Stir in the potatoes, carrots, and leeks and saute gently for 5 minutes, stirring often. Add the water and bring to a boil. Lower the heat and simmer slowly, uncovered for 1 hour. Add the cabbage and garlic and simmer 30 minutes longer. Season to taste with salt and pepper.

Serve hot with Perino's Pumpernickel if desired.

TO PREPARE IN ADVANCE: This soup may be stored in the refrigerator for up to a week or frozen for up to six months.

SPECIAL PACKAGING: You might accompany the soup with an earthenware ovenproof dish or other container for serving. One-quart plastic refrigerator containers or the foil pans described on page 66 would be simplest for giving this soup. If desired, include an airtight container of Perino's Pumpernickel.

THE LABEL: Heat before serving. *If the soup is freshly made, the label should read:* May be stored in the refrigerator for up to a week or frozen for up to six months. *If the soup is frozen, the label should read:* May be kept frozen for up to six months or in the refrigerator for up to a week after it has been thawed.

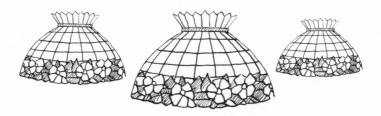

Green Garden Soup
with Pesto à la Penny's Arcade

There's something to admire in people who do not just go along with things as they are. Consider our friends, Penny and Larry Birnbaum. Besides building a 6000-square foot saloon filled with old arcade machines in which to get married, they're one of the very few who feel kitchen-confident enough to invite us to dinner. It's always an adventure. We even invited ourselves once when Penny said she was cooking two geese. We've never even gotten around to cooking *one*. Though the geese (done to a turn and delectable) were the main event, what captured the collective attention of all was this smashing Green Garden Soup. Everybody asked for seconds, a singular occurrence when there is such an abundance of food. Needless to say, we wheedled the recipe out of Penny. It departs from the usual because of its choice selection of greens and because it calls for sweet, dried basil in the Pesto instead of fresh as required by purists. When serving it, Paul places a ball of Pesto on a slice of lemon and sets it afloat. Serve it to raves.

This recipe makes 10 cups of soup before adding the sour cream, sufficient for ten to twelve servings, or two or three gift containers of four to six servings each. The recipe for Pesto makes 2/3 cup.

½ stick (4 tablespoons) butter or margarine
The white part of 2 medium leeks (see directions for cleaning, page 57) cut in ½-inch slices, or 2 medium onions, chopped
1 medium clove garlic, pressed
8 medium zucchini (about 2½ pounds), cut in ½-inch slices
1 (10-ounce) package frozen lima beans, thawed
1 (10-ounce) package frozen peas, thawed
½ cup Spice Islands Chicken Stock Base or about 8 chicken bouillon cubes
6 cups water
Salt and white pepper, to taste
½ to ¾ cup sour cream at room temperature
6 to 8 slices bacon, fried crisp and crumbled, to garnish

Pesto
2/3 cup grated Parmesan or Romano cheese
½ cup firmly packed parsley leaves
2 tablespoons dried sweet basil
3 medium cloves garlic, peeled
2 egg yolks
1 slice bacon, fried crisp and crumbled
1 to 2 teaspoons chopped walnuts or pine nuts

Melt the butter or margarine over medium heat in a heavy 4-quart pot. Saute the chopped leeks or onions, garlic and zucchini until the onion is transparent. Stir in all remaining soup ingredients except for the sour cream and bacon. Let simmer for 30 minutes. Cool slightly, then puree in small batches in the blender until **very smooth and transfer to a clean saucepan or storage container.**

To make the Pesto, combine all the ingredients in an electric blender or, better yet, a Cuisinart food processor and blend for several minutes, stopping the motor often to scrape down the sides of the container with a rubber spatula (the mixture will be very thick). Set aside to serve at room temperature.

Just before serving, bring the soup to a boil over medium heat. Remove from the heat and whisk in the sour cream. (Do not let the soup boil at this point because it could curdle.) Ladle into soup bowls and garnish each serving with a heaping teaspoon of Pesto Sauce and a sprinkling of crumbled crisp bacon.

TO PREPARE IN ADVANCE: The soup may be stored without the sour cream in the refrigerator for up to five days or frozen for up to three months. After thawing slowly bring the soup to a boil in a heavy saucepan and whisk in sour cream just before serving. The Pesto may be stored in the refrigerator for up to five days or frozen for up to four months. The crumbled bacon for the garnish may be refrigerated for up to two weeks or frozen for up to three months sealed in a plastic bag. About

10 minutes before serving, unwrap and heat in a 350° oven for 5 to 10 minutes until crisp.

SPECIAL PACKAGING: The foil containers described on page 66 are especially suitable for freezing and giving, as instructions for serving may be written right on the cardboard lid. Include containers of sour cream, crisp bacon and Pesto Sauce for serving.

THE LABEL: To serve, bring to a boil in heavy saucepan. Remove from heat and whisk—cup sour cream (depends on amount given). Serve immediately. Garnish each serving with 1 heaping teaspoon room-temperature Pesto Sauce and a sprinkling of crumbled bacon. *If the soup is freshly made, the label should read:* The soup and the Pesto Sauce may be stored in the refrigerator for up to five days or frozen for up to three months. *If the soup and Pesto Sauce are frozen, the label should read:* The soup and the Pesto Sauce may be kept frozen for up to three months or in the refrigerator for up to five days after they have been thawed.

Casseroles & One-Dish Meals

There are times when trying to get dinner on the table exactly at 6:00 P.M. is like trying to get five racehorses to forget their differences and cross the finish line simultaneously. For each of us the time comes when life is just too complex to even hope to synchronize soup, salad, meat, two vegetables, as well as a delectable dessert as finale. So it was inevitable that some overworked housewife would invent the one-dish meal: the casserole. Long live the casserole! and all those other handmaidens called convenience foods: packaged, processed, canned, and freeze-dried.

Needless to say, one must have a few fine recipes to work from, and when beginning, you'll find that it doesn't take much more work for you to prepare two casseroles at the same time, rather than just the one. A few of those treasured packages, tucked away in a freezer, could tip the balance from hassled to happy one day when a thousand unexpected intrusions play havoc with the organized plans of even the most organized homemaker.

The benefits of casserole cooking just multiply: a one-dish meal means only one timer to set, one pot to watch, and one pot to wash. It can be put together with ingredients usually kept on pantry shelves, prepared, and even baked, the night before, which actually improves the flavor of many dishes.

The casserole is a far cry from the way food was served 200 years ago—the "French service" way—when everything, absolutely every single course from soup to dessert, came forth from the kitchen at the same moment and overwhelmed the table with its variety of hot and cold abundance. You ate well depending on how fast you were. That was a neat kitchen trick, but then kitchen help was only $3 a month.

When the French economy went bust, "a la Russe" service was adopted. The Russian method was to prepare the food and slice the meat, arrange a complete plate for each course, all beforehand in the kitchen for each invited guest seated at the dining room table. This, of course, had obvious advantages. Each course could be served properly, hot or cold, was presented at its best, and assured each guest a fair share of dinner. Today "Russian service" is the accepted manner of serving throughout the civilized world.

Now where does that leave the casserole? Regardless of French or Russian service, whether it's a step backward or forward, the casserole is here to stay, for it means one person in the kitchen, everything in one dish, and everything easily served all at once, except for the dessert which is prepared and served separately.

Yes, do consider the casserole. It can be your best friend and makes a very welcome gift from one house to another.

Easy Beef Stew with Beer and Walnuts

By any other method, this would be Belgian Carbonnade of Beef. We decided to capitalize on the thousands of dollars that go into food research and simplified the recipe by using convenience foods. In the doing, we simplified the name as well.

When we serve this Easy Beef Stew, Paul hollows out a small round loaf of French bread (if you wish, French rolls may be used for individual servings). He ladles in the meat, and layers it with vegetables (steamed separately), crowning the whole with piquant sauce and nuts. Sliced assorted fresh fruit deck the platter. (We refer to this way of serving as "garbaging up a plate" or, in French, "Garniture Garbage," an inelegant phrase but a step that is vital for the visual appeal needed in dining.) At any rate, this is a hearty stew, perfect for working people as it cooks in a slow cooker or low oven anywhere from eight to ten hours. Accompany with red wine or beer.

This recipe makes about 3 quarts of stew to serve six people. This amount is sufficient for two or three gifts of two servings each. The recipe may be doubled.

> 3½ pounds lean boneless beef (such as chuck or round)
> 1 tablespoon Kitchen Bouquet (brown gravy seasoning)
> 1 (12-ounce) can beer (see Note)
> 1 envelope Lipton onion soup mix
> 1 (¾-ounce) envelope brown gravy mix
> 1 teaspoon Worcestershire sauce
> 1 (10-ounce) can mushroom soup, undiluted
> 4 cups assorted frozen vegetables of your choice (carrots, onions, peas)
> 1 small round loaf of French bread per serving (optional)
> 4 ounces walnut halves or pieces, for garnish

Note: Beer is no stranger to the kitchen, and if fire could be considered a cook's best friend, then beer could be considered her oldest. Stone tablets from more than 7000 years before Christ have been discovered in Mesopotamia with a recipe for beer carved on them. Used as a substitute in recipes calling for water, wine, or milk, a good beer can add subtle new flavor to overly familiar foods.

Trim away all the fat from the beef and cut it into 1½-inch cubes. Place them in a 4-quart ovenproof pot or slow cooker and stir in the Kitchen Bouquet to coat each piece of meat thoroughly—this will tenderize and color the meat. Add the beer, onion soup mix, brown gravy mix, and Worcestershire and stir to blend. Cover the pot tightly and either leave it overnight (8 to 10 hours) in a 200° to 225° oven or cook it for 10 hours in a crockpot set on "low." Stir in the mushroom soup and frozen vegetables and let cook at the same temperature for 30 to 45 minutes longer, just until the vegetables are done.

The stew may be served in individual hollowed-out loaves of French bread. Top each serving with a sprinkling of walnuts.

TO PREPARE IN ADVANCE: After being transferred to containers, the stew may be covered and kept refrigerated for up to five days. If you wish to freeze the stew, do so before adding the mushroom soup and vegetables. The stew may be reheated either in a heavy saucepan over low heat or in a 350° oven for 20 to 30 minutes.

SPECIAL PACKAGING: Set a container of stew in a basket with individual rounds of French bread and walnuts for serving. The foil containers described on page 66, pottery casseroles, or tureens are especially suitable for the stew. A bottle of red wine would also be appropriate.

THE LABEL: Heat in a heavy saucepan over low heat or in a 350° oven for 20 to 30 minutes. Serve the stew hot in hollowed-out rounds of French bread and top each serving with walnut halves. May be stored in the refrigerator for up to five days. Do not freeze.

Yankee Noodle

We naturalized this casserole on the Fourth of July, the day we originated it. It is a lasagna-like dish that utilizes our basic American Style Tomato Meat Sauce, page 133. The sauce is quite agreeable with other pasta as well. If you fear children will not be completely enthralled with the inclusion of spinach, this dish will put the lie to that canard. It is smothered with sauce, pasta, cheese, and olives so that no one flavor predominates. Yankee Noodle has two other characteristics we look for in a casserole: It travels well and reheats perfectly.

This recipe fills three 1-quart casseroles to the brim, making three gifts of three to four servings each.

> 2 (10-ounce) packages frozen chopped spinach
> 1 pound pasta (macaroni spirals, bowknots, or shells)
> 3 large eggs
> 1 (4-ounce) can chopped black olives, drained
> 1 (2-ounce) can sliced mushrooms in broth
> ½ cup chopped parsley
> 1 cup fine dry bread crumbs
> ½ cup grated Parmesan cheese for the filling
> 1 teaspoon salt
> ¼ teaspoon ground cumin
> 10 cups American Style Tomato Meat Sauce, page 133
> ¼ cup Parmesan cheese for the topping

Preheat the oven to 350°. Cook the spinach according to package directions and drain. Cook the pasta according to package directions and drain. Beat the eggs in a large mixing bowl. Stir in the drained spinach, olives, mushrooms and their liquid, parsley, bread crumbs, Parmesan cheese, salt, and cumin. When blended, set aside.

In three 1-quart baking dishes, arrange alternate layers of half the pasta, half the spinach mixture, and half the meat sauce; repeat with remaining halves. Sprinkle grated Parmesan over the top of each casserole and cover with foil. Bake at 350° for 30 minutes until set. Let stand at least 10 minutes before serving.

TO PREPARE IN ADVANCE: This dish is at its best when made in advance and reheated. Let cool to room temperature, cover, and refrigerate overnight. Sprinkle lightly with water and reheat, covered, at 325° for about 30 minutes, just until it is hot clear through. It may be stored in the refrigerator for up to three days or frozen for up to three months. Thaw completely before reheating.

SPECIAL PACKAGING: Quart-size foil baking pans made especially for freezer storage are available at most markets. They come with cardboard lids on which may be written greetings and directions for reheating. When giving as a gift, overwrap in colored cellophane and tie with a ribbon.

THE LABEL: To serve, heat at 325° for 30 minutes or until hot. *If the casserole is freshly made and has not been frozen, the label should read:* May be stored in the refrigerator for up to three days or frozen for up to three months. *If the casserole is frozen, the label should read:* May be kept frozen for up to three months or in the refrigerator for up to three days after it has been thawed.

Pasta Package

Pastaholics! We've coined a new word describing ourselves. In spite of the caloric content, in spite of our interest in nutrition and healthy foods, in spite of knowing that *we are what we eat,* we must admit we adore pasta. This complete meal is mainly a matter of assembling a picnic basket chock full of everything needed to make a sumptuous repast for three or four. We tell ourselves when fixing it just for us, "How can it be bad? Look what it did for Sophia Loren!"

One recipe of American Style Tomato Meat Sauce with Mushrooms will make three gift baskets of three to four servings each.

> 1 quart American Style Tomato Meat Sauce with Mushrooms
>   (page 133)
> 12 ounces loose pasta (linguine, spaghetti, vermicelli),
>   tied with a ribbon around the center
> A 6-ounce wedge imported Parmesan cheese for grating
> Any good red wine
> A loaf of French bread
> A picnic-size, red-checkered tablecloth
> A picnic hamper or other basket

Assemble all the ingredients and pack them decoratively in the basket. Tuck in the directions for reheating the sauce and present to a lucky someone as a perfect busy-day supper.

Dodie's Divine Chili

Margaret (Dodie) Skibitzke is a dear friend who is famous in California for her Texas-style chili. This means it contains no onions, green peppers, or other vege-tables, though she does fudge a bit by adding V-8 juice. No matter. It's a great dish for a crowd and simple to make in either a slow cooker or oven. Beans thicken the chili at the end of the cooking time, so if you omit them (a free hand is best with chili; anything goes, in or out), thicken it with a bit of flour or cornstarch. Cornstarch is best (dissolve in cold water before adding), as it won't impart the raw taste that flour often does.

This recipe makes 12 cups of chili without beans or 14 cups with beans, enough to fill three 1-quart containers of four 1-cup servings and leave a bit for you.

> 4 pounds coarsely ground lean beef
> 4 large cloves garlic, pressed
> ½ cup all-purpose flour
> 1 tablespoon ground cumin (comino)
> 4 to 5 tablespoons chili powder, depending how "hot" you like
>   your chili
> 2 teaspoons salt
> ½ teaspoon ground black pepper
> 1 (46-ounce) can V-8 vegetable cocktail
> 2 teaspoons Worcestershire sauce
> 2 (15-ounce) cans small red beans, drained (optional)
> Grated sharp cheddar cheese, for garnish
> Minced onion, for garnish

Fry the ground beef with the garlic over direct heat until the meat loses its red color and is evenly crumbly. Add the flour and chili powder and stir to blend in the flour; then stir in all remaining ingredients except the beans. Bring the mixture to a boil on top of the stove.

The chili may be cooked in either a slow cooker or a 4-quart (or larger) ovenproof pot. If it is cooked in a slow cooker (crock pot), cook covered on "high" for 2 hours, then reduce heat to "low" for from 6 to 10 hours. If you don't have a crock pot, bake the chili, covered tightly with a lid or aluminum foil, for 6 to 10 hours at 200°.

Spoon excess fat off the surface. If you want chili with beans, drain them and add them to the meat mixture, crushing some of them with the back of a spoon to thicken the chili. Cook, at the same temperature, uncovered, for 2 more hours.

For the very best flavor, let the chili cool completely and reheat before serving.

Serve garnished with grated cheese and onion.

TO PREPARE IN ADVANCE: Chili is at its best made ahead and reheated. Spoon hot chili into refrigerator containers. Let cool completely, then cover. May be refrigerated for up to five days or frozen for up to three months. The chili should be thawed completely, if frozen, and heated slowly to prevent scorching.

SPECIAL PACKAGING: The foil pans described on page 66 are handy gift containers because directions for reheating may be written on their lids. Enclose a wedge of cheddar cheese and an onion for the garnish.

THE LABEL: Heat the chili in a heavy saucepan over low heat or in a 350° oven until hot. Garnish each serving with grated cheese and minced onion. *If the chili is freshly made, the label should read:* May be stored in the refrigerator for up to five days or frozen for up to three months. *If the chili is frozen, the label should read:* May be kept frozen for up to three months or in the refrigerator for up to five days after it has been thawed.

Chili con Carne von Welanetz

To the proliferation of chili recipes already existing, more appear during the Annual Chili Contests held in our country. People combine every conceivable ingredient to create the ultimate chili. A worthy ambition. We, too, have given it our all, as you can see. Our recipe contains everything but the proverbial sink and is served with dollops of sour cream, instead of cheese and onions. It makes a dandy dish to have on hand in the freezer for trouble-free entertaining and gift-giving.

The recipe makes about 4 quarts of chili, enough for four 1-quart gifts of four small servings each.

1 pound well-seasoned pork sausage
2 large onions, chopped
2 large cloves garlic, pressed
1/3 cup minced shallots
4 pounds coarsely ground lean beef
½ cup flour
½ cup chili powder
3 (1-pound, 14-ounce) cans whole tomatoes
1 (12-ounce) bottle Heinz chili sauce
1 (1-pound) can pork and beans
1 (7-ounce) can diced green chiles
1 (9-ounce) can chopped black olives
1 green bell pepper, chopped
1 red bell pepper, chopped
1 cup chopped celery
½ cup minced parsley
1 tablespoon salt
1 teaspoon Lawry's garlic salt
1 tablespoon leaf oregano, crumbled
1½ teaspoons ground cumin
1 teaspoon Spice Islands dried cilantro or 1 tablespoon chopped fresh cilantro
½ teaspoon ground black pepper, or more (to taste)
1 tablespoon Worcestershire sauce
1 (1-pound) can pinto beans, drained and rinsed
Sour cream, for garnish

In a large, heavy 8-quart pot saute the sausage meat over medium heat until it is crumbly. Stir in the onions and garlic and saute until the onions are transparent. Stir in the shallots and cook, stirring, a minute or so longer. Add the ground beef and let cook, breaking up the meat with a wooden spoon until no pink remains and the meat is crumbly.

Remove the pan from the heat. Sprinkle the flour and chili powder evenly over the mixture and stir to blend. Return the pan to the heat. Add the rest of the ingredients, except the beans. Bring the mixture to a boil, then reduce the heat to low and simmer, uncovered, for 3 hours, stirring frequently. Stir in drained beans, crushing some with the back of a spoon to thicken the chili. Continue simmering slowly until you reach the desired thickness. Taste and correct seasoning. Transfer to containers, cool, and refrigerate.

Serve hot, topped with sour cream.

TO PREPARE IN ADVANCE: The flavor of chili is enhanced if it is made a day ahead, chilled, then reheated at serving time. It keeps well for up to five days in the refrigerator or may be frozen for up to three months. To serve, thaw, if frozen, and heat slowly in a heavy saucepan over low heat.

SPECIAL PACKAGING: See Dodie's Divine Chili, page 67. Include a container of sour cream as part of the gift.

THE LABEL: Heat slowly in a heavy saucepan. Garnish each serving with a dollop of sour cream. *If the chili is freshly made, the label should read:* May be stored up to five days in the refrigerator or frozen for up to three months. *If the chili is frozen, the label should read:* May be kept frozen up to three months or in the refrigerator for up to five days after it has been thawed.

Ratatouille Niçoise

At the opposite end of the scale from the first recipe in this section lies Ratatouille Nicoise. If Easy Beef Stew falls under the title of plain good eating, this one must surely fall into the "gourmet" (hate that word!) classification because our method of preparing it is revolutionary. Item: The vegetables are steamed. Item: Wine is used. Item: Liquid and vegetables are combined only during the last few minutes of cooking. The end result is a Ratatouille as it is supposed to look and taste, with each vegetable retaining its own texture and individuality.

This recipe makes 2 quarts or six generous servings of vegetable stew, enough for two to four gifts. The recipe may be doubled.

2 tablespoons olive oil
1 medium onion, finely chopped
2 cloves garlic, minced or pressed
½ teaspoon dried thyme
1 bay leaf
2 (1-pound, 14-ounce) cans whole tomatoes, with their liquid
Salt, black pepper, and cayenne (ground red pepper), to taste
6 zucchini, cut crosswise in ½-inch slices
3 red bell peppers, seeded and cut in 1½-by-½-inch strips
2 green bell peppers, seeded and cut in 1½-by-½-inch strips
2 medium eggplants
1¼ cups dry white wine
2 to 3 tablespoons minced parsley, for garnish
6 lemon wedges from 1 large lemon, for garnish, if the Ratatouille is to be served cold

Heat the olive oil in a large stockpot or stewpot that is large enough, with the lid on, to hold a colander. Saute the onion, garlic, thyme, and bay leaf over medium heat until the onions are transparent. Drain the juice from the tomatoes and add it to the pot. Chop the tomatoes finely and add them, a bit of salt and pepper, and a dash of cayenne. Remove the pot from the heat.

Set a colander inside the pot and in it place the sliced zucchini and the red and green pepper strips. Dice the eggplant in ¾-inch cubes, leaving the skin on, and add it to the colander. Pour the wine over the vegetables, cover the pot, and bring to a boil over medium heat. Steam the vegetables for 45 minutes, then empty the contents of the colander into the other pot ingredients and let simmer together, uncovered, for about 5 minutes, until the mixture thickens slightly. Stir gently once or twice during this period, taking care not to crush the cubes of eggplant. Taste and correct the seasoning. Remove the bay leaf.

For best flavor, let cool completely and refrigerate. To serve, either reheat the Ratatouille gently in a heavy saucepan over low heat or simply serve cold accompanied by wedges of lemon for seasoning. Garnish with chopped parsley.

TO PREPARE IN ADVANCE: This should be made at least one day in advance. It may be stored up to five days in the refrigerator but does not freeze well.

SPECIAL PACKAGING: Earthenware, *terrines,* souffle dishes, oval baking dishes, and many other containers are appropriate. Include a lemon as part of the gift. Slip in a bottle of chilled white wine as well—might as well do it up right!

THE LABEL: Serve hot or cold, garnished with chopped parsley. If serving cold, supply lemon wedges for seasoning. If serving hot, heat in a heavy saucepan over low heat just until hot. May be stored in the refrigerator for up to five days. Do not freeze.

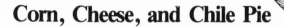

Corn, Cheese, and Chile Pie

In Mexico nothing livens things up more than a mariachi band in the plaza and chile peppers in the kitchen. The Mexicans know this well, as we discovered on a lengthy stay in the lovely, colonial mountain town of San Miguel de Allende. Soon after our arrival, we joined forces with local inhabitants in a series of cooking classes to benefit the local orphanage. It was here that we were first introduced to *pastel de elote,* as this pie is known in Mexico. Our hostess, Dorita Joffroy, served it with steak, salad, and sliced tomatoes. We have simplified it into a one-mixing-bowl, one-baking-dish procedure, find that it's good either hot or cold, and serve it as a main course or vegetable dish. An extremely accommodating casserole.

The recipe makes one pie to serve six as an entree or eight as a vegetable dish. It is baked in a deep 9½-inch pie or quiche dish. The recipe may be doubled or tripled, in which case several pies are baked at the same time.

> 2 teaspoons shortening to grease the baking dish
> 3 large eggs
> 1 (8½-ounce) can creamed corn
> 1 (10-ounce) package frozen corn, thawed and drained, or
>   1 (8-ounce) can corn kernels, drained
> 1 stick (¼ pound) butter or margarine, melted
> ½ cup yellow cornmeal
> 1 cup dairy sour cream
> 4 ounces Monterey Jack cheese, cut in ½-inch cubes
> 4 ounces sharp cheddar cheese, cut in ½-inch cubes
> 1 (4-ounce) can diced green chiles (see Note)
> ½ teaspoon salt
> ¼ teaspoon Worcestershire sauce

Note: Canned chiles vary in flavor, so taste them before adding them to a recipe. If they are mild, season the mixture with a dash or two of cayenne (ground red pepper). If they are very flavorful, treat them as described on page 73, or use less than the specified amount (unless, of course, you love hot dishes).

Preheat the oven to 350°. Grease the baking dish with the shortening. Beat eggs in a large mixing bowl. Add all remaining ingredients and stir until thoroughly blended. Pour the mixture into the baking dish and bake on the center rack of the oven at 350° for 1 hour or until the pie is firm when pressed in the center. If several pies are baked at once, baking time will be longer. Let stand 10 minutes before cutting. Serve warm or at room temperature.

TO PREPARE IN ADVANCE: Cool. May be kept in refrigerator for up to three days or frozen, wrapped in foil, for up to three months. To serve, thaw, if frozen, and heat at 350° for about 20 minutes or until hot. Freezing doesn't harm this pie one bit!

SPECIAL PACKAGING: The dish in which the pie was baked should be part of the gift. Wrap the pie in foil and overwrap in clear or colored cellophane for giving.

THE LABEL: Serve as a main course or vegetable dish. Serves six as an entree, eight as a side dish. To serve, heat at 350° for 20 minutes. *If the pie has not been frozen, the label should read:* May be stored in the refrigerator for up to three days or frozen for up to three months. *If the pie is frozen, the label should read:* May be kept frozen for up to three months or in the refrigerator for up to three days after it has been thawed.

Mexicana Casser-olé

Here is a crustless Mexican-style meat and cheese pie that is perfect for the main course of a brunch. When baked in a 10-inch pie plate it will generously serve six, and the recipe can be doubled easily for a larger south-of-the-border fiesta. Accompany it with assorted fresh fruit and, to drink, equal parts of champagne and freshly squeezed orange juice...a simple but delicious menu for entertaining.

Some words of caution about chiles to the uninitiated. Canned "mild" dark green chiles may not always be as mild as you expect, so we suggest that you taste them before using in a recipe. And, as a precaution, have a glass of milk handy. If the chile threatens to blow off the top of your head, a sip of milk brings quick relief. If the chiles are too fiery for your taste, you can reduce some, or all, of the hotness by stripping out all of the seeds and veins, then soaking in cold water to which a bit of salt and vinegar have been added. This step is almost never necessary if you use our favorite Ortega brand chiles. Be sure to wash your hands with soap after handling any kind of chile. It can be mighty uncomfortable if it gets in your eyes. In that case, milk won't help.

This recipe makes a 10-inch pie of six servings. The recipe may be doubled to make two 10-inch pies or one large pie baked in a 9-by-13-inch pan to serve twelve.

> 1 teaspoon butter or margarine to grease the baking pan
> ½ pound pork sausage
> ½ pound lean ground beef
> 1 large onion, finely chopped
> 1 large clove garlic, pressed
> 1 (4-ounce) can mild green chiles (Ortega), rinsed and seeded
> 9 ounces sharp cheddar cheese, shredded
> 4 large eggs
> ¼ cup all-purpose flour
> 1½ cups milk
> Scant teaspoon salt
> ⅛ to ¼ teaspoon Tabasco sauce, to taste

To Garnish (optional)
2 teaspoons fresh or dried chopped parsley

Preheat the oven to 350°. Grease the baking dish with the butter or margarine.

Break up the sausage and ground beef in a medium skillet and fry over medium heat until cooked and crumbly. Drain off the fat. Stir in the onion and garlic and continue cooking until the onion is transparent. Set aside.

In order, layer the following ingredients in the greased baking dish, spreading each layer evenly: half the chiles, about 1½ cups of the shredded cheese, all of the meat mixture and the remaining chiles.

In a small mixing bowl, beat the eggs and flour together until smooth. Blend in the milk, salt, Tabasco, and pour over the layers in the baking dish. Top with the remaining cheese.

Bake in the center of a 350° oven for 40 to 45 minutes or until a knife inserted in the center comes out clean. Let the pie stand at room temperature for at least 5 minutes before cutting. Sprinkle with chopped parsley and serve warm.

TO PREPARE IN ADVANCE: Let cool to room temperature, then refrigerate for up to three days. Do not freeze. Reheat at 350° for about 20 minutes or until warm through.

SPECIAL PACKAGING: A Pyrex baking dish, along with a wicker or straw holder, available in hardware and department stores, might be part of the gift.

THE LABEL: Six servings. Refrigerate for up to three days. Reheat at 350° for about 20 minutes until warm through.

Vegetables & Accompaniments

"Pease porridge hot, pease porridge cold." The nursery rhymes of Mother Goose have always seemed slightly gruesome to us. This little rhyme is an example. It had its basis in the English famine of 1555 when peasants managed to survive by finally resorting to a hitherto disregarded vegetable which grew wild all over their country. The British, always resistant to new foods, would only submit to this change because it was clearly crisis time, one in which they finally came to appreciate even "pease porridge in a pot nine days old."

We're not chiding the English for this reluctance. All of us in the Western world feel the same with the unfamiliar, to the point, in fact, where we refuse even to sample new food placed before us, regardless of how nutritious it may be. (Did you know, for example, that one cup of peas provides more than half the minimum daily allowance of Vitamin C, half the thiamin, a third of the iron, and a sixth of Vitamin A?) Although dried peas were a common cultivated daily staple in the times of the Roman Empire, they, along with so many other vegetables, vanished during the Dark Ages. Even with their rediscovery in 1555, they remained a novelty until the sixteenth century when green sweet peas (Chinese) captured the fancy of the court.

If you think it was difficult to sell peas, consider the history of tomatoes and potatoes. These two were unknown in Europe until the Spanish brought them back from the Americas. In Spain, they were immediately looked upon with horror. Even here in our Northeastern states, the tomato was shunned until the mid-nineteenth century because it was considered poisonous. There was even one man—or so the story goes—a Mr. Johnson, who on the steps of the Newark, New Jersey, City Hall, attempted to commit suicide by eating a tomato. The crowd ultimately dispersed when he failed to die, and he finally wandered home for dinner.

It took over three centuries for the potato to be accepted and then only out of desperation by a famished Irish population. To their eventual delight, they discovered that with a little over an acre of planted potatoes, they could feed a family of four for a whole year.

Although there are over 250,000 botanical species of plants, only about 300 are grown commercially. The average American restricts his diet to about nineteen, and out of all of these, carrots, peas, tomatoes, and potatoes have the widest acceptance. It would be wise for all of us to experiment with new vegetable dishes now and then, if only to break the monotony of the peas and carrots routine. There are very few varieties of meat as compared to the close to fifty vegetables and fruits in most markets, which are resupplied daily and change every season. They can revolutionize your dinner plates with their shapes, colors, textures, combinations, helping you and your family to indeed "eat with your eyes," to say nothing of the incredible nutritional value they supply. And, best of all, they're usually the best buy in the market.

We would never want to become just vegetarians. The whole world is just too full of good things to try, but do enlarge your vegetable horizons by trying the following, and many other, vegetable accompaniments.

Spanakopita

Did Popeye ever travel to Greece? If so, he must have flipped over Spanakopita, a spinach and cheese pie! The dish consists of dark green, leafy spinach combined with tangy, sharp feta cheese and dill, folded into many buttery leaves of filo dough, the same pastry used to make Dina's Rolled Baklava, page 165. Just because it's hard to pronounce needn't disqualify this marvelous, reheatable vegetable dish from your dining table. It's Greek to the rest of us too.

This recipe makes two 9-inch pies, each serving eight to ten, making two very generous gifts.

For the Pastry
1 pound filo (phyllo) or strudel pastry (see Note 1)
1½ sticks (¾ cup) butter or margarine, melted

For the Filling
4 (10-ounce) packages frozen chopped spinach, thawed
½ stick (4 tablespoons) butter or margarine
2 large onions, finely chopped
2 medium leeks, cleaned and cut into ¼-inch slices (see Note 2)
1 pound Greek or Danish feta cheese, crumbled
12 ounces ricotta cheese
2 bunches green onions, sliced
2/3 cup minced parsley
2 teaspoons dried dill weed
½ teaspoon ground nutmeg
1 teaspoon salt
½ teaspoon freshly ground black pepper
6 large eggs, lightly beaten

Note 1: Filo is leaves of very thin pastry used in Greek cooking. It is available at all Greek and most Italian delicatessens. The whole package should be used at once because the dough dries out quickly once it is unwrapped.

Note 2: See note for cleaning leeks, page 57.

Preheat the oven to 300°. Remove the filo from the refrigerator and allow to come to room temperature. Leave it enclosed in the plastic bag in which it is sealed until you are ready to use it. Melt the butter or margarine and set aside.

To make the filling, place the thawed spinach in a kitchen strainer. Using the back of a spoon, press out as much water from the spinach as possible. Set aside.

Melt the ½ stick butter or margarine in a large skillet over medium heat and saute the onion and leek until transparent. Stir in the drained spinach and cook, stirring often, over low heat until all the moisture has evaporated. Remove the pan from the heat.

Stir in all the remaining ingredients except the eggs. Let cool a minute or two, then stir in the eggs. Set aside.

Open the package of filo and place it on a flat surface. Cover it completely with a sheet of plastic or wide strip of foil and cover with a kitchen towel that has been soaked in cold water and thoroughly wrung out. Do not let the wet towel touch the filo itself. The weight of the towel will keep the filo from drying out while you work. (Another method is to cut open a plastic wastebasket liner so that it lies flat, then place the filo on one end of the liner and fold the other end over the top of the filo and cover with the wet towel.)

Set out two 9-inch pie pans and brush each with melted butter. Remove one sheet of filo at a time and lay it on a flat work surface. Brush quickly with butter, using a wide pastry brush, and place in the pie pan, letting the edges hang over the edge of the pan so that the filo leaves can later be folded on top of the pie. Continue layering and buttering the filo until almost half the filo is used.

Fill the lined pan with half the spinach filling. Top with two or three more layers of filo, buttering in between and bunching them up in the center. Fold in the overhanging edges of the filo leaves. Before baking, cut the pie into 8 to 10 wedges and set aside while you repeat the same process with the remaining filo and spinach filling in the second pie pan.

When both pies have been assembled, place them on a baking sheet and bake at 300° for 40 to 45 minutes until the pies feel firm in the center. Let cool at least 10 minutes before serving.

Serve warm as a vegetable accompaniment with roast meat or poultry or as a main course for luncheon or supper.

TO PREPARE IN ADVANCE: Let cool to room temperature. The pies may be stored in the refrigerator for up to three days or frozen right in their baking dishes for up to three months. To serve, thaw, if frozen, and heat at 300° for about 20 minutes until warm through.

SPECIAL PACKAGING: The baking dish should be part of the gift. Wrap in cellophane and tie with a huge bow.

THE LABEL: Serve as a vegetable accompaniment or as a main course for luncheon or supper. Heat at 300° for about 20 minutes or until warm through. *If the pie has not been frozen, the label should read:* May be stored in the refrigerator for up to three days or frozen up to three months. *If the pie is frozen, the label should read:* May be kept frozen for up to three months or in the refrigerator for up to three days after it has been thawed.

Holiday Spinach Casserole

Isn't stuffing just for holidays, turkeys, and pork chops? We found out otherwise when Suzanne Kroener brought this dish in to share at a holiday menu class. It makes a simple but imaginative vegetable accompaniment. And despite the word "holiday" in the name, it may be served any time since stuffing mix is available all year round. We just included the word because we were first introduced to this casserole during a holiday. It does so well with any simple meat or poultry dish that it manages to turn the simple into the festive.

This recipe makes two gift casseroles, each serving six people. The recipe may be doubled.

> 4 (10-ounce) packages frozen chopped spinach
> 2 cups dairy sour cream
> 1 envelope Lipton's onion soup mix
> 2 sticks (½ pound) butter or margarine
> 3 cups Mrs. Cubbison's herb stuffing mix (don't substitute!)

Preheat oven to 325°. Cook spinach according to package directions until barely tender. Drain thoroughly in a kitchen strainer, pressing out all excess water with the back of a spoon. Combine the drained spinach with the sour cream and onion soup mix in the cooking pan.

Melt the butter or margarine in a medium-size saucepan. Remove from the heat and stir in the stuffing mix. Spread half the stuffing mixture over the bottoms of two shallow 1½-quart baking dishes or one 3-quart dish. Spread the spinach mixture evenly over the crumbs. Top with the remaining crumbs. Bake at 325° 30 to 35 minutes.

TO PREPARE IN ADVANCE: This may be assembled the day before, refrigerated, then baked just before serving. It may also be reheated in a 325° oven for about 20 minutes or until hot. Do not freeze.

SPECIAL PACKAGING: Square or round 8- or 9-inch ovenproof glass cake dishes are right for this. A large glass dish measuring 13 by 9 by 2 inches is right if making the full recipe to serve 12. Other shallow 1½-quart ovenproof dishes or foil containers may be substituted.

THE LABEL: *If giving the casserole unbaked, the label should read:* Bake at 325° for 30 to 35 minutes within 24 hours. May then be stored in refrigerator for up to three days. Heat at 325° for 20 minutes. Do not freeze. *If giving the casserole already baked, the label should read:* May be stored in the refrigerator up to three days. Heat at 325° for 20 minutes before serving. Do not freeze.

Posh Squash

Here is a recipe we found deep in the heart of Dixie at Aunt Fanny's Cabin, a restaurant that was at one time the slave quarters for an enormous plantation. The building has withstood not only time, but also Sherman's fiery march through Georgia. We were prepared for the good Southern meal of fried chicken, Smithfield ham, and squash, but not prepared for the waiters and waitresses dashing off to the old rickety piano and belting out spirituals. It seems there really was an Aunt Fanny Williams who cooked there during the years of slavery. She lived to be a hundred. We like to think her eating Posh Squash helped. This is our version of that dish. It captures the freshness of summer's generous bounty of luscious, yellow squash, grown plump in fields where they soaked up the summer sun and sweet fresh rain.

This recipe will fill four 1-quart gift containers of six servings each.

9 pounds yellow summer squash (crookneck)
1½ sticks (¾ cup) butter or margarine, melted
2 large onions, chopped finely
2 cups cracker meal or fresh toasted bread crumbs
1½ teaspoons ground black pepper
6 eggs, lightly beaten
3 tablespoons sugar
1 tablespoon salt

For the Topping
1½ sticks (¾ cup) butter or margarine, melted
½ cup cracker meal or fresh toasted bread crumbs

Preheat oven to 375°. Wash, but do not peel, the squash, trim the ends, and cut it into 1-inch pieces. Place it in an 8-quart pot and cover with cold water. Bring to a boil and simmer until the squash is tender when pierced with a fork (about 10 to 15 minutes). Drain thoroughly and mash with a potato masher. Add all remaining ingredients to the pot and mix well. Divide the mixture evenly between four 1-quart ovenproof containers.

For the topping, drizzle ¾ cup melted butter or margarine evenly over the tops of the squash casseroles, followed by a sprinkling of bread crumbs or cracker meal. Bake at 375° for 50 to 60 minutes, until puffed and browned on top.

TO PREPARE IN ADVANCE: After baking, let cool to room temperature, then chill. Cover after it is cold. May be stored in the refrigerator for up to three days or frozen for up to three months. Thaw, if frozen, and heat, uncovered, at 350° for 20 to 30 minutes.

SPECIAL PACKAGING: One-quart foil containers with cardboard lids, available at most supermarkets, are quite attractive when wrapped in cellophane. Greetings and directions may be written on the lid and the squash may be reheated right in the container. A thoughtful, though more expensive, container, would be a 4- to 6-cup souffle dish or oval baking dish.

THE LABEL: To serve, heat at 350° for 20 to 30 minutes. *If the squash has not been frozen, the label should read:* May be stored in the refrigerator for up to three days or frozen for up to three months. *If the squash is frozen, the label should read:* May be kept frozen for up to three months or in the refrigerator for up to three days after it has been thawed.

Spaghetti Squash with Cheesy Herb Butter

The rich tradition of Italian cuisine has lacked one thing, and this is it: Spaghetti Squash, a brand new vegetable on the market. Available now only in the fall for a month or two, it is sure to soar in popularity because when it is baked and cut lengthwise, the entire flesh comes out in spaghetti-like strands (honest!). The strands, which look like they were just pressed out of a pasta machine, may be seasoned with almost any sauce, such as our simple butter sauce with garlic and herbs. This wacky but wonderful vegetable is fun to share with friends. Just write a greeting directly on the squash with a marking pen. (It's not recommended for mailing—we have yet to find a stamp that will adhere.)

This recipe makes sauce for a 4-pound spaghetti squash (serving six people), which the recipient will cook himself.

Cheesy Herb Butter
1 stick (¼ pound) butter or margarine at room temperature
¼ cup minced parsley
½ teaspoon Spice Islands Italian herb seasoning
¼ teaspoon garlic salt
¼ teaspoon freshly ground black pepper
1/3 cup grated Parmesan cheese

For Serving
A 4-pound spaghetti squash

Blend together the ingredients for Cheesy Herb Butter and pack into an 8-ounce container. Keep chilled until the squash is to be cooked. At that time allow the butter mixture to come to room temperature.

The squash must be baked just before serving. Preheat oven to 350°. Prick the squash with a fork in about a dozen places and place it on a baking sheet. Bake, whole, at 350° for 45 minutes on one side, then turn it over and bake for another 45 minutes, or until it yields when pressed. Cut the squash in half lengthwise; remove and discard any seeds. Pull out the spaghetti-like strands with two forks and, in a large bowl, toss with the Cheesy Herb Butter until the strands and the sauce are thoroughly combined. Serve immediately.

TO PREPARE IN ADVANCE: The Cheesy Herb Butter may be refrigerated for up to a week or frozen for up to three months. Remove it from the freezer or refrigerator when the squash goes into the oven. The squash must be cooked just before serving.

SPECIAL PACKAGING: The squash itself is the package. Use a marking pen to write a greeting on the outside of the squash and tie the whole thing up with a ribbon. Enclose precise directions for baking. Accompany with a container of Cheesy Herb Butter.

THE LABEL: *See directions for baking the squash in the recipe and include them in detail with your package. Also add:* Squash may be kept for a month in a cool place before using. The Cheesy Herb Butter may be stored in the refrigerator for up to a week or frozen for up to three months. Allow it to come to room temperature before adding it to the squash.

 # Vegie Squares

This is such a current, contemporary, mod dish. Perfect for your friendly neighborhood vegetarian. Or as a snack on your way to the gym. Even your Yoga instructor would approve. What else can we say? Only that it's a super vegetable dish, snack, or an hors d'oeuvre, satisfying, easy to whip out of freezer and into your microwave oven for quick thawing. Out with the heavy, caloric stuff and in with Vegie Squares, stage right, center, bow!

This recipe makes from thirty-six to forty-nine squares depending on how large you cut them. The baking dish and one recipe will make one gift or cut the squares and wrap in foil packets for six or seven small gifts.

> Butter or margarine to grease the baking pan
> 2 bunches scallions (green onions), finely sliced
> ¼ stick (2 tablespoons) butter or margarine
> 1 (10-ounce) package frozen chopped spinach, thawed, thoroughly
>   drained, and minced
> ¼ cup minced parsley
> ½ teaspoon salt
> ⅛ teaspoon ground black pepper
> 6 large eggs
> ¼ cup dairy sour cream
> ½ cup soft bread crumbs (see Note)
> 3 ounces (about ¾ cup) natural Swiss cheese, grated
> ¾ cup grated Parmesan cheese
> Paprika

Note: The easiest way to make soft bread crumbs is to put 1-inch pieces of fresh bread, a small handful at a time, into an electric blender or food processor. Turn the motor on and presto, instant bread crumbs. In fact, if you have a Cuisinart food processor, use it for all the processes involved here—slicing scallions, mincing spinach and parsley, making bread crumbs, and grating cheese.

Preheat the oven to 350°. Grease a 9-inch square baking pan with butter or margarine.

In a large heavy skillet, saute the scallions in the butter or margarine until they are limp. Add the spinach and cook for 1 minute longer. Remove from the heat and stir in the parsley, salt, and pepper.

In a medium mixing bowl, beat the eggs until well combined, then stir in the sour cream, bread crumbs, Swiss cheese, and ½ cup of the Parmesan cheese. When well blended, stir in the spinach-onion mixture and pour into the prepared pan. Smooth the top with a rubber spatula and sprinkle evenly with the remaining ¼ cup Parmesan and a sprinkling of paprika for color. Bake at 350° for 20 minutes or until a knife inserted in the center comes out clean. Let cool slightly, then cut into squares and serve warm as a vegetable, an hors d'oeuvre, or accompaniment to soups.

TO PREPARE IN ADVANCE: When cool, store the squares in the baking pan or package six to eight squares in foil. May be stored in the refrigerator for up to four days or frozen for up to four months. Thaw, if frozen, and heat at 325° for 5 to 10 minutes until warm.

SPECIAL PACKAGING: A square 8- or 9-inch Pyrex baking dish is ideal for baking these, though any dishes of a similar size may be substituted. The dish might be included as part of the gift. We often give these in small foil packets with directions for reheating written on with the special pen described on page 41.

THE LABEL: Serve as an hors d'oeuvre, vegetable, or accompaniment to soup. Heat at 325° for 5 to 10 minutes until warm. *If the squares are freshly baked, the label should read:* May be stored in the refrigerator for up to four days or frozen for up to four months. *If the squares are frozen, the label should read:* May be kept frozen for up to four months or in the refrigerator for up to four days after they have been thawed.

 # The World's Best Baked Beans

Although we respect the culinary arts, you may have noticed that we're not purists, locked into the rules of the game. After all, it's only the joy of cooking that counts, and the end result. And so we come, as we must, to The World's Best Baked Beans, a modest claim, for these are not ordinary baked beans, nor are they particularly economical, but they are exceedingly good.

The addition of bourbon and coffee is what provides the indefinable something different, a trick we learned from a student of ours who frequently sprang out of his seat to teach us his own recipes. One day he brought some Vermont baked beans to class, and they were marvelous, though the students were dismayed to find included among his long list of ingredients fresh pigs' and calves' feet! Working along the lines of his basic recipe, we made a few necessary substitutions and evolved this simple recipe. Serve with salad and French bread, or give away in a beanpot.

This recipe makes about 3 quarts of baked beans, enough to fill three 1-quart containers of four to six servings each or six 1-pint containers of two to three servings each.

½ pound bacon, fried crisp and crumbled
½ pound pork sausage, cooked and drained
2 tablespoons bacon fat
2 (3-pound, 7-ounce) cans B&M baked beans
6 ounces sharp cheddar cheese, grated
2/3 cup chili sauce
1/3 cup bourbon
1 medium onion, minced
1 tablespoon Poupon Dijon mustard
1 tablespoon Worcestershire sauce
2 teaspoons instant coffee
1 small clove garlic, pressed

Preheat oven to 350°. Fry the bacon until it is crisp and reserve the fat. Cook and drain the pork sausage. Crumble the bacon and combine it, the sausage, and 2 tablespoons of the bacon fat with all remaining ingredients in a 4-quart ovenproof casserole or beanpot. Bake uncovered at 350° for about 1½ hours, stirring every 30 minutes.

TO PREPARE IN ADVANCE: Transfer to storage containers and cool. May be stored in the refrigerator for up to a week or frozen for up to four months. Thaw, if frozen, and heat at 350° in an ovenproof container, stirring often, for 30 to 40 minutes (depending on the amount) until hot through. Add water or broth if the beans become dry.

SPECIAL PACKAGING: A beanpot would be a delightful gift container. Souffle dishes or other ovenproof serving dishes are equally suitable.

THE LABEL: Heat at 350°, stirring often, until hot through. Add water or broth if beans become dry. *If the beans are not frozen, the label should read:* May be stored in the refrigerator for up to a week or frozen for up to four months. *If the beans are frozen, the label should read:* May be kept frozen for up to four months or in the refrigerator for up to a week after they have been thawed.

Breads & Muffins

"Open thine eyes and thou shalt be satisfied with bread" (Proverbs 20:13). The process of baking bread has not changed very much in 5000 years. We know the ancients baked bread because loaves have been found well preserved in Egyptian tombs and in the ashes of Pompeii. Bread can truly be considered the staff of life, and in 3000 B.C. in Egypt, four loaves of bread and a few jugs of beer were happily accepted in return for a hard day's work.

If you consider the delicate, fluffy white loaves of bread found on our market shelves today as a modern invention, it's not so! They were enjoyed 2000 years ago in Athens, where the populace not only enjoyed a variety of shapes, but baking artisans prepared floral designs, flavored them, dusted them with poppy seeds, and sometimes mixed in nuts.

After the fall of the Roman Empire, about all a man could do each day was feed his family. In the Dark Ages there were no more Roman plates or handsomely designed silver utensils. Eating became a matter of hand to mouth, or rather from hand to trencher to mouth, a trencher being a slice of stale bread used to catch and absorb the juices of whatever was served on it. Depending upon your status or your hunger, you could either give this trencher to the poor or eat it at the end of your meal. "Breaking bread" was a literal fact of life.

After the French Revolution, the common man wanted his bread to be as white as that of the rich. And bakers quickly found the way, by adding unwholesome additives and bleaching grain to a point where it was almost rendered poisonous. The reason early bread was not white was that in milling the flour by stonemills, the germ of the grain was crushed at the same time as the endosperm. It was the oil from the germ that gave flour its characteristic yellow color.

In the middle 1800s Hungarians developed a method of rolling flour with iron rollers. This method allowed the germ to remain uncrushed and, when sifted, it was swept off with the bran. Consequently, flour was not only whiter than before, but it could also be stored for a longer period of time. This pleased everyone, including the consumer, and rolling became standard practice. However, the discarded germ was a source of highly nutritious substances which were lost and which our commercial baking industry today adds artificially.

Grain is the principal food of both men and animals. Half of the world's daily intake of calories is supplied by it. Bread has been made from every conceivable vegetable and grain, but primarily from wheat, rice, oats, corn, barley, and rye. These six grains alone occupy over half of all the land under cultivation. The reason that the potato took three centuries to become accepted was that it made very poor bread.

If you find additives abhorrent, put on your apron, roll up your sleeves, bury your hands deep in warm, living yeast dough, and prepare yourself for one of life's great pleasures. It's time to start "leaven" it up!

Frances Pelham's Plum-Crazy Bread

If you don't particularly relish the idea of facing purple bread for breakfast, be assured that Plum-Crazy Bread is not purple. The plums, true, are, but in the baking they turn the loaf into a rich brown color. You need to be forewarned though. Its preparation provides a measure of excitement as there's an unexpected foaming and gurgling at the time you stir the baking soda into the plums and melted butter. And then it turns a terrible gray brown. The first time we made it, we thought we had blown it somewhere along the way because the reaction was very much like what happens in our sink when we pour in the drain opener. The color and foaming are only temporary, however, simply a part of the interesting chemistry of this particular formula.

Frances Pelham, our dear friend who cooks up her own kitchen storms in Palm Springs, California, is open and generous about sharing her recipes, as are all accomplished cooks. This is one of hers. It knows no season (because the plums come in a can) and is especially delicious served warm, accompanied with a crock of whipped cream cheese for spreading.

This recipe makes a 9-by-5-inch loaf. It may be doubled, in which case the bread may be baked in either two 9-by-5-inch pans or three 8-by-4-inch pans.

1 (1-pound, 13-ounce) or 2 (1-pound) cans purple plums, drained
1 stick (¼ pound) butter or margarine
2 teaspoons baking soda
Shortening and flour for the pans
2 cups sifted all-purpose flour
1 cup sugar
½ teaspoon salt
½ teaspoon ground cinnamon
½ teaspoon ground cloves
½ cup seedless raisins
¾ cup chopped walnuts

For Serving
Whipped cream cheese

Preheat oven to 350°. Remove the pits from the plums and mash plums, using an electric blender, a Cuisinart food processor, or a simple potato masher. Place the pulp in a saucepan over medium heat; add the butter or margarine and cool, stirring until melted. Remove from the heat and transfer to a large mixing bowl. Stir in the baking soda. The mixture will foam and take on an unappetizing charcoal brown color at this point—don't worry about it. (We told you this was crazy bread!) Let the mixture cool to lukewarm.

While waiting for the mixture to cool, set out the remaining ingredients and prepare the baking pan(s) by greasing the inside heavily with shortening and dusting with flour. When the mixture is barely warm to the touch, add all the remaining ingredients. Mix well, then pour into the prepared pan(s).

Bake the bread at 350° for 70 to 80 minutes (check smaller pans after 50 minutes). Test by pressing the center to see if it is firm; if not, continue baking and test again in a few minutes. Let the bread cool for one hour in the baking pan; then turn out onto a rack to cool completely.

For the most delicious flavor, serve the bread warm accompanied by whipped cream cheese.

TO PREPARE IN ADVANCE: When cool, wrap the bread tightly in foil or plastic wrap. May be stored at room temperature for up to five days, in the refrigerator for three weeks, or in the freezer for up to six months. For best flavor, heat the bread wrapped tightly in foil in a 300° oven until it is warm through, depending on the temperature of the bread and the amount to be heated.

SPECIAL PACKAGING: Foil bread pans are handy for baking and giving. Simply wrap them in clear or colored cellophane and tie with a ribbon. Frances found some breadboards at a gourmet shop in the shape of gingerbread boys, which she uses when serving spice breads. Wrapping the bread on a breadboard in cellophane and accompanying it with a container of whipped cream cheese would make an elaborate presentation.

THE LABEL: Heat, wrapped in foil, at 300° until warm. Serve with whipped cream cheese. *If the bread is freshly baked, the label should read:* May be stored at room temperature for up to five days, in the refrigerator for up to three weeks, or frozen for up to six months. *If the bread is frozen, the label should read:* May be kept frozen for up to six months, at room temperature for five days, or in the refrigerator for up to three weeks after it has been thawed.

Glazed Apple Loaf

This Glazed Apple Loaf accommodates itself to any hour. Serve it sliced for breakfast, as a snack at tea time, or for dessert with a dollop of whipped cream and a sprinkling of nutmeg. The glaze is not fundamental to the taste. It just provides a nice touch for gift loaves. With or without its mantle of white, it will stay fresh for a long time without losing flavor.

This recipe makes one large (9-by-5-inch), two medium (8-by-4-inch), or six small (5-by-3-inch) loaves.

Shortening and flour for the pans
3 cups sifted all-purpose flour
1 teaspoon salt
1 teaspoon baking soda
1½ cups vegetable oil
2 cups sugar
3 large eggs
1 tablespoon vanilla
4½ teaspoons ground cinnamon
½ teaspoon ground nutmeg
3 cups peeled, cored, and diced apples
1 cup (about 5 ounces) diced pecans

For the Glaze (optional)
2 cups powdered sugar
½ stick (4 tablespoons) butter or margarine, melted
2 to 3 teaspoons fresh lemon juice or brandy
Pecan halves to decorate (optional)

For Serving (optional)
Sweetened whipped cream
Sprinkling of grated nutmeg

Preheat oven to 350°. Use shortening to grease bread pan(s). Dust the insides of the pan(s) with flour and shake out any excess.

Sift together the flour, salt, and soda and set aside. In a large mixing bowl, beat the oil, sugar, eggs, vanilla, cinnamon, and nutmeg until well blended. Add the dry ingredients and mix until smooth. Fold in the apples and pecans.

Divide the batter evenly among the pans. Bake in the center of a 350° oven 45 to 60 minutes for the small pans, about 90 minutes for the medium pans, up to 2 hours for the large pan until the loaves feel firm when pressed in the center. Let cool 10 minutes in the pan, then turn out on a rack to cool completely. Leave plain or decorate tops with the optional glaze.

To make the glaze, press the powdered sugar through a kitchen strainer with the back of a spoon into a small mixing bowl. Stir in the melted butter or margarine and 2 teaspoons lemon juice or brandy. Beat until smooth and creamy. If the mixture is too thick, add more lemon juice or brandy. Pour the glaze decoratively over the loaves. Press pecan halves into the glaze for decoration, if desired.

Serve in thin slices. This is especially delicious topped with a dollop of sweetened whipped cream and a sprinkling of grated nutmeg.

TO PREPARE IN ADVANCE: Wrap the cooled loaves carefully in foil to protect the glaze. The loaves keep well at room temperature for up to a week if wrapped airtight. They may be refrigerated for up to three weeks or frozen for up to four months. To freeze, place directly into the freezer, unwrapped. When solidly frozen, wrap carefully in foil to protect the glaze.

SPECIAL PACKAGING: The foil-wrapped loaves may be wrapped decoratively in cellophane and tied with a ribbon.

THE LABEL: Serve, sliced thinly, for breakfast, tea, or dessert. If desired, top with sweetened whipped cream and a sprinkling of nutmeg. *If the bread is freshly baked, the label should read:* May be stored for up to a week at room temperature or for two weeks in the refrigerator, or frozen for up to four months. *If the bread is frozen, the label should read:* May be kept frozen for up to four months, at room temperature for a week or in the refrigerator for up to two weeks after it has been thawed.

Twin Carrot Loaves
with Lemon Carrot Glaze

Peter Rabbit would stand on his ear if he knew carrots could taste like this. We prefer to bake and use these loaves as a bread because they have a finer crumb and are more lightly spiced than our 24-Karat Cake. And the small amount grated into the icing proclaims to all the world that these are carrot, carrot (you're baking two of them, right?) loaves.

This recipe makes two 9-by-5-inch loaves for two gifts.

Shortening and flour for the pans
2½ cups sifted all-purpose flour
1½ teaspoons baking powder
½ teaspoon baking soda
½ teaspoon salt
1 teaspoon ground cinnamon
1½ cups vegetable oil
2½ cups sugar
1/3 cup hot water
4 large eggs, separated
1½ cups grated carrots (about ½ pound)
¼ teaspoon cream of tartar or 1 teaspoon fresh lemon juice
  (see Note)
1 cup diced pecans

For the Glaze
¾ cup powdered sugar
1 tablespoon fresh lemon juice
¼ cup grated carrot

Note: When beating egg whites, always do so in a grease-free bowl and make sure the whites are at room temperature. Add either cream of tartar or fresh lemon juice before you begin beating. If you follow these rules, the whites will beat to the highest possible volume, which is important when making cakes, souffles, etc.

Preheat oven to 350°. Grease two 9-by-5-inch loaf pans with shortening and dust with flour. Shake out excess.

Sift together the flour, baking powder, soda, salt, and cinnamon. Set aside.

In the large bowl of an electric mixer, beat the oil, sugar, water, and egg yolks until the mixture is creamy. Add the carrots alternately with the dry ingredients while beating. When both have been added, stir in the pecans.

Beat the egg whites with cream of tartar or lemon juice until they hold stiff peaks when the beater is lifted. Fold half the whites into the batter, mixing thoroughly. Fold in the remaining whites gently until no lumps of white can be seen. Divide the mixture between the prepared pans. Bake at 350° for 60 to 70 minutes until firm when pressed in the center. Remove from the oven and let rest in the pans for 15 minutes before turning out on a rack to cool slightly before glazing.

To make the glaze, sift the powdered sugar by pressing it through a kitchen strainer with the back of a spoon into a small mixing bowl. Stir in lemon juice and grated carrot and beat until smooth and pourable. Drizzle the glaze over the loaves while they are still warm.

TO PREPARE IN ADVANCE: The flavor and texture of this bread is best if it is made at least 24 hours before serving. Wrapped in foil, it will stay moist and fresh for up to a week at room temperature. It freezes perfectly for up to three months. Let it freeze solidly before wrapping in foil—this will protect the glaze.

SPECIAL PACKAGING: Wrap the glazed loaves in see-through plastic wrap and then in clear cellophane and tie with a ribbon.

THE LABEL: Serve at room temperature. *If the bread is freshly baked the label should read:* May be stored, wrapped in foil, for up to a week at room temperature or frozen for up to three months. *If the bread is frozen, the label should read:* May be kept frozen for up to three months or at room temperature for a week after it has been thawed.

Zucchini Walnut Bread

Zucchini as a bread ingredient? What next? A long-time student, Nomi Wagner, brought us a loaf of moist zucchini bread. It had a rich brown color, similar to carrot bread, except that it was flecked with traces of green instead of orange. In making Nomi's recipe, we threw in some ground walnuts and an extra sprinkle of cinnamon for luck. And lucky it was! Out of the oven emerged this light spicy loaf that's fantastic with fruit salads or perfect as a snack—anytime.

This recipe makes two 8-by-4-inch loaves (baked in foil pans) or six 5-by-3-inch loaves.

Shortening and wax paper for the pans
2 cups sugar
1 cup vegetable oil
3 large eggs
1 tablespoon ground cinnamon
1 teaspoon baking powder
1 teaspoon baking soda
1 teaspoon vanilla
½ teaspoon ground ginger
½ teaspoon salt
3¼ cups sifted all-purpose flour
3 cups shredded, unpeeled zucchini (about 3 medium zucchini)
1 cup walnuts, ground (see Note)

For Serving
Whipped cream cheese (optional)

Note: The easiest way to grind nuts is in an electric blender or Cuisinart food processor, using the steel blade.

Preheat the oven to 325°. Grease two 8-by-4-inch or six 5-by-3-inch loaf pans generously with shortening. Line the bottom of each pan with wax paper and grease that.

Combine all the ingredients except the flour, zucchini, and walnuts in the large bowl of an electric mixer. Beat for about 2 minutes until blended, scraping side of the bowl often with a rubber spatula. Fold in the flour until blended, then fold in the zucchini and the walnuts.

Divide the mixture evenly among the prepared pans. Bake on the center rack at 325° until a wooden toothpick inserted in the center of the loaves comes out clean and the centers feel firm to the touch. This will be about 1 hour, 15 minutes for the large loaves and 1 hour for the small loaves. Let cool 5 minutes in the pans, then turn out on racks to cool completely.

Serve the bread warm with whipped cream cheese if desired.

TO PREPARE IN ADVANCE: When the loaves are cool, wrap them airtight in plastic wrap or aluminum foil. May be stored at room temperature for up to three days, in the refrigerator for up to a week, or in the freezer for up to three months. For best flavor, serve warm. Heat the bread wrapped tightly in foil in a 300° oven until it is warm through, depending on the temperature of the bread and the amount to be reheated.

SPECIAL PACKAGING: Foil bread pans are handy for baking and giving. Simply wrap them in clear or colored cellophane and tie with a ribbon.

THE LABEL: Heat, wrapped in foil, at 300° until warm. Serve warm with whipped cream cheese if desired. *If the bread is freshly baked, the label should read:* May be stored at room temperature for up to three days, in the refrigerator for up to a week, or in the freezer for up to three months. *If the bread is frozen, the label should read:* May be kept frozen for up to three months, or at room temperature for up to three days, or for up to a week in the refrigerator after it has been thawed.

Lemony Lemon Nut Bread

There are times when a recipe has such universal appeal that it quickly becomes a classic and its reputation spreads rapidly via the cookbooks of women's clubs across America. Such is the case with this superb lemon bread. Our daughter Lisa, who tends to be somewhat of an adventurous hostess, serves little sandwiches of it filled with whipped cream cheese to her friends and accompanies this with a crock of pate! The children may think the combination a trifle peculiar but eat it with no apparent pain. The combination is nothing to encourage but the bread is. Do give it a try. You'll find it has a fine moist texture that stays fresh for a long time and makes a delightful gift.

This recipe makes one 9-by-5-inch loaf. Double the recipe to make two loaves. Use one loaf for a generous gift or slice the bread thin, spread with cream cheese, and cut into tiny tea sandwiches to make several gifts.

Shortening and wax paper for the pan
1 cup sugar
1/3 cup melted butter or margarine
1 tablespoon lemon extract
2 large eggs
1½ cups sifted all-purpose flour
1 teaspoon baking powder
1 teaspoon salt
½ cup milk
Grated rind of 1 large lemon
½ cup chopped pecans

For the Glaze
1/3 cup fresh lemon juice (1 large lemon)
1/3 cup sugar

Preheat the oven to 350°. Grease the bread pan and line the bottom with wax paper. Grease the wax paper.

In the large bowl of an electric mixer, beat the sugar, melted butter, and lemon extract for 1 minute. Beat in the eggs, one at a time. Sift the flour, baking powder, and salt together and add them alternately with the milk while beating. Fold in the lemon rind and nuts. Transfer the mixture to the prepared pan. Bake for 60 minutes or until the bread feels firm when pressed in the center. Remove from the oven and let cool for a few minutes. Meanwhile, combine the lemon juice and 1/3 cup sugar. Drizzle over the bread while it is still warm. Let the bread cool completely before turning it out of the pan. Wrap tightly in foil and refrigerate for 24 hours before cutting.

Serve the bread in thin slices.

TO PREPARE IN ADVANCE: May be stored tightly wrapped in foil in the refrigerator for up to three months or frozen for up to one year. Sandwiches may be stored for up to three days in foil packages in the refrigerator.

SPECIAL PACKAGING: The foil-wrapped loaf might be wrapped decoratively in cellophane and tied with a ribbon. You may wish to include a breadboard as part of the gift. A container of whipped cream cheese could accompany the loaf. Tiny tea sandwiches might be presented on a small serving plate or in a basket inside a handkerchief or napkin.

THE LABEL: *If the entire freshly baked loaf is the gift, the label should read:* A moist tea bread. Serve in thin slices. May be stored in the refrigerator for up to three months or in the freezer indefinitely. *If frozen, the label should read:* Keep frozen for up to a year or refrigerate for up to three months after it has been thawed. *If a package of tea sandwiches is the gift, the label should read:* Sandwiches to serve with afternoon tea or coffee. May be stored, wrapped in foil, for up to three days in the refrigerator.

Orange Bread Grand Marnier

Here is a variation of the Lemon Nut Bread, in which we substitute Grand Marnier for the briskness of the lemon. If you scan through this volume, you'll note our obvious infatuation for this orange Cognac, our first choice when a recipe calls for orange liqueur. Its primary appeal lies in what it does for the things we stir up in our kitchen. It adds vigor, power, poetry, not always discernible if you rely solely on fruit from the orchard. In this case, it coalesces with the orange juice and rind to heighten the citrus goodness of the loaf.

This recipe yields a 9-by-5-inch loaf for one gift. Double the recipe to make two loaves. To make many small gifts, slice thin, spread with whipped cream cheese and form into tea sandwiches.

Shortening and wax paper for the pan
2/3 cup milk
1 tablespoon vinegar
½ cup (1 stick) butter or margarine, at room temperature
1 cup sugar
2 eggs, beaten
2 cups all-purpose flour
1 teaspoon salt
1 teaspoon baking soda
3 tablespoons grated orange rind (zest)
1 teaspoon vanilla
¼ teaspoon almond extract

For the Glaze
½ cup freshly squeezed orange juice
2 ounces (¼ cup) Grand Marnier

For Serving
Whipped cream cheese

Preheat oven to 350°. Grease loaf pan and line the bottom with wax paper; grease the wax paper. Add vinegar to milk and set aside for 5 minutes. In a large mixing bowl, cream the butter or margarine with the sugar and eggs for about 5 minutes until very light and fluffy.

Sift together the flour, salt, and soda. Add alternately to the creamed mixture with the milk. Once both have been added, beat in the rind, vanilla, and almond extract.

Pour the batter in the pan and bake at 350° for 1 hour or until the bread springs back when pressed in the center. Do not overbake.

Combine the orange juice and Grand Marnier. While the bread is still hot, pierce it deeply all over with a skewer and spoon the liquid over it. Let cool in the pan. Remove from the pan, then wrap in foil. Store overnight in the refrigerator before cutting.

Serve as a bread at room temperature. It makes tea sandwiches when sliced thin and spread with whipped cream cheese.

TO PREPARE IN ADVANCE: Wrapped tightly in foil, the loaf will keep for several months in the refrigerator or may be stored in the freezer for six months. Sandwiches may be stored for up to three days wrapped in foil in the refrigerator.

SPECIAL PACKAGING: The foil-wrapped loaf might be dressed up with cellophane and a fancy bow or presented on a breadboard along with whipped cream cheese and a spreader.

THE LABEL: A moist tea bread to serve with whipped cream cheese. *If the entire freshly baked loaf is the gift, the label should read:* May be stored in the refrigerator for up to two months or in the freezer for six months. *If given frozen, the label should read:* Keep frozen for up to six months or in the refrigerator for two months after it has been thawed. *If tea sandwiches are given, the label should read:* Sandwiches to serve with afternoon coffee or tea. May be stored, wrapped in foil, for up to three days in the refrigerator.

James Beard's Buttermilk White Bread

James Beard, the sage of American cooking, has written a book, *Beard on Bread,* published by Alfred Knopf, that is a joy for those who want to get involved with the tactile pleasures of this art. There's enchantment in breadmaking. And it all begins with the fermentation that takes place when yeast, sugar, and water commingle. Additional subtle changes take place in the texture as the bread is kneaded. There's a mysterious ascent, a punch, and a rise upward once more. In fact, it puts on quite a performance. It all comes nicely together to produce that tantalizing aroma, a long line of ready eaters, and that glorious rush from oven to table. Life can indeed be a joy once you learn the basics, so here is Beard's recipe. If you want to make home-baked bread more than just an occasional treat, this simple but honest loaf is ideal for all beginning bakers.

This recipe makes one 9-by-5-inch loaf.

> 2 packages active dry yeast
> 1 tablespoon granulated sugar
> ½ cup warm water (100° to 115°, approximately)
> 4 cups unbleached hard-wheat flour
> 1 tablespoon salt
> 3 tablespoons melted butter
> 1 to 1½ cups buttermilk

Combine the yeast, sugar, and water and allow to proof (see page 98). Mix the flour, salt, melted butter, and buttermilk together, work into a smooth dough, and then add the yeast mixture. Beat well for 2 minutes, then remove to a well-floured board and knead for approximately 10 minutes, until the dough is supple, smooth and satiny. (The dough can also be prepared in an electric mixer equipped with a dough hook. Combine all the ingredients, knead with the dough hook for approximately 5 to 6 minutes, and then remove the dough to a floured board for about 2 minutes of kneading by hand.) Place the dough in a buttered bowl and turn to coat the dough with butter. Cover and set in a warm spot to rise until more than doubled in bulk. Punch down the dough, remove to a floured board, and knead for 2 minutes. Form into a loaf about 9 by 5 inches by patting flat to a rather rough rectangle, folding in the ends, and then folding in the sides. Pinch the seams together well. Put in a buttered 9-by-5-by-3-inch bread pan, cover, and place in a warm, draft-free spot to rise until more than doubled in bulk. Bake in the center of a preheated 375° oven for about 40 minutes. For rolls, bake at 375° for 18 to 20 minutes. Remove from the pan, and bake for another 5 to 8 minutes on its side to give a crisp brown crust. Cool on a rack before slicing.

TO PREPARE IN ADVANCE: May be stored in a plastic bag in the refrigerator for up to five days or frozen for up to three months.

SPECIAL PACKAGING: What could be more tempting than a warm loaf of crusty bread presented on a breadboard with a crock of butter?

THE LABEL: Dig right in! If not eating immediately, the loaf may be stored in a plastic bag in the refrigerator for up to five days or in the freezer for up to three months.

Crunchy Granola Bread

Ever see a rabbit test the air? Your nose, too, will positively quiver when you catch the fragrance of this marvelous bread toasting. It's an excellent yeast bread for first-time breadmakers because it requires no kneading. As for the granola, you can either use the recipe on page 21 or construct your own from ingredients purchased at a health food store or local market. Be as liberated as you wish in the nut selection. Lightly salted sunflower seeds, pine nuts, or walnuts are particularly delicious. Buy prepackaged granola if you want to save yourself this extra step. Our favorite brand contains shredded coconut and dates, though any kind will do. Just be sure to buy the granola that furnishes the most nutrition by comparing the table of daily minimum requirements on the packaging.

This recipe makes one large 9-by-5-inch loaf. For best results, make only one loaf at a time.

> 1½ tablespoons butter or margarine for the pan
> 1½ cups hot tap water
> 2 tablespoons honey
> 2 packages active dry yeast
> 2 tablespoons vegetable oil
> 1½ teaspoons salt
> 3½ cups all-purpose flour
> 2 cups any type granola cereal (our recipe for granola, see page 21)
>
> ¾ cup chopped nuts of your choice
> ½ cup seedless raisins
> 2 teaspoons butter or margarine

Use the 1½ tablespoons butter or margarine to grease the bread pan. Warm a large mixing bowl by rinsing it with hot water. Add 1½ cups of hot tap water to the bowl; stir in the honey until dissolved. Use a thermometer to check that the mixture is between 110° and 115°. If it is above 115° let it cool for a few minutes before proceeding. Sprinkle the yeast over the surface of the water. Allow it to rest for a few minutes until you can see the yeast actively moving beneath the surface of the mixture. This procedure is called proofing the yeast — it's one way a baker can test to see that the yeast is alive. (If the yeast remains inactive, stir in one beaten egg — it will revive the yeast. It's true!) Add the oil and salt; stir to dissolve. With a large wooden spoon, stir in the flour, granola cereal, nuts, and raisins. Mix until thoroughly blended. Cover the bowl with a towel and set it in a warm place such as a turned off gas oven for 30 minutes. The dough will rise during this time to almost double in volume.

Preheat the oven to 350°. Beat with a wooden spoon to collapse the dough, scrape it into the greased bread pan, and pat it into a loaf shape. Cover again with a towel and place in a warm spot for 15 minutes.

Bake the loaf at 350° for 45 minutes. Remove it from the oven, brush the melted butter or margarine over the top crust, and turn out on a rack to cool.

This bread has the finest flavor when served sliced, toasted, and spread with butter.

TO PREPARE IN ADVANCE: After the loaf has cooled, wrap it airtight in foil or seal tightly in a heavy plastic bag. May be stored in the refrigerator for up to a week or frozen for up to three months. As a general rule, breads may be refrozen.

SPECIAL PACKAGING: Wrap clear cellophane around the outside of the foil or bag. Tie with a ribbon.

THE LABEL: Slice and serve toasted with butter. *Whether or not the bread has been frozen, the label should read:* May be stored in the refrigerator for up to a week or frozen for up to three months.

Cinchy Pineapple Cinnamon Rolls

A little gratitude would not be out of order for the companies who manufacture all the convenience foods lining our market shelves. They make recipes like this one possible. It's our version of a Pillsbury Bake-off winner, in which two convenience foods (crescent rolls and frosting mix) are used to make a fruity sweet roll of which any continental chef would approve. It is a trifle messy to handle at one point but so easy that our eight-year-old Lisa bakes batches for houseguests or family on weekends. The rolls keep beautifully, actually improve with age, and are ideal for weekend breakfasts of omelettes and fresh orange juice spiked with chilled champagne.

This recipe makes twenty to twenty-four glazed sweet rolls, which will probably be enough for four gifts. If your kids make them though, you may not have many left!

    20 to 24 frilled paper liners for muffin cups
    1 (8-ounce) can crushed pineapple
    2 (8-ounce) cans Pillsbury refrigerator crescent rolls
    ¼ cup sugar
    2½ teaspoons ground cinnamon
    2 large eggs, lightly beaten
    1 (8-ounce) package Pillsbury coconut-pecan frosting mix

    For the Glaze
    1 cup powdered sugar
    2 to 3 tablespoons of the syrup from the crushed pineapple

Preheat the oven to 375°. Place paper liners in muffin pans.

Drain the crushed pineapple in a kitchen strainer over a small mixing bowl that will catch the syrup. Press out as much of the syrup as possible with the back of a spoon. Reserve both the fruit and the juice.

Separate the crescent dough as illustrated into eight rectangles instead of sixteen triangles as directed on the package. Place four of the rectangles together to form one large rectangle measuring about 13 inches by 7 inches. Press the edges and perforations to make a smooth continuous piece of dough. Repeat with the remaining four rectangles to make a total of two large rectangles.

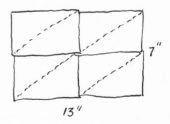

Mix together the sugar and cinnamon. Sprinkle evenly over the surface of the rectangles. In a small mixing bowl combine eggs, dry frosting mix, and drained pineapple. Blend well and spread this mixture evenly over the rectangles to within ¾ inch of the edges. Starting with a 13-inch side, roll up the rectangle like a jelly roll. When completely rolled, pinch the edge to seal. Repeat with the other rectangle. Sorry, this is a little messy but worth it.

Cut each roll into ten to twelve even slices and place each slice with the cut side down into a paper-lined muffin cup. Bake at 375° for 20 to 25 minutes until golden. Remove from the oven and let cool slightly in the pans while you make the glaze.

To make the glaze, blend the powdered sugar with enough of the reserved pineapple syrup to make an icing of drizzling consistency. When the rolls have cooled to lukewarm, drizzle the glaze from the end of the spoon decoratively in swirls over the top of each roll.

The rolls may be served warm or at room temperature. Warm is best.

TO PREPARE IN ADVANCE: The rolls improve in flavor if made at least one day ahead of time. May be wrapped airtight in aluminum foil and stored at room temperature for up to five days, in the refrigerator for up to a week, or frozen for up to four months. Thaw if frozen and heat, wrapped in foil, at 325° for about 15 minutes until warm.

SPECIAL PACKAGING: Almost any small basket would make a great gift container.

THE LABEL: Heat, wrapped in foil, at 325° for 15 minutes before serving. *If the rolls are freshly made, the label should read:* May be stored tightly wrapped in foil at room temperature for up to five days, in the refrigerator for up to a week, or frozen for up to four months. *If the rolls are frozen, the label should read:* May be kept frozen for up to four months, at room temperature, wrapped in foil, for up to five days, or in the refrigerator for up to a week.

Glorious Pineapple Bran Muffins

We added pineapple, raisins, and whole wheat to the Promised Land lure of milk and honey, and came up with these richly coated bran muffins. They're highly nutritious and superdelicious. A great gift for the health nuts on your gift list.

This recipe yields twenty to twenty-four muffins, depending on the size of your muffin tins, enough for three gifts of six muffins each. The recipe is easily doubled if you have enough tins for baking.

For the Coating
½ stick (4 tablespoons) butter or margarine at room temperature
1/3 cup firmly packed dark brown sugar
2 tablespoons honey
1 tablespoon cold water

For the Muffin Batter
½ cup sifted all-purpose white or whole wheat flour
⅝ cup sifted cake flour (½ cup plus 2 tablespoons)
2/3 cup sugar
½ teaspoon salt
½ teaspoon soda
½ teaspoon ground cinnamon
2 large eggs
¼ cup vegetable oil
4 tablespoons (¼ cup) honey
¼ cup well-drained crushed pineapple
3 cups All-Bran cereal
1½ cups buttermilk
½ cup seedless raisins

Preheat oven to 400°. To prepare the coating, cream the butter or margarine with the sugar in a small mixing bowl until the mixture is very light and creamy. Add the honey and cold water and continue beating until very fluffy. Spread the inside of each muffin cup evenly with about 2 teaspoons of this mixture.

To prepare the batter, sift flours, sugar, salt, soda, and cinnamon together into a large mixing bowl. Add the eggs, oil, honey, pineapple, bran, and buttermilk and beat until the batter is well blended. Stir in the raisins. Fill the prepared muffin pans ¾ full. Bake at 400° for about 20 minutes until the muffins are firm to the touch. Turn out of the pans immediately onto racks to cool.

Serve at room temperature.

TO PREPARE IN ADVANCE: When cool, wrap tightly in aluminum foil. May be stored at room temperature for up to three days, in the refrigerator for up to one week, or in the freezer up to three months.

SPECIAL PACKAGING: A small basket or serving plate might be included as part of the gift.

THE LABEL: Serve at room temperature. May be stored, wrapped in foil, at room temperature for up to three days, in the refrigerator for up to a week, or in the freezer for up to three months.

Our Version of Perino's Pumpernickel

Restaurants these days have devised novel ways of helping customers wile away the time that stretches between getting service, menu, and dinner. Some bring coffee with the menu. Some bring out the bread and butter. Some seek to fill the void with chatter. Perino's, the award-winning restaurant in Los Angeles (opened in 1930), has found the perfect foil to dilute potential customer complaints. Diners there are welcomed with baskets of crispy, cheese-covered pumpernickel.

Now, regardless of whether we have all the time in the world or not, we didn't have this recipe, so we picked up the challenge of trying to duplicate it. It was a tough challenge because the slices were so thin and evenly coated. After every possible kind of experimentation with slicers, loaves, and baking temperature, we discovered that spreading soft butter or margarine on the cut end of the bread and using a hot, wet knife enabled us to cut a thin, even slice every time. The buttered slices were then thickly coated with grated Parmesan and baked until crisp and curly. Enjoy them along with us. They stay crisp indefinitely in airtight tins.

We are giving directions to make about thirty ⅛-inch slices of toasted pumpernickel, for three gifts of ten slices each.

> 1 1-pound loaf of unsliced pumpernickel, black bread, or Westphalian rye (actually, any good rye bread can be used)
> 2 sticks (½ pound) butter or margarine, at room temperature
> 1½ cups finely grated Parmesan cheese

Preheat oven to 300°. Cut the loaf in half crosswise. Butter one cut end generously with soft butter or margarine. Hold a long thin knife under hot running water and immediately use it to cut a slice of bread no more than ⅛ inch thick from the end.

Press the buttered side of the bread into the Parmesan cheese, coating it densely, and place on a baking sheet. Continue buttering, slicing, and coating in the same manner until the baking sheet is filled with slices. Then bake at 300° for 15 to 20 minutes until the bread is crisp and curled on the edges. Remove from the oven and cool. Continue making slices in the same manner until all ingredients are used.

TO PREPARE IN ADVANCE: When cool, may be stored in an airtight container at room temperature for up to two months.

SPECIAL PACKAGING: This is divine to give along with almost any kind of soup. Some kind of airtight tin is most practical.

THE LABEL: Serve at room temperature as an appetizer or accompaniment to soups. May be stored at room temperature for up to two months in an airtight container.

Preserves, Relishes & Chutneys

What do you suppose Sir Isaac Newton did with that apple that fell on his head? No doubt, he picked it up, wiped it off, and ate it. When it's time for nature to drop her fruit and reseed the earth with apples she, unfortunately, does it all at once. At that time, about the only way Mrs. Newton had of preserving apples was to dry them, weather permitting. (However, there was also the possibility, if she knew about it, of making them into relishes and chutneys, perhaps the world's oldest preserves, dating way back to early China and India.) At any rate, it would be another 150 years before mechanical refrigeration would be invented and another 160 years before freezing techniques were developed.

Let's move up to 1809 when mankind was given another great invention. That year Napoleon Bonaparte awarded a prize of $250,000 (current United

States dollars) to a Frenchman who for fourteen years labored to discover a method for preserving perishable foods. His name was Nicholas Appert, inventor of hermetically sealed jars. Can you imagine what a boon this was to the nutrition of mankind? It was Napoleon's secret weapon. He could march an army quickly almost anywhere without the necessity of driving herds of cattle, flocks of geese and poultry along with them and without having to forage through the winter snows for vegetables.

It also opened the world's waterways to long voyages of discovery. Until that time each ship that went to sea was a floating farmyard. Remember the animals on the boat from the *Swiss Family Robinson* and the poor plight of the sailors with scurvy in *Moby Dick?* Somehow, now in Mr. Appert's funny little glass jars, vitamins could be retained all winter long anywhere you went.

In America today we open about 29 billion jars and cans a year — everything from peas to baby food to tuna. And according to the Glass Container Manufacturers Institute of Washington, more than one billion of these jars are put up by homemakers. The process is so simple; anyone can do it. And everybody enjoys the result.

For example, is there anything in this world that can make a mouth water more quickly than the sight of strawberry jam on buttered toast? As jam, strawberries are crushed and mixed with sugar. As jelly, they are crushed into juice and mixed with sugar. As conserve, they are combined with other fruits and sugar. As a preserve, they are bottled whole in a sugar syrup. But for a simple diet dessert, you can eat as many as a dozen fresh strawberries to get 100 percent of the recommended daily allowance of Vitamin C; one cup contains only 55 calories.

And strawberries are just one out of a great number of fruits and vegetables that can be preserved to last from one season to another.

So nature in her clever way has permitted us to fall irresistibly in love with her abundant harvest, and in return we willingly become husbands and protectors of huge mortgaged orchards, spraying for damaging insects, artificially heating our citrus groves all night during killing frosts, and jealously enforcing border inspection laws.

If Napoleon Bonaparte could have kept his secret, he might have conquered the world.

Sangría Jam

We are indebted to the Spanish. Consider Isabella whose jewels launched Columbus our way. Now comes this fruit-flavored sensation inspired by its liquid Spanish counterpart — and by the fact that we broke one of a pair of antique wine glasses. Out of the destruction came a sort of redemption. We filled the remaining glass with the red wine-lemon-orange jam and gave it away as a "one of a kind" present. This jam is especially good for breakfast, slathered over toasted English muffins.

This recipe makes 4 cups of jam, enough to fill four ½-pint wine glasses or other containers. (Please read "About Jellies and Jams," page 230, before beginning this recipe.)

> ½ bottle Certo liquid fruit pectin
> 1½ cups red burgundy
> 1 tablespoon grated orange rind (see Note)
> ¼ cup fresh orange juice
> 2 tablespoons fresh lemon juice
> 2 tablespoons Triple Sec, Cointreau, or Grand Marnier
> 3 cups sugar

Note: One kitchen tool we would hate to do without is a zester (see illustration), an inexpensive gadget used to remove the outer peel (zest) of citrus fruits in long thin strips. We would like to include it as part of the gift when grated rind is called for in the recipe.

Remove the label and the enclosed recipe booklet from around the Certo bottle so you can see the line marking half a bottle.

Combine all the ingredients except Certo in the top of a double boiler. Place over boiling water and stir the mixture for 3 to 4 minutes until the sugar is thoroughly dissolved. Remove from the heat, add the Certo, and stir for 1 minute.

To prevent breakage, warm the glasses by rinsing with hot water, dry, and place a metal spoon in each before filling. Pour the jam over the spoon to within ¼ inch of the top of the glass. Remove the spoons and seal with paraffin, if desired (directions are on page 231). If you do not wish to seal the jam, simply cover the glasses tightly with plastic wrap and store in the refrigerator.

TO PREPARE IN ADVANCE: Sealed with paraffin, this jam will keep beautifully on the pantry shelf without losing quality for at least two months. It will keep indefinitely in the refrigerator.

SPECIAL PACKAGING: Any odd wine glasses you might have are suitable — a great way to get rid of them! Tie a bow around the stem of the glass. For other ideas, see "Containers for Jellies and Jams," page 232.

THE LABEL: Divine on toasted English muffins. *If the jam is sealed with paraffin, the label should read:* May be stored in a cool, dark place for up to two months. Refrigerate after opening. *If the jam is sealed only with plastic wrap, the label should read:* May be stored in the refrigerator indefinitely.

Champagne Jelly

If we had any fewer ingredients, we might not have a recipe. But the crucial one, champagne, happened to be in the refrigerator at a time when Paul's mother was helping us bake some Monkey Bread. Our thoughts turned to a proper accompaniment for the bread now baking in the oven. It was serendipity! Too flat to drink but not too preposterous to jell, we turned the champagne into jelly, poured some into jelly jars, and the rest into a champagne glass, ready to turn over to a friend.

This recipe makes 3¼ cups of jelly, enough to fill three to six champagne or wine glasses for giving. (Please read "About Jellies and Jams," page 230, before beginning this recipe.)

> 2 cups champagne (flat champagne is fine)
> 3 cups sugar
> ½ bottle Certo liquid fruit pectin

Mix the champagne with the sugar in the top of a double boiler. Place over boiling water and stir for 3 to 4 minutes until the sugar is dissolved. Remove the pan from the heat and immediately stir in the Certo.

To prevent breakage, warm the wine or champagne glasses, rinsing with hot water, dry, and place a metal spoon in each before filling. Pour the jelly over the spoon to within ½ inch of the top of the glass. Remove the spoon and seal the jelly with paraffin, if desired (directions, page 231), or simply cover with plastic wrap. Refrigerate until set.

TO PREPARE IN ADVANCE: Sealed with paraffin, the jelly will keep for up to two months in a cool, dark place. It lasts indefinitely in the refrigerator.

SPECIAL PACKAGING: Here's your chance to get rid of odd wine and champagne glasses. Tie a ribbon around the stem.

THE LABEL: *If the jelly is sealed with paraffin, the label should read:* May be stored in a cool, dark place for up to two months. Refrigerate after opening. *If the jelly is sealed only with plastic wrap, the label should read:* May be stored in the refrigerator indefinitely.

Lancaster Lemon Butter

There's a lot to be said for detours. One rainy Sunday noon, late in summer, we were contentedly driving the long way around to luncheon at an historic Pennsylvania inn, which had already lured us a hundred miles off our planned vacation route. Driving through lush, winding farm roads in the heart of the Amish country, we suddenly came up behind two polished black carriages. The one directly in front of us was drawn by a shiny brown mare, steaming in the lightly falling warm rain. Young Amish couples were courting — the boys dressed in black and their girls in traditional purple and white. Not able to pass and in no mood to hurry, we slowed to twelve miles an hour and joined the procession. It was easy to let ourselves imagine that time had slipped back into a bygone century and that our yellow, imported car was, in fact, a handcrafted carriage made by the local blacksmith. All too soon we found ourselves back in the present as our caravan approached our destination, the Moselem Springs Inn near Lancaster, Pennsylvania.

Lunch was everything our research had promised, and more. We were given a cozy table by a window overlooking the veranda, beyond which the rain still fell lazily. Distant thunder rumbled and rolled as if trapped within those green hills. Our conversation centered around the menu with its down-to-earth cooking — home-smoked meats, preserves, relishes, hot breads, and cold apple cider so typical of hearty Pennsylvania Dutch fare.

Our greatest reward was the discovery of a simple, yet thoroughly delicious, lemon-flavored spread which was served with cinnamon graham crackers. We bought some to take as a gift to Paul's mom, and she liked it so well that she successfully duplicated it in her kitchen. It makes a marvelous after-school treat for kids. They can make it easily and serve it to themselves and to their chums.

This recipe will make 2 cups of spread, enough for two ½-pint or four 4-ounce gift containers.

> 1 pound "soft" margarine, packaged in 2 (8-ounce) tubs
> ½ cup powdered sugar
> 2½ teaspoons lemon extract
>
> *For Serving*
> 2 (16-ounce) boxes cinnamon-flavored graham crackers

Transfer the margarine to a small mixing bowl. Blend in the confectioner's sugar and lemon extract. Pack into containers and chill.

Serve as a spread on cinnamon-flavored grahams.

TO PREPARE IN ADVANCE: This will keep for several months in the refrigerator. It is so simple to make and lasts such a long time that there is no advantage in freezing it.

SPECIAL PACKAGING: A small basket will hold a container of lemon butter along with a ribbon-tied package of graham crackers and a spreader.

THE LABEL: A sinful snack to serve as a spread with cinnamon graham crackers. May be stored in the refrigerator for up to two months.

Sugar Plum Jam

The artistry that Tchaikovsky put into the *Nutcracker Suite* with his Sugar Plums is the same kind we achieved in our kitchen one fine summer day. The afternoon called for a languid occupation, but instead we found ourselves knifing through a basket of garden-fresh plums from the market. We merged the pulp with dark Jamaican rum and orange rind to create this shimmering jam. Should the opportunity arise, it can double as a crepe filling. But it must be made with fresh plums, which are in season during the summer months from June to September. The work will be easy, and time will fly as it always does when you're with your best friend. It is, however, very simple to make, even without a best friend to help, and you'll hug yourself for planning ahead when you open pantry doors to see the good things stocked there, waiting, like a secret Swiss account, to be withdrawn when the right moment arrives.

This recipe makes approximately 9 cups of jam, enough to fill nine 8-ounce jelly glasses or other containers. (Please read "About Jellies and Jams," page 230, before beginning this recipe.)

> ½ bottle Certo liquid fruit pectin
> 4 cups pitted and chopped unpeeled purple plums
> 7 cups sugar
> ½ cup fresh lemon juice
> Grated peel (zest) of 1 large orange
> ¼ cup dark Jamaican rum

Remove the label and the enclosed recipe booklet from around the Certo bottle so you can see the line marking half a bottle.

Combine the plums, sugar, lemon juice, and orange rind in an 8-quart saucepan or kettle. Place over medium-high heat. Bring the mixture to a rolling boil that you cannot stir down and boil hard for 1 minute. Remove the pan from the heat and stir in the Certo and the rum. Skim the foam off the surface; then continue to stir and skim for 5 minutes. The jam will begin to thicken slightly during this time; this is important to prevent the fruit from floating. At the end of 5 minutes, ladle the jam immediately into containers and seal, if desired, or cover with plastic wrap.

TO PREPARE IN ADVANCE: If sealed with paraffin, this jam will stay at peak quality for at least two months in a cool dark place. Stored in the refrigerator, it will keep indefinitely.

SPECIAL PACKAGING: The color of this jam is exquisite, so clear glass containers are a must. See "Containers for Jellies and Jams," page 232.

THE LABEL: Use as a jam or crepe filling. *If the jam is vacuum sealed, the label should read:* May be stored in a cool dark place for up to six months. Refrigerate after opening. *If the jam is sealed with paraffin, the label should read:* May be stored in a cool, dark place for up to two months. Refrigerate after opening. *If the jam is sealed only with plastic wrap, the label should read:* May be stored in the refrigerator indefinitely.

Year-Round Strawberry Preserves

The grocer's dirge, "It's not in season," needn't deter you from making this jam. It can be made any time because the recipe calls for frozen sliced strawberries. Add orange liqueur to take it out of the "ho hum" category. (Does anyone ever view strawberries with such detachment?)

This recipe fills 6 ½-pint jars. (Please read "About Jellies and Jams, page 230, before beginning this recipe.)

> 3 (10-ounce) packages frozen sliced strawberries
> ¼ cup water
> 1 (1¾-ounce) package Sure-Jell powdered fruit pectin.
> 6 cups sugar
> 1/3 cup Grand Marnier, Cointreau, or Triple Sec
> 3 tablespoons fresh lemon juice

Thaw the strawberries according to package directions. Combine them with the water and pectin in a heavy 6-quart pot (not aluminum). Bring the mixture to a boil over high heat, stirring occasionally. Boil for 1 minute. Stir in the sugar and bring to a full, rolling boil that you cannot stir down. Boil hard for 1 minute. remove the pan from the heat and immediately stir in the liqueur and lemon juice. Let stand for 5 minutes, stirring occasionally. Skim off any foam from the surface. Pour the preserves into containers. Seal, if desired and let cool undisturbed.

TO PREPARE IN ADVANCE: If sealed with paraffin, this jam will stay at peak quality for at least six months in a cool dark place. Stored in the refrigerator, it will keep indefinitely.

SPECIAL PACKAGING: Glass canning jars would be most suitable. Other 8-ounce containers might be used, such as condiment jars and souffle dishes.

THE LABEL: *If the jam is vacuum-sealed, the label should read:* May be stored in a cool, dark place for up to six months. Refrigerate after opening. *If the jam is sealed with paraffin, the label should read:* May be stored in cool, dark place for up to two months. Refrigerate after opening. *If the jam is sealed only with plastic wrap, the label should read:* May be stored in the refrigerator indefinitely.

Frandy's Spiced Pear Jam

During the season when there is a superabundance of pears, Frandy Hopkins, a student in our class, peels and cores, chops and mashes a sufficient number of pears to make her famous jam. Like a country cook, she bubbles and boils the fruit pulp, knowing that the fine perfume of allspice and cinnamon will do much to enhance the future history of the breads, muffins, or rolls of friends who fall heir to one of these jars.

This recipe makes 7 cups of jam to fill seven ½-pint canning jars or other gift containers. (Please read "About Jellies and Jams," page 230, before beginning this recipe.)

3 pounds of fully ripe pears (6 to 7 pears) to make 4 cups of prepared fruit
3 tablespoons fresh lemon juice
¾ teaspoon ground cinnamon
½ teaspoon ground allspice
1 (1¾-ounce) package Sure-Jell powdered fruit pectin
½ cup white raisins brought to a boil in 1/3 cup red wine (optional)
5 cups sugar
7 or 8 cinnamon sticks, 2 to 3 inches in length (optional)

Peel, core, and chop or mash the pears. Measure 4 cups of fruit and place in a 5- to 6-quart heavy saucepan. Stir in the lemon juice, cinnamon, allspice, Sure-Jell, and the optional wine-soaked raisins. Bring to a hard boil. Add the sugar all at once and bring to a full rolling boil that you cannot stir down. Let boil hard for 1 minute, stirring constantly. Remove from the heat. Skim and stir the jam for 5 minutes to cool slightly. Place a cinnamon stick in each glass, if desired, and pour the jam into containers to within ⅛ to ½-inch of the top. Seal, if desired, or cover and refrigerate. Let cool undisturbed.

TO PREPARE IN ADVANCE: If vacuum-sealed in canning jars and stored in a cool, dark place, the jam will stay at peak quality for up to six months. Sealed with paraffin, it will keep for two months. It may be stored indefinitely in the refrigerator. Refrigerate the jam after opening.

SPECIAL PACKAGING: Canning jars are ideal. Any kind of small serving dishes or condiment jars would be suitable.

THE LABEL: *If the jam is vacuum-sealed, the label should read:* May be stored in a cool dark place for up to six months. Refrigerate after opening. *If sealed with paraffin, the label should read:* May be stored in a cool, dark place for up to two months. Refrigerate after opening. *If the jam is sealed only with plastic wrap, the label should read:* May be stored in the refrigerator indefinitely.

Cranberry-Pineapple Jam

If you, like us, have a passion for cranberries, you can lengthen its brief season. One way is by freezing. The plastic bags in which they're purchased are perfect freezer wrappers. When available in the markets, buy several, use one bag, freeze the other. The second way is to prepare some jam, like the elegant preserve that follows. It can be used also as a relish to accompany roast turkey or ham at holiday time. It's perfect for giving—anytime.

This recipe makes nine cups of jam, enough to fill nine ½-pint canning jars. (Please read "About Jellies and Jams," page 230, before beginning this recipe.)

> 4 cups (1 pound) cranberries
> 1½ cups water
> 1 (1-pound, 4-ounce) can crushed pineapple in syrup
> 8 cups sugar
> ½ bottle Certo liquid fruit pectin
> ½ cup fresh lemon juice
> 1 tablespoon grated orange rind

Wash and pick over the cranberries. Chop them either by hand, in a Cuisinart food processor, or by putting them through the coarse blade of a meat grinder.

Place the cranberries and the water in a 5-quart saucepan (not aluminum). Bring to a boil and let simmer for 5 minutes over medium heat. Add the pineapple with its syrup and the sugar. Bring the mixture to a hard rolling boil and let boil for 2 minutes.

Remove from the heat and stir in pectin, lemon juice, and orange rind. Let stand 25 minutes, then pour either into canning jars and seal or into containers for refrigerator storage. Let cool undisturbed.

TO PREPARE IN ADVANCE: Stored in vacuum-sealed canning jars, this jam will keep well for six months in a cool, dark place. May be stored for two months before refrigerating sealed with paraffin. Refrigerate after opening. It may be stored indefinitely in the refrigerator.

SPECIAL PACKAGING: This jam can double as a relish, so small serving dishes would be appropriate if it is to be used for that purpose. Otherwise, canning jars are your best bet.

THE LABEL: *If the jam is vacuum sealed, the label should read:* May be stored in a cool, dark place for up to six months. Refrigerate after opening. *If the jam is sealed with paraffin, the label should read:* May be stored in a cool, dark place for up to two months. Refrigerate after opening. *If the jam is sealed only with plastic wrap, the label should read:* May be stored in the refrigerator indefinitely.

Christmas Cranberries

People who read cookbooks straight through as if they're absorbing novels are a race apart. We joined their number in 1963 when we chanced across *The Blueberry Hill Menu Cookbook* by the late Elsie Masterton, published by Thomas Crowell. We never met Elsie, but got to know her and her Vermont winters and summers, springs and falls. She was some of the best company we ever had in our kitchen. Among the more than a thousand cookbooks on our shelves, we treasure this volume of hers from which comes this slightly tart cranberry relish. It has become a cherished holiday tradition in our home and makes a wonderful gift as well. (We have changed the wording of the recipe to fit the format of this book.)

This recipe makes 3½ to 4 cups of relish, enough to fill two 1-pint or 4 half-pint gift containers.

> 2 cups sugar
> ½ cup water
> 3 whole cloves
> 1 medium stick cinnamon
> 4 cups (1 pound) cranberries, washed and picked over
> ½ thin-skinned orange including the rind, finely chopped
> ½ cup Cognac or brandy

In a heavy-bottomed saucepan, combine the sugar and water. Bring to a boil and boil for 3 minutes without stirring. Add the cloves, cinnamon stick, cranberries, and orange. Cook, stirring occasionally, over low heat for 4 to 5 minutes until the cranberries begin to burst. Remove the pan from the heat and stir in the Cognac. Let cool, then remove the cinnamon stick. Place in containers, cover, and refrigerate. Serve at room temperature.

TO PREPARE IN ADVANCE: When cool and covered with plastic wrap, it may be stored in the refrigerator for up to a month or in the freezer for up to six months.

SPECIAL PACKAGING: Any kind of small serving dish is appropriate.

THE LABEL: Serve at room temperature with roast meats. May be stored in the refrigerator for up to a month or frozen for up to six months.

Christmas Pepper Jelly

Our unique dark green jelly speckled with red causes a sensation whenever it is served, either as a topping for cream cheese and crackers or as a lively accompaniment to meat. We created this special holiday version especially for gift-making. It's the handiest of all hostess gifts because it's quick to make and keeps indefinitely.

Warn eaters that the jelly is an exuberant combination of hot and sweet, as in the words of the popular Mexican lament, "La Llorona," "I am like a green chili pepper, hot but delicious . . . "

This recipe makes about seven ½-pint gifts. (Please read "About Jellies and Jams," page 230, before beginning this recipe.)

> 1 cup green bell pepper, seeded and chopped
> ¼ cup rinsed and seeded canned jalapeno pepper
> 1¼ cups apple cider vinegar
> 6 cups sugar
> ½ cup red bell pepper, seeded and finely diced (if not available, omit)
> 1 bottle Certo liquid fruit pectin
> 8 or 9 drops green food color
>
> *For Serving*
> Cream cheese or cheddar cheese spread
> Crackers

Place the green peppers and jalapenos in the container of an electric blender with ½ cup of the vinegar and blend until smooth. Pour the mixture into a 4-quart saucepan. Rinse the blender container with the remaining vinegar and add it to the green peppers. Stir in the sugar and the diced red peppers. Bring the mixture just to a hard boil that you cannot stir down. Remove from the heat and let stand for 5 minutes. Skim the foam carefully off the top, leaving as many of the red pepper pieces on the surface as possible. Add the Certo and the green food color. Stir until thoroughly blended.

Pour immediately into selected gift containers and seal or refrigerate.

TO PREPARE IN ADVANCE: Covered with plastic wrap, the jelly will keep indefinitely in the refrigerator. Sealed in vacuum jars, it may be stored in a cool, dark place for up to six months. Sealed with paraffin, it may be stored in a cool, dark place for up to two months. Refrigerate after opening.

SPECIAL PACKAGING: This jelly is usually served with cream cheese and crackers; therefore, matching containers for the jelly and cream cheese would be appropriate. See section on Containers, page 232. The jelly looks beautiful in individual, white souffle' dishes tied with a green and red plaid ribbon.

THE LABEL: Serve as a condiment with cream cheese and crackers or with any kind of roast meats. *If the jelly is sealed in vacuum jars, the label should read:* May be stored in a cool, dark place for up to six months. *If the jelly is sealed with paraffin, the label should read:* May be stored in a cool, dark place for up to two months. *If the jelly is sealed only with plastic wrap, the label should read:* May be stored in the refrigerator indefinitely.

 # Drunken Mincemeat

There is an element of surprise in the English language. While there is no egg in eggplant, there is meat in mincemeat. This one is an honest-to-goodness, old-fashioned mincemeat, the kind our mothers made. The longer you keep it around, the better it gets. We make it with brandy and sherry, as is traditional, but also add a splash of dark rum and orange liqueur, a minor addition that lifts this recipe into the majors. Another cut of beef, such as brisket, may be substituted for the tongue. Keep the mincemeat in a covered crock at room temperature, and check it once a week. If the top of the mixture looks dry, pour on more booze. You can never add too much. And at its first public appearance, in pie or tart, complete the perfect partnership by combining it with an equal measure of freshly grated apple and chopped nuts.

This recipe yields almost 2 gallons of mincemeat, enough for twelve or more 1-pint gifts. Each gift, when combined with grated apple and walnut, will make a 9-inch pie.

2 pounds lean beef chuck, boneless
1 (2½-to-3 pound) beef tongue
1 pound beef suet
2 (15-ounce) packages seedless raisins
1 (15-ounce) package golden seedless raisins
1 (15-ounce) package seeded (muscat) raisins
1 (11-ounce) package currants
1 (16-ounce) jar orange marmalade
8 ounces dried figs, chopped
1 cup diced candied citron
1 cup diced candied orange peel
½ cup diced candied lemon peel
Grated rind of 1 large lemon
2½ cups sugar
2 teaspoons salt
2 teaspoons each ground nutmeg, cinnamon, and allspice

1 teaspoon ground cloves
½ teaspoon ground mace (optional) (see Note)
1 bottle (fifth) brandy or cognac
1 bottle (fifth) pale dry sherry
½ cup dark rum
½ cup or more orange-flavored liqueur (Grand Marnier, Triple
   Sec, Cointreau, etc.)
More brandy or sherry, as needed

Note: Mace is the outer covering of a nutmeg. It is one ground spice that can quickly turn rancid. Store in the refrigerator and taste to check freshness before using in recipes.

Place the beef chuck and tongue in a saucepan large enough to hold them comfortably. Cover them with cold water and bring to a boil over high heat. Reduce the heat, cover the pan, and simmer for 3 hours or until both meats are very tender when pierced with a fork. Drain and reserve the broth for another use.

Plunge the tongue in cold water to loosen the skin; then pat dry. Slit the underside lengthwise and peel away the covering from the tongue. Grind both meats and the suet, using the coarse blade of a meat grinder, into a large mixing bowl (if you do not have a meat grinder, chop the meat finely). Add all remaining ingredients except for the booze. Mix well. Add the Cognac, sherry, rum, and orange liqueur — the mixture will be soupy. Pack into a clean crock or Rumtopf pot, and cover tightly. Use foil underneath the lid, if the container has one, to provide a good seal. Let stand at room temperature for two weeks or longer before using. After ten days or so, check the container regularly to see if the liquid has evaporated. Add more brandy alternately with sherry as the mincemeat absorbs moisture.

To make filling for a 9-inch mincemeat pie, combine 2 cups mincemeat with 1½ cups fresh grated and peeled apple and ½ cup broken walnuts. Or, use the mincemeat "straight" for Delectable Mincemeat Bars with Vanilla Glaze, page 162.

TO PREPARE IN ADVANCE: If regularly soused with more booze, this mincemeat will keep for 3 months at room temperature. After that, it may be stored in the refrigerator for a year or longer.

SPECIAL PACKAGING: Any kind of 1-pint (2-cup) container is the right size for mincemeat to make one 9-inch pie.

THE LABEL: Mincemeat for one 9-inch pie. To use, add 1½ cups freshly grated apple and ½ cup chopped walnuts. May be stored in the refrigerator for up to one year; add brandy or sherry if the mixture needs moisture.

Favorite Chutney

A delightful, spicy aroma permeates every room in the house when we set our outrageously good chutney on to simmer, conjuring up visions of Englishmen, far from home, adapting themselves to the clime and fare of another land. The ingredients for our recipe may be found in local markets nearly all year round, so it may be made whenever the mood strikes. The result is a rich, dark chutney, with a mild but tangy taste. It may be used as a condiment for curries or simply as a relish for meat, chicken, or shellfish. This particular recipe makes a host of hospitality gifts with a minimum of effort.

This recipe makes 8 pints (16 cups), which, depending on the size of your containers, will be sufficient for up to sixteen gifts.

> 3 firm pears, peeled, cored, and thinly sliced
> 1 large firm cantaloupe, peeled, seeded, and cut into ¾-inch cubes
> 1 pound tart (Pippin) apples, peeled, cored, and chopped
> 8 dried apricot halves, chopped
> 1 (8-ounce) can crushed pineapple in heavy syrup
> 6 firm tomatoes, peeled and chopped (see Note)
> 3 large onions, peeled and chopped
> 1 large clove garlic, peeled and minced
> 4 fresh hot red peppers, seeded and chopped, or 8 dried chile
>   pods, seeded and crumbled
> 1 green bell pepper, seeded and chopped
> 3 cups firmly packed dark brown sugar
> 2½ cups cider vinegar

> ....

> ½ cup golden raisins
> ¼ cup dried black currants
> ¾ cup broken walnuts
> 1 tablespoon mustard seed
> ¼ teaspoon powdered ginger
> ¼ teaspoon powdered cloves
> ½ pound (8 ounces) candied or crystallized ginger, chopped

Note: To peel a tomato, place in boiling water for 30 seconds. The skin will then slip off easily.

Combine all the ingredients down to the dotted line in a heavy 8-quart pot. Bring the mixture to a boil, lower the heat and simmer for 1 hour, stirring frequently. Add the remaining ingredients and simmer 45 minutes longer. Stir often at the end of the cooking time—the mixture tends to burn as it thickens.

Pack it into sterilized jars (see "Containers for Jellies and Jams," page 232) or other containers while hot. If desired, seal with vacuum lids or paraffin — but sealing is unnecessary if the chutney is to be stored in the refrigerator.

For best flavor, serve at room temperature.

TO PREPARE IN ADVANCE: Chutney will keep indefinitely in the refrigerator. If you prefer, it may be sealed in sterilized jars (see directions, page 232). Vacuum-sealed chutney will keep beautifully in a cool, dark place for at least six months; paraffin-sealed chutney will keep for up to two months in a cool, dark place.

SPECIAL PACKAGING: Canning jars are ideal if the chutney is to be sealed. If the chutney will be stored in the refrigerator, it does not require sealing, so any kind of serving container is suitable.

THE LABEL: Serve as a curry condiment or meat relish. *If the chutney is sealed in vacuum jars, the label should read:* May be stored in a cool, dark place for up to six months. Refrigerate after opening. *If the chutney is sealed with paraffin, the label should read:* May be stored in a cool, dark place for up to two months. Refrigerate after opening. *If the chutney is sealed only with plastic wrap, the label should read:* May be stored in the refrigerator indefinitely.

Fresh Mint Chutney Taj Mahal

Sometimes you ask a question and hit the jackpot. Take this chutney recipe. We owe it all to a desk clerk in Minneapolis who was good enough to recommend the Taj Mahal Restaurant to us. We were served an outstanding chicken tandoori that came with a fragrant mint chutney. Debbie Chaddah, co-owner of the restaurant (the only East Indian one in Minnesota), entertained us with stories about cooking and curries and recollections of the Bombay heat, rain, and smells. We walked back to the hotel, elated by our discovery of this new recipe which she gave us. It takes only minutes to prepare in a blender and freezes perfectly. We make it whenever we have an abundance of fresh mint. It's divine not only with curries, but with roast or barbecued lamb and as a quick summer snack atop cream cheese and crackers.

This recipe makes 2 cups of chutney. A little bit of it goes a long way, so this amount will be sufficient for four 4-ounce (½-cup) gifts.

20 large sprigs of fresh mint (approximately 100 mint leaves)
2 medium onions, coarsely chopped
4 teaspoons whole coriander seeds
8 hot green chiles (jalapenos) (see Note)
2 teaspoons salt
4 tablespoons fresh lemon juice
4 tablespoons cold water

Note: We use canned jalapenos, rinsed and seeded. This chutney is definitely "hot," so use fewer chiles if you prefer a milder flavor.

Wash the mint well. Remove the leaves and discard the stalks. Place the mint in an electric blender with all other ingredients. Blend at low speed until the mixture is running smoothly through the blades. Stop the motor once or twice to scrape down the sides with a rubber spatula. Blend at high speed until the chutney is smooth — 3 or 4 minutes will do it. Transfer to containers and refrigerate for 24 hours to ripen before serving.

TO PREPARE IN ADVANCE: The chutney may be stored for up to a week in the refrigerator and may be frozen for up to three months.

SPECIAL PACKAGING: Small jars, such as those containing baby food, mustard, olives, or maraschino cherries, are ideal for giving. Soak off labels in warm water.

THE LABEL: A cool yet fiery condiment to accompany roast lamb or cream cheese with crackers. *If the chutney is freshly made, the label should read:* May be stored in the refrigerator for up to one week or frozen for up to three months. *If the chutney is frozen, the label should read:* May be kept frozen for up to three months or in the refrigerator for up to five days after it has been thawed.

Pickles

When is a pickle not just a pickle? When it becomes the beauty secret of one of history's most glamorous women. Sounds fantastic, doesn't it?

History has recorded that since the moment Cleopatra first heard the secret of pickle power a day never passed without her eating some. She considered them to be an elixir of both beauty and health. It's not unusual that she should have such secret knowledge; after all, her country was famous for the art of preserving. The Egyptians also had a thriving export trade in fish and meat pickled in salt brine. It's a matter of historical importance that they were responsible for developing many methods of preserving still in use today, even though they knew nothing about bacteria.

All of history is packed with pickle pusses. Even Emporer Tiberius included pickles on his daily menu for health. They were standard fare for Caesar's legions and Napoleon's armies; even the man for whom America was named, Americus Vespucci, was once a pickle dealer in Spain.

In approximate figures, Americans this year will eat 10 billion pickles, about five pounds per person. Each area seems to have its favorite. The sweeter ones, for example, are preferred in the South; spicy sweet in New England; a good, mixed selection in the Midwestern plain states, and on the West Coast the kosher dill and the Polish dill are by far the most popular. If you're an average American, you can expect to have pickles served at least once a week.

Americans, however, aren't the world's only pickle lovers. The French take national pride in their little finger-size *cornichons*. Latin Americans prefer pickle peppers. In India, bamboo shoots are pickled. And when you tire of cucumbers, large or small, you can always switch to tiny green tomatoes, pickled beets, cauliflower, okra, string beans, cherries — everything from Peter Piper's pickled peppers to pig's feet.

The end of World War I was almost the precise moment in the history of man when the scales were tipped on our old enemy, hunger. The year 1918 saw the mass production and sales of refrigerators, canned foods, and the introduction of frozen foods. Until that time we prepared for long hungry winters by drying and pickling our fruits and vegetables, and salting our meat and fish. This whole process is called curing (as if all fresh foods had a "killing" illness). As man became more sophisticated in preserving his harvest, certain preserves became a tradition. The purpose, of course, in every instance of preservation was to produce a condition which would inhibit decaying agents from multiplying.

Modern nutritionists have told us that Cleopatra wasn't very far wrong when she ate pickles to remain beautiful and to retain her health. A project at Michigan State College headed by Dr. F. W. Fabian, Research Professor of Bacteriology, has found that pickles contain Vitamin A, Vitamins B-1, B-2, and a very large amount of Vitamin C. Cleopatra may have been the first to believe that "you are what you eat" when she began the trend so many years ago.

Super-Crisp Pickle Chips

There isn't a cook alive who doesn't love to share the good things that come out of her kitchen. We, too, are a part of this happy community of compulsive kitchen gift-givers. After all, isn't that what this book is all about? But we do have one tiny admission to make. As bountiful as the season is and as generous as we long to be, we find ourselves extremely loath to part with the Super-Crisp Pickle Chips gracing our shelves—just because we might run out of them!

It all began back when Paul's mother (now *she* was magnanimous!) sent us a bottle of these indescribably crisp pickles. The recipe had come to her through a friend in Oak Ridge, Tennessee. Up until that time, we had no idea that pickles could be so crunchy. Now we make them often, and it becomes quite an event when we "break" out a bottle of Super-Crisps for our charcoal-grilled hamburgers. (After all, if one "breaks" out a bottle of champagne, should Super-Crisps be far behind?) Maybe you'll be more generous than we, though it's not likely. After making the recipe, however, if you, too, find yourself reluctant to part with your precious hoard, do as we do — give away the next best thing: the recipe.

This recipe makes nine to ten pints of pickles. Depending on the size of the jars you use, this amount will be sufficient for nine to twenty gifts.

> 2 (11.5-gram) bottles calcium hydroxide (see Note)
> 8 pounds unpeeled cucumbers
> 3 tablespoons mixed pickling spices
> 9 cups sugar
> 2 quarts white vinegar
> ¼ cup coarse salt (kosher salt)

Note: Calcium hydroxide is available at well-stocked pharmacies. It is a highly refined form of slaked lime, a product used for pickling in the rural sections of the United States for generations. Soaking cucumbers in water to which some form of lime has been added gives them incomparable crispness. The chemical does not actually dissolve in water, so any residue of chemical will be thoroughly washed away in the numerous rinsings. Do not worry about getting the mixture on your hands — it is not caustic.

Place the calcium hydroxide in a large crock or stockpot of at least 8-quart capacity made of any material except aluminum or cast iron. Add 2 gallons of water and mix according to the directions on the bottle. Wash and trim the ends from the cucumbers. Cut into ¼-inch slices. Add the sliced cucumbers and let stand undisturbed for 24 hours.

The next day drain the cucumber slices in a colander and rinse two or three times with cold water. Wash the crock or stockpot with soap, rinse it, and fill it with cold water. Soak the cucumber slices in the water for 3 hours to remove any last traces of chemical residue. Drain thoroughly.

Tie the spices in a piece of cheesecloth or other clean cloth, leaving enough space so they can move about inside the bag. Mix the sugar, vinegar, and salt in a large pot (again, not aluminum or cast iron) and heat, with the spice bag, just to the boiling point. Add the well-drained cucumber slices and remove from the heat to cool. Stir often during the next 24 hours.

On the third day, bring the mixture to a boil and simmer for 10 to 15 minutes until the cucumbers begin to look transparent. Using a slotted spoon, transfer the slices to hot, sterilized jars (see page 232). Fill the jars with boiling liquid to within ⅛ inch of the top, seal, and let cool undisturbed. Store in a cool place and allow to mellow for one week before serving.

TO PREPARE IN ADVANCE: These pickles will keep at peak quality for six months in sealed jars if stored in a cool dark place. Store in the refrigerator after opening. Do not freeze.

SPECIAL PACKAGING: It is important to use quality canning jars with self-sealing lids (see page 232). After the pickles have cooled and the seal is tight, clean any residue of syrup from the outside of the jar. The ring may be removed to use again. Wrap the jars in clear cellophane and tie with a bow.

THE LABEL: May be stored for up to six months in a cool, dark place. Refrigerate after opening.

Jeanne Lesem's Frozen Sliced Sweet Dill Pickles

These are really sensational crisp cucumber slices combined with thin onion rings and seasoned with dill. They're heavenly on charcoal-grilled hamburgers and great to take as a hospitality gift when you know your hostess is barbecuing. They are reminiscent of the dilled onion rings served at Alice's Restaurant on the pier in Malibu, California.

The recipe comes from Jeanne Lesem's *The Pleasures of Preserving and Pickling* published by Alfred A. Knopf. If you wish to delve deeply into jam, jelly and pickle-making, this is the book for you. It's a treasure trove of information and imaginative recipes.

This recipe makes about 4 cups of frozen dills, enough for four 8-ounce or eight 4-ounce gifts.

1 pound 3-inch-long unwaxed cucumbers, sliced ⅛-inch thick
   (about 4 cups packed)
¾ pound 2-inch-diameter yellow onions, sliced ⅛-inch thick
   (about 2 cups packed)
4 teaspoons table salt
2 tablespoons water
¾ to 1 cup sugar (we use ¾ cup)
½ cup cider vinegar
1 teaspoon dried dill weed (or more to taste)

Mix the prepared cucumbers, onions, salt, and water in a 2-quart bowl (not aluminum), and let stand about 2 hours. Drain, but do not rinse.

Return the vegetables to the bowl, and add the sugar, the vinegar, and the dill. Let stand, stirring from time to time, until sugar has dissolved completely and liquid covers the vegetables. Pack in glass or plastic freezer containers (leave 1 inch of head space), seal tightly, and freeze.

Defrost either in the refrigerator or at room temperature. Defrosting time will vary greatly, depending on the size of the freezer containers and the temperature.

Jeanne serves these on open sandwiches of thinly sliced pumpernickel spread with cream cheese. We adore them on charcoal-grilled hamburgers or spoon them into a lettuce cup to use simply as a small condiment on plates when serving most any kind of sandwich.

TO PREPARE IN ADVANCE: These may be kept in the freezer for up to six months. Use them within three or four days after thawing.

SPECIAL PACKAGING: You can use any kind of glass or plastic container suitable for giving. Be sure to leave at least an inch of room in the containers because the contents will expand when frozen and could break the container if packed too full.

THE LABEL: Pile on hamburgers or thinly sliced pumpernickel spread with cream cheese. *If the pickles are frozen, the label should read:* May be kept frozen for up to six months. Defrost either in the refrigerator or at room temperature. *If the pickles have been thawed, the label should read:* Use within three or four days.

Emerald Watermelon Pickles

Let nothing you dismay from tackling the job of making this pickle. Not even the matter of the 40 pounds of melon. Solve this problem by planning ahead. A summer picnic among a handful of friends ought to net you enough to begin. Or you may cut the recipe in half. But if you're going to go ahead and make these pickles anyway (not a big production but they do require tending over a three-day period) you may as well make the full amount because they keep indefinitely.

Paul's mom, who originated this recipe, finds that using spice oils instead of whole spices prevents the pickles from discoloring. She also adds green food coloring to the half-inch squares to attain a close approximation to the square-cut emeralds in the name.

Our cookbook author friend, Ruth Mellinkoff, uses her watermelon pickles in a utilitarian way when she serves rumaki, the chicken liver-bacon hors d'oeuvre. She secures the rumaki with watermelon pickles instead of the usual pineapple chunk at the end of the skewer, thus creating an elegant color/flavor contrast.

This recipe makes 15 pints of pickles, which is enough for fifteen 1-pint or thirty ½-pint gifts. This may sound like a lot of pickles; however, making the full amount is hardly more difficult than making just a few jars. You will enjoy having them on hand for so many gift occasions.

> 12 pounds of prepared watermelon rind cut from 35 to 40 pounds
>   of watermelon (see Note 1)
> 12 pounds granulated sugar
> 1 quart white vinegar
> ¼ teaspoon oil of cinnamon (see Note 2)
> ¼ teaspoon oil of cloves (see Note 2)
> Green food color

Note 1: If possible, buy watermelons which have been cut so that you can see that they have good thick rinds, at least ½-inch thick. Some watermelons have much thinner rinds.

Note 2: We specify spice oils because they have a finer flavor and do not discolor the pickles as do whole spices. Spice oils are available at well-stocked pharmacies. You might even have some oil of cloves if you have a first-aid kit—it's used for toothaches.

Remove all the green skin and the red meat from the watermelon rind—a vegetable peeler may be used to remove the green skin, a grapefruit knife works well to remove the red meat. Cut the rind into ½-inch or large cubes and place them in a large pot or crock, cover with cold water, and allow to stand in the refrigerator for 24 hours.

The next day, drain the rind and rinse with cold water; drain again. Place the cubes in a pot large enough to hold them (not aluminum or cast iron). Cover with cold water and bring to a boil slowly; then lower the heat and simmer for 5 minutes. Drain, rinse well with cold water, and let stand in a colander until cool. Dry on paper towels.

In the same pot, combine the sugar, vinegar, spice oils, and enough green food color to give the mixture a brilliant green color. Stir in the rind cubes and let stand at room temperature, stirring often, for the next 24 hours.

On the third day, bring the mixture to a hard boil. Reduce to a simmer and cook until the fruit is tender when pierced with a toothpick. This will take about 20 minutes. Using a slotted spoon transfer the cubes to hot sterilized jars (see page 230   ). Fill the jars with boiling syrup to within ¼ inch of the top and seal (see directions page 231   ). Let cool undisturbed to room temperature. Store in a cool place for a week before serving to allow the flavors to mellow.

TO PREPARE IN ADVANCE: Stored in a cool, dark place, such as a garage, these pickles will stay at peak quality for six months. We have kept some for a year and could hardly notice any loss of quality. Store in refrigerator after opening. Do not freeze.

SPECIAL PACKAGING: It is important to use quality canning jars with self-sealing lids (see page 231). After the pickles have cooled and the seal is tight, clean any residue of syrup from the outside of the jar. The ring may be removed to use again. Wrap the jars in clear cellophane and tie with a bow.

THE LABEL: May be stored in a cool, dark place for up to six months. Refrigerate after opening.

Russian Ruby Eggs

Something has been added to the established procedure of pickling beets. The something extra, in this case, is a dozen hard-cooked eggs. This recipe came to us from Verlie Hite, who is the hostess at the Mexican restaurant near our California home, where we often dine on burritos and chilled guacamole.

Verlie tells us there is a stunning transformation in these eggs as they absorb color and spice during their steeping, which can last as long as a month or longer. After a decent interval in their rosy residence, say, in two days' time, the whites of the egg are only slightly tinged with pink; after a week, the white has become a brilliant shocking pink; after a month, even the yolk has gone pink, making them eminently qualified to rate as Russian Ruby Eggs! The quartered eggs and whole beets can add flame and seduction to the cool greens that make up your dinner salads.

This recipe will fill two 1-quart containers, with six eggs each. The recipe may be doubled or tripled.

> 1 (1-pound) can whole beets, with liquid
> 1½ cups white or cider vinegar
> 1 cup sugar
> 2 tablespoons mixed pickling spices
> 12 hard-cooked eggs, peeled (see Note)

Note: After the eggs are cooked, plunge them immediately into ice water or cold tap water to facilitate peeling. We've found that eggs that are not too fresh are easier to peel.

Drain the canned-beet liquid into a small saucepan with the vinegar and sugar. Set the beets aside. Wrap the mixed pickling spices in a small piece of cheesecloth or other clean cloth and tie with a string, leaving a bit of air space. (Verlie uses a metal tea caddy). Place the spice bag in the saucepan and bring the liquid to a boil. Lower the heat and simmer, covered, for 20 minutes.

Place the peeled eggs in a 2-quart jar or divide among other nonmetal gift containers. Pour the hot liquid over the eggs and top with the reserved beets. The beets will keep the eggs from floating. Refrigerate for at least 24 hours before serving. The eggs will have a vivid ruby color after three days.

TO PREPARE IN ADVANCE: We know these will keep in the refrigerator at least a month and probably indefinitely.

SPECIAL PACKAGING: Old-fashioned canning jars make lovely containers for these elegant eggs.

THE LABEL: May be stored in the refrigerator for up to a month.

Lucky Pickled Black-Eyed Peas

Both of us have Southern ancestors who believed that eating black-eyed peas on New Year's Day brought good luck for the new year, a rather powerful incentive for rushing right out and making this dish. Be that as it may, we waited until two years ago to serve it and had one of the best years ever. You can bet that it's now become a von Welanetz tradition, if indeed two years of anything can be termed "tradition." It may not have been the peas, but we're not about to take any risks, either with ourselves or with friends we care about. Bless yourself and others. Spread the good fortune about. Gift friends and hostesses with this easy-to-duplicate recipe, made even easier by the use of black-eyed peas in a can.

This recipe makes 3 cups of pickled peas to fill three 8-ounce or six 4-ounce gift containers.

> 2 (15-ounce) cans black-eyed peas or about 1½ cups dried black-eyed peas, cooked and drained
> ½ cup vegetable oil
> ¼ cup red wine vinegar
> 1 large clove garlic, flattened
> ½ small onion, thinly sliced and separated into rings
> 1 tablespoon minced parsley
> ½ teaspoon salt
> ¼ teaspoon ground black pepper

Flatten the garlic by peeling it, placing it on a hard surface, and pressing it with the flat side of a knife until the clove bursts. Leave whole.

Combine all ingredients in a mixing bowl or refrigerate container. Refrigerate for at least 24 hours before serving. Remove the garlic clove after 24 hours.

TO PREPARE IN ADVANCE: May be stored in the refrigerator for up to two weeks.

SPECIAL PACKAGING: The amount of good luck does not depend on the size of the serving. Any attractive small containers are suitable.

THE LABEL: An old superstition says that eating black-eyed peas on New Year's Day brings good luck. May be stored in the refrigerator for up to two weeks.

Sauces, Mustards & Marinades

Sauces to enhance, or more often, to hide the flavor of fish and meat date far beyond our European ancestors, all the way back to prehistoric China. The name *catsup* itself is from the Siamese *kachiap*.

Bottled sauce-making was a well-established trade by the end of the fourteenth century, when vendors on Paris streets would sell their well-known cameline sauce, yellow sauce, and green sauce. Cameline was basically cinnamon; green sauce was ginger and green herbs; yellow sauce was ginger and saffron. At the same time among the isles of Greece, banqueters feasted on spitted goats, periodically basted with aromatic sauces and brushed with brooms of mint.

The first settlers to this country brought their favorite spices with them for the very same reasons they used them in the kitchens of their former homelands: it was the best possible way to mask tainted fish, overripe or salted beef.

The whole world was in love with sauces in the eighteenth century, and great men would scheme to have one named after them. The most illustrious of them all was the financier, Monsieur Bechamel, who won such favor in the French court of Louis XIV that he was awarded the position of Lord Steward to the royal household. Clearly he didn't create this sauce (he wasn't a chef), but the honor came through his position as superintendent of the royal kitchens.

What an incredible tribute to have France's mother sauce, or "sauce mere," carry one's name into history! The variations of this basic white sauce seem to be endless. By the simple addition of grated cheese, you have sauce Mornay. Substituting chicken, beef, or hot vegetable broth for milk, you have sauce veloute. Add heavy cream, and you have sauce supreme; or sauce aurore, by the addition of tomato paste and a teaspoon of powdered mustard seed, turns it into an excellent garnish for broiled meats.

The invading Romans of the first century B.C. taught the French the art of making mustard, used not only for cooking but medicinally as well. We still use mustard packs to relieve congestion and break up a cold. The powdered black mustard seed, when mixed with water or vinegar, produces the same tangy sauce used by Greeks and Romans long ago. The addition of other herbs and spices, like tarragon, bring new surprising flavor.

All meat is naturally tender until it is cooked, but as we apply heat, the fibers of the muscles tighten, and a process sets in called "shrinkage." Next to buying very expensive and well-marbled meat, there are only three ways to tenderize: cook slowly over low heat, pound and tear the fibers with a heavy mallet (as with Swiss steak and schnitzel), or marinate (Spanish for pickle). Marinades tenderize by softening muscle tissue with their high-acid content. When selected seasonings have been added to the marinade, it will deliciously flavor even the lowliest cuts of meat.

The many uses of sauces were well established before Mr. Heinz went into business in 1869. The advent of refrigeration in the 1800s did away with the need to salt and preserve winter meats, and most markets today insist that freshness is the keystone of their success. But sauces still linger on, and it would as unthinkable for an American not to use catsup on a hamburger as it would be to remain seated when the National Anthem is sung.

Secret Steak Sauce

Oh, how we were tempted to keep Paul's Secret Steak Sauce secret, saving it for some nebulous future to manufacture in our dotage. But, we thought, why should we delay, for isn't it in the telling that a secret becomes tantalizing? And then (as we kept right on thinking) why not make the Secret Steak Sauce a part of everybody's future? And, why not make that future *now*. So here it is, dear friends, in all its glory. The only secret about it now (and you don't have to tell a soul if you don't want to) is that is requires no cooking at all! We send it your way with all our love and one caution: Take heed: It's so good, it can become addictive.

This recipe makes approximately 7 cups of sauce. Depending on the size of your containers, it is enough for three to six gifts.

> 1 (12-ounce) bottle Heinz chili sauce
> 1 (14-ounce) bottle catsup
> 1 (12-ounce) bottle Sun Brand mango chutney
> 1 (10-ounce) bottle Worcestershire sauce
> ¼ cup Cognac or brandy
> 1 tablespoon Dijon mustard
> 1 teaspoon sugar
> 1 tablespoon anchovy paste (optional—but not if you like
>   anchovies!)
> 5 drops red food color (optional)
> 2 drops green food color (optional)

Combine the ingredients in an electric blender. Blend at low speed until smooth. Funnel into gift containers.

Serve as an accompaniment to steaks, hamburgers, roasts, etc.

TO PREPARE IN ADVANCE: This may be stored indefinitely on the pantry shelf.

SPECIAL PACKAGING: Many kinds of bottles may be used, but the most convenient ones for this recipe are those left over from the catsup, chili sauce, chutney, and Worcestershire called for in the recipe.

THE LABEL: A tangy steak and all-purpose meat sauce. May be stored indefinitely at room temperature.

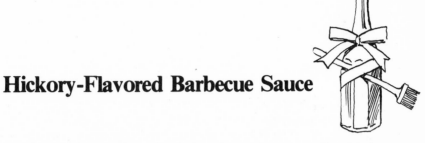

Hickory-Flavored Barbecue Sauce

Perhaps it's Paul's interest in chemistry that helps him perform so well as kitchen magician when concocting sauces. As you may have noticed, his name appears with regularity in this section. Here you have his favorite barbecue sauce, a five-minute marvel that belies its no-cooking, no-labor-lost background. A gift bottle of this will go a long way toward enhancing meat or poultry. It is especially superb on what all Americans regard with undiminished affection—hamburgers, thick and juicy and covered with sauce.

This recipe makes about 3 cups of sauce which is enough to fill two 12-ounce containers. The recipe may be doubled, tripled, or quadrupled. We recommend making it in large quantity because it disappears quickly at our house.

1 (20-ounce) bottle catsup
¼ cup cider vinegar
4 teaspoons firmly packed dark brown sugar
1 tablespoon Kitchen Bouquet gravy seasoning
1 tablespoon Worcestershire sauce
1 teaspoon salt
1 teaspoon onion powder
½ teaspoon imitation smoke flavor (see Note)
¼ teaspoon garlic powder

Note: Imitation smoke flavor is available in the spice section of most markets. Always use it sparingly— too much can spoil a recipe.

Combine all ingredients in a blender, pitcher, or mixing bowl. Mix until well combined. Use a funnel to transfer the sauce to bottles for storage. Let the flavor mellow for 24 hours before serving. Shake before using.

TO PREPARE IN ADVANCE: This may be stored indefinitely on the pantry shelf. The mixture will separate on standing, so be sure to shake the bottle before pouring.

SPECIAL PACKAGING: Save old wine bottles and corks for this, or bottles that once contained catsup, Worcestershire sauce, etc. Soak off labels and apply your own.

THE LABEL: Shake before using on hamburgers or barbecued meats. May be stored indefinitely at room temperature.

Merlin's Magical Meat Marinade

Merlin (alias Paul) has been at work in his laboratory concocting the perfect marinade, and we both agree this is it. Make the magic work for you. Here is a pungent, garlic-scented marinade that will promote ordinary steaks, chops, hamburgers, and even roasts to the upper echelons. It is magic because of its startling effect. It tenderizes quickly. It is simple to reproduce. It requires no cooking. Don't even bother with an apron. Best of all, it makes a wonderful present for the man of the house to prepare, funnel into flask-shaped bottles, and bestow on one and all.

This recipe makes five ½-pint gifts of marinade.

> 4 cups Kikkoman soy sauce
> ¼ cup (4 tablespoons) onion powder
> ½ teaspoon garlic powder
> ½ cup bottled Kitchen Bouquet or Gravy Master
> 2 tablespoons plus 2 teaspoons Spice Islands Beau Monde or
>   Schilling's Bon Apetit

Combine the ingredients in a mixing bowl and let stand for 1 hour at room temperature. Stir and pour through a funnel into containers for giving.

To use as a marinade, place meat in a shallow glass dish. Pour ½ cup marinade over each steak or ¼ cup for each chop or hamburger. Allow to stand, covered, at room temperature for two hours, turning once. One cup of marinade is sufficient for a roast, which should be allowed to stand, covered, for eight hours, turning several times. Cook the meat as usual. Heat the remaining marinade to serve as an aromatic sauce.

TO PREPARE IN ADVANCE: There is nothing in this which can spoil, so make it whenever you're in the mood (Merlin prefers the full moon!). Store the containers on the pantry shelf, ready for last-minute giving.

SPECIAL PACKAGING: The marinade has a rich deep brown color which shows off beautifully in clear, flask-shaped brandy bottles. See suggestions for other bottles, page 213 .

THE LABEL: Shake or stir with wand before using. Marinate a roast, two steaks, or four chops in a shallow glass dish at room temperature for two hours (eight hours for roast). Cook meat as usual. Heat leftover marinade to serve as sauce. May be stored indefinitely at room temperature.

American Style Tomato Meat Sauce with Mushrooms

We think we're decisive, with good judgment and taste, except, it seems, when it comes to deciding which is our favorite of all pasta sauces. When we're asked, we find ourselves facing a bewildering array of savory sauces. How to decide which one to include in our book? Well, having taught classes for a number of years on the art of making homemade pasta with a variety of sauces from meat, to tomato, to fish, we decided to let our students make the choice. And this one ranks high, no doubt because it is so versatile. Use it to make lasagna or Yankee Noodle, **page 66**. Best of all, put it in a container, include some uncooked pasta, a wedge of Parmesan cheese and wine, and present it to your best friend. You will provide him with a feast that will long linger, like the memory of some sunny isle in the blue Adriatic.

This recipe makes 3 quarts of rich sauce, enough for three 1-quart gifts of three to four servings each. It takes 10 cups of sauce to make one recipe of **Yankee Noodle**. One quart of sauce is sufficient for **one pound of pasta**.

1 pound pork sausage
2 pounds lean ground beef
6 medium onions, finely chopped
4 to 6 large cloves garlic, minced or pressed
1 cup minced parsley
¾ pound fresh mushrooms, cleaned and thickly sliced (See Note, page **42**)
1 (1-pound, 14-ounce) can solid-pack tomatoes
1 (12-ounce) can tomato paste
1 bottle (fifth) dry red table wine
¼ cup Madeira or sherry
1 tablespoon Worcestershire sauce
1 ¼-inch slice fresh lemon
2 teaspoons salt, to taste
1½ teaspoons dried oregano
1 teaspoon dried sage
½ teaspoon dried thyme
½ teaspoon dried sweet basil
½ teaspoon coarsely ground black pepper
¼ teaspoon fennel seed

For Serving
Any kind of cooked pasta, buttered
Grated Parmesan cheese

Slowly brown the sausage in a heavy 6-quart pot, mashing with the back of a spoon until crumbly. Pour off the fat. Add the ground beef to the pan and saute slowly, breaking it up with a spoon until the meat has lost its red color and is crumbly. Stir in the chopped onions and garlic and continue cooking until the onion is transparent. Add all remaining ingredients.

Simmer the sauce uncovered over medium-low heat, stirring often, for 2 to 3 hours until it is the desired thickness. Skim off excess fat. Transfer to containers and let cool completely at room temperature. Cover and refrigerate. When chilled, remove congealed fat from the surface.

Serve hot over any kind of cooked, buttered pasta. Accompany with grated Parmesan.

TO PREPARE IN ADVANCE: The flavor of this sauce is enhanced if it is made at least a day ahead and heated before serving. It may be stored for up to five days in the refrigerator and for up to four months in the freezer. If frozen, thaw completely. Heat slowly in a heavy-bottomed saucepan.

SPECIAL PACKAGING: We enjoy giving this sauce in a picnic basket with imported pasta and a wedge of fresh Parmesan from an Italian delicatessen. We also include a red-and-white checkered picnic-size cloth, Italian bread, and breadsticks.

THE LABEL: Serve over cooked, buttered pasta with lots of grated Parmesan. Heat slowly in a heavy-bottomed saucepan over low heat. *If the sauce is freshly made, the label should read:* May be stored in the refrigerator for up to five days or frozen for up to four months. *If the sauce is frozen, the label should read:* May be kept frozen for up to four months, or in the refrigerator for up to five days after it has been thawed.

Poppy Seed Salad Dressing for Fruit Salads

California is the land of fruits and nuts, and everybody makes the most of it. Where else are there young women, garbed like gypsies, walking into business offices to sell health food lunches (that include fruits and nuts) out of wicker baskets? The most wonderful salad they sell is an unbeatable alliance of lettuce, farmer's cheese, fresh strawberries, dates, sunflower seeds, pecans, and a containerful of poppy seed dressing. Why not make up your own gift basket with fresh fruit and berries of the season, some alfalfa sprouts, and salad greens of any description. Slip in a bottle of this sweet-sour onion dressing and beat the path to stardom.

The recipe makes about 3 cups of dressing, enough for three 8-ounce gift containers or six 4-ounce containers.

> 1 small white onion
> 1½ cups sugar
> 2/3 cup cider vinegar
> 2 teaspoons dry mustard
> 1½ teaspoons salt
> 2 cups vegetable oil
> 2 to 3 tablespoons poppy seeds

Use an electric blender or Cuisinart food processor to make this. Cut the onion coarsely and blend at medium speed until you have onion juice. Add the sugar, vinegar, mustard and salt.

With the motor running, pour the oil slowly through the top until all the oil is in and the mixture is very thick. Add the poppy seeds and blend a few seconds longer.

Transfer to containers and store in a cool place or in the upper part of the refrigerator away from the coils.

If the dressing gets too hot or too cold, it may separate. If so, pour off the clear part into the blender or food processor and blend again, adding the poppy-seed mixture very slowly until all is recombined.

TO PREPARE IN ADVANCE: This will keep for up to a month in a cool, dark place and indefinitely in the refrigerator. Do not freeze.

SPECIAL PACKAGING: Set a container of dressing in the middle of a basket of lettuce, fruit, and nuts for a salad.

THE LABEL: Use the dressing over fruit, lettuce and nut salad. May be stored for up to a month in a cool, dark place, or indefinitely in the refrigerator. Do not freeze.

Garlic or Herb-Flavored Wine Vinegar

When we present bottles of this wine vinegar to friends, we send it along with a fourteenth-century legend. It seems that during the Plague, four beggars were promised their freedom from a French prison if they would perform the grim task of burying the dead. All four lived to a ripe old age to tell their tale again and again, attributing their survival from the Black Death to eating cloves of garlic and consuming bottles of sour wine. In honor of these legendary four, we spear four large cloves of garlic on a wooden skewer and insert into an empty wine bottle. We fill the bottle with wine vinegar, either red or white, seal with a cork and melted wax. To make a more elegant gift, we tie a bow around the neck of the bottle with a length of narrow ribbon and attach the streamers with a notary seal. See illustration.

If you wish, you may substitute fresh garden herbs for the garlic, but then there'd be no legend.

The directions are for one bottle of vinegar. It is easy to make dozens while you are at it, if you have bottles, jug vinegar, etc. The amount of wax will seal several bottles.

A clean wine bottle (fifth) with cork
Enough red or white jug wine vinegar to fill the bottle
4 large cloves of peeled garlic impaled on a bamboo skewer or
    about 4 long sprigs of fresh tarragon, basil, or dill

For Sealing
¼ bar paraffin melted with 1 crayon, *or* 2 to 3 sticks sealing wax
    from a stationery store, *or* leftover candles melted with
    crayons for color

Place the skewered garlic or the herb sprigs inside the bottle and fill to within 1½ inches of the top with vinegar. Insert the cork all the way into the bottle.

Place the wax and crayon in an empty 6-ounce juice can or other small metal container. Set the can in a small amount of water over low heat. Stir often until melted. Dip the top of the bottle into the wax to coat the cork and mouth of the bottle and let cool until set. Redip several times, if necessary.

TO PREPARE IN ADVANCE: Let the vinegar age in a cool, dark place for at least two weeks. The bottles may be stored at room temperature for up to four months or in the refrigerator indefinitely.

SPECIAL PACKAGING: Decorate the bottles with ribbon and seals as illustrated.

THE LABEL: May be stored in a cool dark place for up to four months or in the refrigerator indefinitely.

Tangy Tarragon Mustard

We have a great affection for tarragon. In fact, Bearnaise (a kind of hollandaise with herbs) was one of the first successful sauces we learned to make in our kitchen when we were first married. We doused everything with it. Sometimes it went toward masking minor cooking mishaps. We've become good friends over the years, and we haven't gotten our fill of it. We were overjoyed, therefore, when we found tarragon used in a French mustard. In time, however, there was a lamentable decline in the imported product, and the milder mustard proved not to our liking. We like mustard to be hot, and this recipe is hot. If you don't like hot mustard, this is not for you. It has a kick and a half that will lift your spirits right through the rest of the twentieth century!

This recipe makes about a cup of mustard, enough to fill two 4-ounce containers. Do not double the recipe.

¼ cup Coleman's dry mustard
1 tablespoon sugar
1/3 cup dry white wine
¼ cup white wine vinegar
½ teaspoon salt
3 egg yolks
½ teaspoon dried tarragon leaves, crumbled

Combine the dry mustard and sugar in the top of a glass double boiler. Mix well to remove any lumps from the mustard. Stir in the wine, vinegar, and salt. Let stand, uncovered, at room temperature for an hour or two to allow the flavor to mellow.

Blend in the egg yolks and place the mixture over hot, but not boiling, water. Whisk constantly for about 5 minutes until slightly thickened. Transfer immediately to a small mixing bowl to stop further cooking. Stir in the tarragon. Spoon the mustard into containers and cover immediately with plastic wrap.

Serve sparingly as a sandwich spread or with roast or charcoal-grilled meats.

TO PREPARE IN ADVANCE: May be stored, covered, for up to three weeks in the refrigerator. If the mustard is for your own use, it may be frozen for up to three months. Use within a few days after thawing—the mustard will separate easily after it has been frozen.

SPECIAL PACKAGING: Small crocks, mustard jars, or even custard cups are ideal gift containers.

THE LABEL: Use sparingly as a sandwich spread or an accompaniment to roast or charcoal-grilled meats. May be stored in the refrigerator for up to three weeks.

Sweet Champagne Mustard

This is such a choice gift item that we simply had to include it in this volume, although it already appears in our book, *The Pleasure of Your Company*, published by Atheneum. We get quite lyrical about the amazing smoothness of this hot, sweet mustard, unlike anything to be found here or abroad. To use one of our family expressions, "It's to die over!" Frances Pelham, our cooking buddy, is responsible for its creation and for the way it's served, in style, in an 18-inch champagne glass that towers over the ham and roast beef sandwiches she's prepared in homemade biscuits.

This recipe makes about 1¾ cups of sauce, enough for two or three small gifts.

2/3 cup Coleman's dry mustard
1 cup sugar
3 large eggs
2/3 cup Regina champagne-stock vinegar or white wine vinegar

In the top of a glass double boiler, combine the dry mustard and sugar. Beat with a whisk to remove any mustard lumps. Beat in the eggs and the vinegar.

Place over boiling water and beat constantly for 5 to 7 minutes until the mixture has thickened and appears slightly foamy. Pour immediately into another container to stop the cooking. Spoon into gift containers, cover with plastic wrap, and let cool.

Serve with roast ham or any kind of cold cuts.

TO PREPARE IN ADVANCE: The mustard will keep, covered, for at least three weeks in the refrigerator. Do not freeze.

SPECIAL PACKAGING: Small crocks or mustard pots are ideal. Cover with plastic wrap held in place with a rubber band. Tie a ribbon over the rubber band. This would be a marvelous accompaniment to a platter of sandwich makings, such as sliced ham and roast beef, sliced cheese, sweet butter, and rye bread.

THE LABEL: Caution, it's hot! Serve with roast ham or any cold cuts. May be stored in the refrigerator for up to three weeks. Do not freeze.

Mustard Dill Sauce

Friends and students are continually asking us to decipher the ingredients of dishes they have enjoyed in restaurants. Since we love eating out, we relish this type of investigation. Here is a sharp and snappy sauce that will reward your diligence of adding the oil drop by drop when making the recipe. It perks up sandwiches and seafood and was fashioned after a sauce served at a restaurant which specializes in open-face sandwiches and salads after the Scandinavian manner.

This recipe makes about 1¾ cups of sauce, enough for two or three small gifts.

> ½ cup Poupon Dijon mustard
> 2 teaspoons Coleman's dry mustard
> 1/3 cup sugar
> ¼ cup white wine vinegar
> 1 tablespoon olive oil
> ¾ cup commercial or homemade mayonnaise
> 2 tablespoons dried dill weed

Combine the two mustards, sugar, and vinegar in a medium mixing bowl. Beat rapidly with a wire whisk. Add the oil (very gradually), a few drops at a time, while whisking. When all the oil is in, the mixture will have a thin-mayonnaise consistency. Beat in the mayonnaise and dill.

Serve cold with open-face sandwiches, cold cuts, or cooked shellfish.

TO PREPARE IN ADVANCE: May be stored, covered, in the refrigerator indefinitely. Do not freeze. If the sauce separates, simply beat it briskly with a whisk until it is smooth again.

SPECIAL PACKAGING: A small dish or crock of the sauce might accompany a platter of either cold cuts or cheeses for sandwich making or cooked chilled shellfish for dipping.

THE LABEL: Use as a sandwich spread or dipping sauce for shellfish. May be stored indefinitely in the refrigerator. Do not freeze. If the sauce separates, beat it rapidly with whisk until smooth.

Herb Blends & Seasoning Salts

In kitchen use, both herbs and spices are considered spices, though, of course, technically speaking, this is not true. But rather than conjugate Latin or confuse ourselves with botany and the precise way these items are used, we prefer this simpler geographical definition: "Any aromatic plant products used in the preparation of food and native to the tropical parts of China and India are spices. All others native to a more temperate climate are herbs." There is, however, another definition that we enjoy and that is Christopher Marlowe's where he defines "spice" as the plural of "spouse."

But we digress.

"India," "China," and "spices" — those three words are like golden threads woven through the whole fabric of Western history. To understand the incredible influence spices have had on all our lives would take a lifetime — and certainly more space than we have here.

For countless ages there was this Silk Road, this Golden Road, the Spice route. It traveled West from China winding through breathless eagle-high mountain passes down through scorching deserts, threading through Persia to its final destination on the shores of the Mediterranean. This was the world's oldest trading road. It carried, at a rate of less than ten miles per day, such exotic luxuries as musks, aloes, pearls, precious stones, and spices, including cinnamon, cloves, and pepper. (Spices were so precious they were seldom used in the kitchen; until the Greco-Roman Empire, their primary use was for medicine.) On the return trip East, woolen cloth was transported, as well as eunuchs, swords, and white women slaves. This was the only possible land route between Asia and the continent of Europe, and since it passed through Arab lands, the Arabs naturally became traders and grew wealthy beyond belief, forming their first monopoly.

Egypt had great need of this trade route for incense (such as frankincense and myrrh) to fumigate their temples, and for spices (especially cinnamon) to embalm and preserve their dead.

As for the Greek and Roman legions, when they established new empires and founded huge cities, such as Alexandria, they created a dilemma: the larger the city, the further away the farms, and the supplying of fresh food became almost impossible. For those who could afford it, Asian spices and incense were the answer. Incense masked the stench of crowded humanity, spices masked the flavor of decaying meat, and both spices and herbs preserved winter foods.

As the Roman Empire flourished and grew, the need for spices became greater and the Arab taxes became heavier. At one point in Arab history, the levied tax was one-third of every shipment leaving their country. But about 40 A.D. the Roman Emperor Claudius handsomely rewarded a Greek merchant who discovered (through studying the change in wind direction) a way to make a complete round trip to the Orient in one year, rather than the two years it usually took. The West had found a way past the Arabic curtain. A sea route was the answer, the only answer, to satisfy mankind's growing dependence on spices.

And, of course, when Columbus set sail westward with his three ships, his main purpose was to discover a sea route to India and cinnamon. When he bumped into America, he believed he had done it and named the inhabitants Indians. He made three more trips, still searching for the riches of the fabulous East, and though he died in disappointment, he had opened up the way West. The names of other explorers who followed are famous, among them, Vasco da Gama, who found a seaward passage from Western Europe to India that ultimately destroyed the Arab stranglehold on trade and the Portuguese navigator, Magellan, who in 1520 sailed through the Straits of Patagonia, later to be named after him, and discovered the Philippines and the Moluccas, which we know today as the Spice Islands.

We no longer require spices to mask offensive odors, but after thousands of years of using them to flavor and enhance our food, cooks have unanimously decided that it is better to live with them than without them. And the whole world is at work to supply them to us in their infinite varieties.

Aromatic Summer Salt

Paul devised this delicate all-purpose seasoning salt, a happy marriage of mint and other summer herbs. We like to give it away, crushed, powdered, ready for sprinkling in containers called "dredgers" used for pepper or confectioner's sugar. Dredgers are available at hardware stores and often have a brightly colored enamel finish. The large holes in the cap allow the kosher salt to flow through freely on whatever you feel would benefit from this special blend. It is especially good on tomatoes, eggs, salads, and steamed vegetables.

This recipe makes one cup of seasoning salt, enough for two 4-ounce gifts.

2 tablespoons plus 2 teaspoons onion powder
4 teaspoons garlic salt
4 teaspoons dried parsley
2 teaspoons dried sweet basil
2 teaspoons dried marjoram
2 teaspoons dried mint leaves
½ teaspoon curry powder
¾ cup coarse salt (kosher salt)

Place all ingredients except the coarse salt in an electric blender, electric coffee mill, or mortar and pestle. Grind to a powder. Mix with the salt and transfer to containers. If you prefer a finer salt, grind the salt with the other ingredients or use table salt in place of kosher salt.

TO PREPARE IN ADVANCE: This will keep indefinitely.

SPECIAL PACKAGING: There are many containers that would be suitable: salt cellars with large holes, muffaniers, hand-decorated dredgers, or, easiest of all, empty spice bottles with shaker tops.

THE LABEL: An all-purpose seasoning salt.

A Salt for All Seasons

Here is a wonderful seasoning salt that we discovered quite by chance while setting out to duplicate a nationally distributed product. We tasted our happy accident, pronounced it great, and quickly closed the book on further research.

It's especially good when broiling or barbecuing steaks. But take heed for if your steak is not thick, you should sear both sides before sprinkling with any kind of salt. Salt on the surface of raw meat draws juices outward! To keep juices and flavor in, cook both sides of the meat long enough to seal the surface. If over an inch thick, you may go ahead and salt the steak before cooking because the salt will only draw the moisture from the outside one-quarter inch.

This is an all-season salt so don't stop with steak. Use it also on radishes, celery, chicken, tuna salad. It's even great for tossing over your left shoulder when you need some extra good luck.

This recipe makes about 1½ cups of seasoned salt, enough to fill three empty spice bottles with shaker tops or other 4-ounce containers.

¼ teaspoon dried sweet basil
¼ teaspoon dried marjoram
¼ teaspoon dried tarragon
¼ teaspoon dried thyme
1¼ cups salt
4 teaspoons paprika
2 teaspoons onion powder
2 teaspoons Spice Islands Beau Monde seasoning
1 teaspoon black pepper
1 teaspoon garlic powder
1 teaspoon dry mustard
1 teaspoon curry powder
1 teaspoon sugar
¼ teaspoon cayenne (ground red pepper)
¼ teaspoon nutmeg
¼ teaspoon chili powder

Combine the basil, marjoram, tarragon, and thyme with ¼ cup of the salt in an electric blender or Cuisinart food processor and blend until the herbs are pulverized. Transfer to a 3-cup bowl or measuring cup and stir in the rest of the salt and all remaining ingredients. Stir until well blended. Pour the seasoned salt through a funnel into containers for giving.

Use as you would commercial seasoned salts for coating roast meats and poultry, seasoning vegetables and salads, etc.

TO PREPARE IN ADVANCE: The salt, if tightly sealed, may be stored indefinitely on the pantry shelf.

SPECIAL PACKAGING: Save empty spice bottles with shaker tops for this. Remove the label and add your own. Colored enamel dredgers (see illustration) are equally suitable.

THE LABEL: Sprinkle on meats and poultry before roasting and use for seasoning vegetables, salads, etc.

Parisian Spice

The mystery is no more. This is Parisian Spice, a judicious blend of thyme, cloves, allspice, and nutmeg. Although it is still called for in many recipes, as far as we know there has been nothing marketed under this name for a long time. Now you can make your own supply. Give it away in small amounts. A little goes a long way, as it is used sparingly to enhance meat loaf, pate, and stock.

The recipe makes a little more than one cup of spice blend. It is used sparingly, so this amount is enough for four 2-ounce gifts.

> 1 cup coarse salt (kosher salt)
> 1 tablespoon dried thyme leaves
> 2 teaspoons ground cloves
> 2 teaspoons ground allspice
> 2 teaspoons ground nutmeg

Combine the ingredients and store in tightly covered containers.
Use sparingly for seasoning pate, meatloaf, soup, sauces, etc.

TO PREPARE IN ADVANCE: This spice mixture, like most herbs, may be stored almost indefinitely if tightly covered in a cool, dark place. For best flavor use within one year.

SPECIAL PACKAGING: Save tiny bottles for giving, such as empty spice bottles, pill bottles, etc. Antique stores and garage sales are good sources. Include a container of this when giving Chicken Liver Pate Maison along with the recipe for making the pate.

THE LABEL: Use sparingly to season pate s, meatloaf, soups, and sauces. Store in an airtight container in a cool, dark place. Use within one year for best flavor.

Bouquet Garni

Bulbs, cookies, lights, tinsel adorn most Christmas trees, but one of the most unusual ornaments we've ever used was given to us the first Christmas we were married. As her contribution to our tree-trimming party, a friend brought a little shallot basket (see illustration) which she had filled with tiny cheesecloth parcels of herbs. We were enchanted! At the end of its stint on our tree in the living room, it went on to seasoning soups and stocks in our kitchen. If shallot baskets are not readily available, tiny flowerpots or clear plastic cubes make good substitutes.

This recipe makes enough for six or seven gifts.

> Cheesecloth
> Herbs of Provence, page 146, or a combination of 8 parts dried
>   parsley flakes, 1 part crumbled bay leaf, and 1 part dried
>   thyme
> String
> Miniature rickrack

Cut 4-inch squares out of a double thickness of cheesecloth. Place about ½ teaspoon mixed herbs in the center of each square and tie securely with string, forming tight bundles. Tie miniature rickrack over the string for decoration. Pack into containers for giving.

TO PREPARE IN ADVANCE: Store in an airtight container. Herbs quickly lose their flavor when exposed to air, so if the bouquets are not simply for decoration, they should be used within a month or two.

SPECIAL PACKAGING: Tiny metal shallot baskets from France (see illustration) or miniature flowerpots make perfect containers. The little baskets, which make imaginative tree ornaments, are available wherever gourmet supplies are sold.

THE LABEL: An herb mixture for seasoning soups, stocks, and sauces. Remove the rickrack before using, then drop the bundle into simmering liquid. Discard before serving. Store in an airtight container. Use within two months for best flavor.

Herbs of Provence

The intriguing quality emanating from roasts and poultry often comes from a very small, but important, element: the addition of a choice selection of herbs. For that reason, herb mixtures make delightful and practical gifts. This particular blend is fashioned after one that comes from herbs grown and used in Provence, imported to us, however, in eleven-ounce crocks! The only long-term value in buying such an import would be to use the very attractive rustic crock as a flowerpot, since buying herbs in this quantity, as you know, is a very poor investment because of short shelf life. But for those of you who want to gratify your palates, and your friends', here is Herbs of Provence, a fresh and fragrant mixture to use, not only in our Cream Cheese with Garlic and Herbs in the Manner of Boursin, page 26, but also to rub into roasts and poultry before roasting and on steaks before barbecuing.

This recipe makes ½ cup of mixed herbs, enough for two 2-ounce gifts. The recipe is easily doubled, tripled, or quadrupled.

3 tablespoons dried marjoram
3 tablespoons dried thyme
3 tablespoons dried summer savory
1 tablespoon dried sweet basil
1½ teaspoons dried rosemary, crumbled
½ teaspoon crushed sage
½ teaspoon fennel seeds

Combine the herbs, mix well, and pack into airtight containers.

TO PREPARE IN ADVANCE: All dried herbs should be stored in airtight containers in a cool, dark place. For best flavor, they should be used within six months.

SPECIAL PACKAGING: Keep your eye out for tiny containers such as pottery crocks from art fairs, clear plastic cubes, etc.

THE LABEL: An all-purpose herb blend to flavor soups, stocks, roast meats, and cheese spreads. Store in an airtight container. Use within six months.

Cookies

"Speak for yourself, John" — that romantic fragment of history from colonial Nieuw Amsterdam would have been lost forever if John Alden only could have mustered the courage to give Priscilla a *speculaas koekjes.*

Speculaas in the Netherlands means bishop. In the third century in Amsterdam there was a bishop who gave three impoverished maidens their dowry out of his own pocket. To this day, December 5 is set aside to honor this loving man, and young girls and boys of marrying age exchange molded cookies in their own likeness with their sweethearts.

After America was settled and firmly established, such old-world traditions presented themselves at each and every table. And your reputation was made by how well you could bake. The English showed off their teacakes; the Scottish, their shortbreads; and the Dutch, their *koekjes,* which, ultimately, was transformed into the American "cookies."

Is it possible that nothin' says lovin' like something from the oven? Cookies *are* a gift of love, whether it's a basket to a new neighbor, a full cookie jar and glass of milk for children when they come home from school, or a full tin under someone's tree at Christmas.

There are dozens, hundreds, of cookies that are easy to make, satisfying, and delicious. There's no longer any need to be a great baker to make delicious ones. Modern electrical equipment, automatic ovens, and more leisure time to putter in the kitchen make filling the lunch box and the gift basket a pleasure.

There are really only six basic types:

1. *Molded.* A thick dough, shaped and rolled in your hands into balls, logs, or crescents.

2. *Rolled.* A thick dough rolled with a rolling pin to about ⅛ inch and cut into shapes with a cardboard pattern, cooky cutter or pastry wheel.

3. *Bar Cookies (totally American).* These are a cross between a cake and a cookie. (James Beard has traced the Bangor brownie back to 1907.) This is a soft dough turned into a shallow pan, baked, and cut into bars, or baked in special molds or cups.

4. *Pressed Cookies.* Dough is forced through special cooky shapers or pastry tubes into selected shapes.

5. *Refrigerator.* A very stiff dough, shaped into rolls, sliced, and baked days later.

6. *Drop Cookies.* Just as the name implies, this is a soft dough that is simply pushed off a spoon and dropped onto baking sheets.

Cookies are a quiet but eloquent way of "speaking for yourself." Why not go turn the oven on?

Spicy Lithuanian "Mushroom" Cookies

Time and patience. You need both to make these cookies. Patience is what you need to fashion stems and caps out of the well-kneaded, honey-spiced dough. Time is what you need to make them mellow. Allow at least three days. But they're well worth it. The mushroom caps are dipped into a white sugar coating and sprinkled with poppy seeds. When giving, package them with an assortment of other cookies in a flowerpot or in a rustic basket on a bed of Easter grass or sphagnum moss.

This recipe makes about four dozen "mushrooms." They are time-consuming to make, so be stingy with them by including a few with other assorted cookies. Three to five per gift will be ample to yield up to sixteen gifts.

½ cup honey
¼ cup sugar
2 tablespoons firmly packed dark brown sugar
¼ stick (2 tablespoons) butter or margarine
1 large egg
1½ teaspoons ground cardamon
1½ teaspoons ground cinnamon
1½ teaspoons ground ginger
1½ teaspoons ground cloves
1½ teaspoons ground nutmeg
1½ teaspoons fresh grated lemon rind
1 teaspoon fresh grated orange rind
2¾ cups sifted all-purpose flour
¾ teaspoon baking soda
¼ teaspoon salt
2 tablespoons cream or milk

For Decorating

2 cups powdered sugar
3 tablespoons water
Poppy seeds

Preheat oven to 350°. Heat the honey in a 2- to 3-quart saucepan over medium heat until it bubbles around side of pan. Remove from the heat and stir in the sugars, butter, egg, spices, and grated rinds.

Sift the flour, baking soda, and salt into a medium-size mixing bowl. Add the honey mixture alternately with the cream or milk stirring with a wooden spoon until blended. Turn the dough out onto a floured board or pastry cloth. Knead the dough adding flour to the board as often as necessary to prevent sticking, for 5 or 6 minutes, until the dough is easy to handle and not at all sticky. It should be firm enough to hold the impression of your finger. Let the dough rest at room temperature for 20 minutes.

Divide the dough into four equal parts. Make mushroom "stems" from one-quarter of the dough by shaping into four rolls, each about 12 inches long and about ⅜ inch in diameter. Cut into 1-inch lengths. Shape one end of each piece into a point with your fingers. Place the stems on their sides 1½ inches apart on an ungreased baking sheet. Bake at 350° for about 7 minutes until firm. Cool on wire racks.

Make "caps" by shaping remaining dough into ¾-inch balls. Hold a ball in the palm of your hand and make an indentation about ½ inch deep in each with handle of a wooden spoon, twisting it in and out. This is where the stem will later be inserted. Place the caps, indented side down, on an ungreased baking sheet, spacing them about 1½ inches apart. Bake for about 12 minutes until the cookies are lightly browned on the bottom. Cool on wire racks.

Press the powdered sugar through a coarse kitchen strainer to remove any lumps. Blend it with 1 tablespoon of the water until smooth. Add the remaining 2 tablespoons water, 1 teaspoon at a time, beating well after each addition.

Enlarge indentations in caps if necessary with a small pointed knife. Dip one end of each stem in frosting and insert in caps. Dry the cookies, cap side down.

Dip the top of each cap in frosting, allowing any excess to drip back into the bowl. While still wet, sprinkle the frosted caps with poppy seeds. Place the cookies, stems down, onto oven racks in a turned-off oven where they may dry undisturbed for several hours or overnight. Pack in airtight containers and allow the flavor to mellow for three or four days before serving.

TO PREPARE IN ADVANCE: Make these at least three days before serving to allow the flavor to mellow. May be stored in airtight containers at room temperature for up to six weeks or in the freezer for up to six months. They may be refrozen. (A friend made these and kept them for a year in an airtight jar at room temperature. They were still fragrant and perfect to use as ornaments.)

SPECIAL PACKAGING: Rustic baskets containing sphagnum moss make these "mushrooms" look like the real thing. Glass or china flowerpots are also appropriate.

THE LABEL: These may be eaten or used as ornaments. May be stored in an airtight container at room temperature for up to six weeks or frozen for up to six months. They may be refrozen.

Glazed Oatmeal Crisps

Breathes there a man with soul so dead who never to himself hath said, "Hmm, not bad." These cookies contain very little flour and yield a paper-thin, delicate disk, much loved by cooky *aficionados*.

It's a cooky with a difference. A glaze is formed while baking and appears, not on top, but underneath the cooky, making it a simple matter to peel off the foil-lined baking sheet.

This recipe yields fifty to sixty 3-inch cookies, enough for four gifts.

> 1 egg, beaten
> 3 tablespoons plus 1 teaspoon all-purpose flour
> 1 stick (½ cup) butter or margarine, at room temperature
> 2 teaspoons vanilla extract
> 1 cup any kind of oatmeal
> 1 cup sugar
> ½ teaspoon salt
> ½ teaspoon baking powder

Preheat oven to 350°. In a medium-size mixing bowl, beat the flour, shortening, egg, and vanilla with a spoon. Add the oatmeal, sugar, salt, and baking powder and beat until blended and smooth.

Drop the mixture by small teaspoonsful, three inches apart, onto foil-covered cookie sheets. Bake one sheet at a time in the center of the oven for 10 to 12 minutes until the cookies have browned lightly. When cool, carefully remove the cookies from the foil.

TO PREPARE IN ADVANCE: After the cookies have cooled, they may be stored in an airtight container at room temperature for up to a week or frozen for up to three months. We find it easiest to freeze them because they take only minutes to thaw.

SPECIAL PACKAGING: See "Containers," page 212. These cookies are not quite as fragile as lace cookies, so they may be stacked in wide-mouth jars or other cylindrical containers.

THE LABEL: May be stored in an airtight container at room temperature for up to a week or frozen for up to three months. These cookies may be refrozen, and they thaw quickly.

Cloud Nine Meringue Cookies

It's the neatest trick of the century! These Cloud Nine Cookies are really forgotten cookies, suitable for those of us mildly afflicted with bouts of amnesia. Heat your oven, mix ingredients, spoon onto bake sheets, put into oven, turn off oven, go to bed. When you wake up the next morning, you have forty-eight overnight sensations: four dozen crisp, pink meringues, infused with chocolate, nuts, and a touch of mint.

This recipe makes about four dozen 1-inch cookies. Depending upon the size of your containers, you will have two to four gifts.

> Whites of 2 large eggs at room temperature
> ¼ teaspoon cream of tartar
> 2/3 cup regular or superfine sugar (see Note)
> 1 (6-ounce) package chocolate morsels
> 1 cup chopped pecans, almonds or walnuts
> 1 teaspoon creme de menthe (optional)
> ½ teaspoon peppermint extract
> 4 or 5 drops red food color

Note: Superfine sugar is best to use when making meringues because it dissolves easily. Regular granulated sugar will do — just don't be tempted to add it quickly.

Preheat oven to 350°. Use an electric mixer or a whisk to beat the egg whites and cream of tartar until they do not slide when the bowl is tilted. Gradually add the sugar one tablespoon at a time, constantly beating — take your time here! Once all the sugar is in, beat one more minute and stop! You should have a stiff glossy meringue. Fold in the remaining ingredients all at once. Drop the mixture by large teaspoonsful onto two (no more) foil-covered cookie sheets. Place the cookie sheets in the preheated oven, close the door, and turn off the oven immediately. Leave the cookies in the oven overnight and do not open the door to peek — not even once! The next morning your cookies will be done to perfection.

TO PREPARE IN ADVANCE: May be stored in airtight containers for up to one week. If stored longer, the meringue loses crispness. Do not freeze.

SPECIAL PACKAGING: These must be stored airtight. Use small candy tins if possible.

THE LABEL: These won't last long, so enjoy! Store in airtight containers at room temperature.

Crisp Lemon Cookies

It's the Age of the Lemon. Manufacturers are adding it to everything from soap to furniture polish. Long before the current craze, cooks were using its zest in a multiplicity of ways, and never any better than in these Crisp Lemon Cookies. Our dough is made with fresh lemon juice and grated rind, rolled into balls, pressed, and baked into superthin wafers. Great with ice cream sundaes or puddings!

This recipe yields about five dozen 2½-inch cookies. It is not necessary to bake them all at once — the dough may be refrigerated for up to three days.

> 1¾ cups sifted all-purpose flour
> 1 scant teaspoon baking soda
> 1 scant teaspoon cream of tartar
> ½ teaspoon salt
> 2 sticks (½ pound) butter or margarine, at room temperature
> 1 cup superfine sugar
> 1 egg, beaten
> The finely grated rind (zest) from 2 medium lemons
> 1 tablespoon fresh lemon juice

Sift together flour, soda, cream of tartar, and salt, set aside. Place the butter or margarine in the bowl of an electric mixer and beat until creamy. Gradually add the sugar, beating until the mixture is very light and fluffy. Beat in the egg, lemon rind, and juice, then add the dry ingredients just until blended. Chill the dough, wrapped in plastic wrap, overnight in the refrigerator.

Just before baking, preheat the oven to 325°. Form the chilled dough into balls, ¾ inch in diameter. Place the balls three inches apart on a lightly oiled cookie sheet. Hold a wet cloth over the bottom of a drinking glass, dip into fine sugar, and use the glass bottom to press the balls into thin wafers. Redip the cloth in sugar before flattening each cookie.

Bake at 325° for 7 to 9 minutes or until the cookies are lightly browned around the edges. Let cool before removing from the sheet.

TO PREPARE IN ADVANCE: These may be stored in airtight containers at room temperature for up to a month. They freeze perfectly for up to six months and thaw quickly.

SPECIAL PACKAGING: Any airtight container is suitable.

THE LABEL: May be stored in an airtight container for up to a month at room temperature or frozen for up to six months. These cookies may be refrozen, and they thaw quickly.

Sheila Ricci's Viennese Crescent Cookies

Sheila is a delightfully outspoken Englishwoman with a merry disposition who has taken a familiar, old recipe and adapted it to her own healthy standards by substituting ground nuts for part of the flour called for. Take another tip from this lady and present a batch of these elegant cookies in a basket lined with a lacy English napkin.

Sheila once conducted a cooking class of her own, sending out invitations which read, "Wednesday from ten to God knows when." It was titled, "Nothing in the freezer except your ironing." She believes that food should be as fresh as possible and never frozen, so we beg her forgiveness for our note in the "To Prepare in Advance" section that states her cookies can be frozen. She prefers serving them fresh to her students right before class with coffee, which is the way we were introduced to them.

This recipe makes four dozen cookies, which is enough for four gifts of one dozen each.

2 sticks (½ pound) butter, at room temperature
¾ cup sugar
2½ cups sifted all-purpose flour
1 cup (about 5 ounces) ground almonds, black walnuts, pecans or other nuts
1½ teaspoons vanilla or almond extract
Powdered sugar

In the large bowl of an electric mixer beat the butter and sugar together until light and fluffy. Alternately add the flour and ground nuts while beating. When the dough is well mixed, beat in the vanilla or almond extract. Form the dough into 1-inch balls and chill for 30 to 60 minutes.

Preheat the oven to 350°. Form each ball of dough into a crescent shape like an apple section with your fingers. Bake on a cookie sheet at 350° for about 15 minutes until the bottoms start to brown. Remove from the oven. While the cookies are still warm, sprinkle them with powdered sugar through a kitchen-strainer to dust them heavily. Let cool.

TO PREPARE IN ADVANCE: After the cookies are cool, they may be stored in an airtight container at room temperature for up to two weeks or in the freezer for up to six months.

SPECIAL PACKAGING: Sheila would surely give these away in a small basket lined with a perky, freshly ironed napkin from her freezer! (She's the one who has only ironing in her freezer.)

THE LABEL: May be stored in an airtight container at room temperature for up to two weeks or frozen for up to six months.

Old-Fashioned Cut-Out Cookies

We hesitate to use the word *indestructible* in describing this dough, since it, like all things, must one day come to a timely end. But it is a good dough for children. Handling does little to damage it and in that sense, it is indestructible. So let them squeeze, smash, roll to their heart's content, then shape with cookie cutters, and bake. They may either eat and enjoy its old-time bakery goodness or hang it from the tree as an ornament, a fitting momento of their joyful kitchen fling.

This recipe makes about three dozen 2½-inch cookies; however, the yield will depend on the size of the cookie cutter you use. The recipe may be doubled.

> 2 sticks (½ pound) butter or margarine, at room temperature
> 1½ cups sugar
> 3 large eggs
> 1 tablespoon vanilla
> 1 teaspoon almond extract
> 3 cups sifted all-purpose flour
> 1 teaspoon baking powder
> ½ teaspoon salt
>
> *For Decorating (optional):*
> Colored sugar, nuts, or candies

In the large bowl of an electric mixer, cream the butter with the sugar until light and fluffy. Beat in the eggs, vanilla, and almond extract. Sift together the flour, baking powder, and salt, and add to the butter-egg mixture, beating until smooth. Form the dough into two patties. Wrap each in plastic wrap and chill for at least 3 hours.

Preheat oven to 375°. Roll the dough out, one patty at a time, on a floured surface. If crisp, thin cookies are wanted, roll the dough a bit less than ⅛ inch thick; if soft, thicker cookies are wanted, roll up to ½ inch thick. Cut into shapes. Decorate cookies with colored sugar, nuts, or candies as desired.

If the cookies are to be used as ornaments on a Christmas tree, insert the large end of a toothpick through the cookie and leave there during the baking.

Bake at 375° until very delicately golden, about 8 to 10 minutes. Watch carefully that they do not overbrown. Remove toothpick when the cookies come out of the oven. When cool, thread with yarn or narrow cord.

TO PREPARE IN ADVANCE: These cookies keep for up to three weeks in an airtight container. They may also be frozen for up to six months. If they are to be used only as decorations, they may be kept indefinitely.

SPECIAL PACKAGING: These cookies make wonderful gift tags. Write the name of the recipient and decorate with frosting available in tubes.

THE LABEL: Eat or use as ornaments. May be stored in airtight containers at room temperature for up to three weeks or frozen for up to six months. If they are to be used for ornaments, they will last indefinitely.

Ruth Mellinkoff's Stuffed Dates Baked

This recipe is a bit like those Chinese boxes that nestle one inside the other, until you come to the last, and the treasure you're seeking. In this case, the last cover of all is the roof of your mouth. But it all begins with a walnut half, stuffed inside a date, encased in cookie dough, covered with vanilla icing. The recipe is from *The Just Delicious Cookbook* by our dear friend Ruth Mellinkoff.

This recipe makes about four dozen, enough for four gifts of one dozen each.

> 4 dozen pitted dates
> Walnut halves
> ½ stick (¼ cup) butter
> ¾ cup firmly packed brown sugar
> 1 large egg
> 1 teaspoon vanilla
> 1¼ cups sifted all-purpose flour
> ½ teaspoon salt
> ¼ teaspoon baking powder
> ½ teaspoon baking soda
> ½ cup commercial sour cream
>
> *For the Icing (Optional)*
> ¼ cup melted butter
> 1 cup sifted powdered sugar
> 1 teaspoon vanilla
> A little milk

Stuff each date with a walnut half. Break nuts in pieces, if necessary, but be sure to use the entire walnut half in each date. Set aside.

Cream butter and sugar until fluffy. Beat in egg and vanilla. Sift dry ingredients together, then add them alternately with the sour cream.

Dip each stuffed date in the prepared batter, covering all sides. Place on greased cookie sheets. Bake at 400° for about 8 to 12 minutes until lightly browned. Watch that they don't burn.

To make the vanilla icing, combine butter, sugar, and vanilla. Add milk a very little at a time until an icing of spreading consistency is obtained. Frost the cookies when cool.

TO PREPARE IN ADVANCE: The unfrosted cookies may be stored in an airtight container at room temperature for up to three days or frozen for up to three months. Ice them only after they have been defrosted and before you plan to serve them or give them away.

SPECIAL PACKAGING: Place these in frilled paper candy cups in airtight tins to keep them fresh.

THE LABEL: *If the dates are frosted, the label should read:* Please eat as soon as possible. *If the dates are freshly baked and are not frosted, the label should read:* May be stored in an airtight container for up to three days or frozen for up to three months. *If the dates are frozen, the label should read:* May be kept frozen for up to three months or stored in an airtight container at room temperature for up to three days after they have been defrosted.

Pecan Lace Cookies

We only use imperatives when dealing with these cookies. Make them! It will be an hour to remember. Spectacular enough to rate high in taste, there is also the matter of ease in preparation. What better combination of reasons to make this our unanimous first choice in the cooky kingdom. Pack them into airtight tins to keep them crisp. When giving these away, you might as well include the recipe and save a stamp.

This recipe yields about three dozen 2½-inch cookies, enough for three gifts of one dozen cookies each.

> ½ stick (¼ cup) melted butter or margarine
> ¼ cup firmly packed dark brown sugar
> ¼ cup light Karo syrup
> ½ cup unsifted all-purpose flour
> ½ cup finely chopped pecans
> 2 teaspoons vanilla

Note: Don't make these when it's raining or a storm is threatening! They'll never get crisp.

Preheat oven to 350°. Melt butter or margarine in a small, heavy saucepan. Add the brown sugar and corn syrup. Cook, stirring constantly, over high heat until the mixture comes to a boil. Remove from the heat. Add the flour and pecans all at once and stir until smooth. Blend in the vanilla.

Drop the mixture by level teaspoonful on foil-covered cookie sheets, placing them about 3 inches apart to allow room for spreading. Bake at 350° for 7 to 10 minutes or until the cookies are a rich golden brown.

Remove the cookies from the oven. Let cool for 2 to 3 minutes just until the cookies are firm. Immediately use a spatula to transfer the cookies to paper towels, which will absorb any excess butter. Work quickly so the cookies don't stick to the foil. If they harden too much, return the pan to the oven for a few seconds. When cool, pack in airtight tins between layers of wax paper.

TO PREPARE IN ADVANCE: These will probably keep for weeks in an airtight tin, but, try as we may, we never have any around that long. They are irresistible! They freeze between layers of wax paper.

SPECIAL PACKAGING: Airtight candy tins are ideal to preserve the crispness and prevent breakage of these fragile cookies.

THE LABEL: May be stored in airtight containers at room temperature for up to two weeks, or frozen for up to four months.

Florentines

Now that we've used up all the superlatives for Pecan Lace Crisps, we hasten to include Florentines. These might just be the most elegant holiday cooky around, an elegance matched only by the city for which it is named. Similar to Pecan Lace Crisps, it has one happy addition: the European touch of candied fruit. They will add immeasurably to the pleasures of your holiday table. If you wish, the back of each cooky may be coated with chocolate.

The recipe yields about thirty-six 2½-inch cookies or three gifts of one dozen each. We enjoy giving an assortment of cookies and include only six of these when other cookies are given at the same time.

½ cup sifted all-purpose flour
2/3 cup mixed candied fruit (orange, lemon, and citron)
½ cup chopped candied cherries
½ cup chopped walnuts
½ cup chopped blanched almonds
1/3 cup sliced almonds
1 stick (¼ pound) butter or margarine
½ cup firmly packed dark brown sugar
2 tablespoons light corn syrup

Preheat the oven to 325°. In a small mixing bowl combine the flour, fruits, and nuts. Stir until evenly coated.

In a heavy 2- or 3-quart saucepan, combine the butter or margarine, brown sugar, and corn syrup. Stir the mixture over medium heat until the butter is melted and blended with the other ingredients—do not boil. Remove the pan from the heat and stir in the fruit and nut mixture.

Drop the batter by teaspoonsful, 3 inches apart, on a foil-lined cookie sheet. Press the mounds of batter with your fingers into flat round patties. Bake in the center of the oven for 15 to 20 minutes until the cookies have spread and browned lightly around the edges. Let cool for 3 to 4 minutes until the cookies are just firm enough to lift with a spatula. Transfer them to paper towels to absorb excess butter. Let cool completely. Serve as is or coat with chocolate.

To coat the backs of the Florentines with chocolate, follow directions for making the chocolate coating on page 175. Brush chocolate on the backs of the cookies and refrigerate until the chocolate has set. Serve at room temperature within 24 hours.

TO PREPARE IN ADVANCE: Florentines may be stored in an airtight container at room temperature for up to a week; however, any humidity will make them lose their crispness. They may be frozen with or without the chocolate coating for up to one month. We prefer coating them with chocolate within 24 hours of serving.

SPECIAL PACKAGING: These are especially lovely included in an assortment of cookies on a doily-lined serving plate.

THE LABEL: May be stored in an airtight container at room temperature for up to a week or frozen for up to one month.

Luscious Little Lemon Pastries

A trinity of textures—rich crust, lemon filling, powdery topping—conspire to make this a pastry for those in love with fresh lemon flavor. It's important to dust the top heavily with powdered sugar for visual appreciation and to compensate for the tanginess of the filling.

Baked in a 9-by-13-inch pan, this recipe makes twenty-four squares, enough for four gifts of 6 squares each. Baked in two 9-inch spring-form pans, the recipe makes twenty-four pie-shaped wedges.

Nonstick spray coating for pan (optional)

For the Butter Crust
1 stick (¼ pound) butter
½ cup powdered sugar
2 cups sifted all-purpose flour
Dash of salt

For the Lemon Topping
4 large eggs
2 cups sugar
¼ cup unsifted all-purpose flour
1/3 cup fresh lemon juice
2 teaspoons fresh grated lemon rind
About ½ cup powdered sugar

Preheat the oven to 350°. It will be easier to remove the pastries from the pan after baking if you spray the baking dish lightly with nonstick spray.

Combine the crust ingredients in the bowl of an electric mixer and beat until smooth. Press the dough with your fingertips onto the bottom of a 9-by-13-inch pan or, if you want pie-shaped wedges, a 9-inch spring-form pan. Bake in the center of the oven for 15 minutes until lightly browned.

Let cool slightly while you make the topping. Beat the eggs and sugar in the bowl of an electric mixer until very creamy. Add the flour, lemon juice, and lemon rind. Beat until well blended and pour over the warm crust. Return the pan to the oven and bake 25 minutes longer until the topping has set. Let cool. Sprinkle an even heavy layer of powdered sugar over the top of the cooled pastry by pressing the sugar through a kitchen strainer with the back of a spoon. Cut into squares or wedges. Serve at room temperature.

TO PREPARE IN ADVANCE: May be wrapped in foil or packed into airtight containers and stored for up to a week at room temperature. These freeze perfectly for up to six months and may be refrozen.

SPECIAL PACKAGING: Candy tins are ideal. Small foil packages of pastries may be overwrapped in colored cellophane and tied with a ribbon. These pastries are especially nice to include as part of a cooky assortment on a serving plate.

THE LABEL: May be stored in airtight containers at room temperature for up to a week or frozen for up to six months.

Frosted Fudge Brownies

Now about this matter of brownies. The controversy still rages as to whether they should be rich and solid or light as a cloud. This is the way we like them: moist and fudgy, and frosted while still warm with a thick swirl of chocolate frosting. But you can have it either way, says Carolyn Irvine, from whom this recipe came. It all depends on how much the batter is beaten. Barely mix for fudgy brownies or beat well if you like them cake-like. Texture notwithstanding, these brownies have an evanescent quality. They never remain too long in this world into which you have brought them.

This recipe makes sixteen 2¼-inch squares, enough for two gifts of eight brownies each. Double recipe to bake in two pans.

Shortening for the pan
2 ounces (2 squares) unsweetened chocolate
1 stick (¼ pound) butter or margarine
2 large eggs
1 cup sugar
½ cup unsifted flour
1 teaspoon vanilla
⅛ teaspoon salt
1 cup diced walnuts or pecans

For the Icing
1 ounce (1 square) unsweetened chocolate
1 tablespoon butter or margarine, melted
1 cup unsifted powdered sugar
1½ tablespoons water

Preheat the oven to 350°. Grease a 9-by-9-inch baking pan with shortening.

Melt the chocolate with the butter over low heat in a heavy-bottomed saucepan or double boiler (chocolate burns easily!). Set aside.

Place the eggs in a medium-size mixing bowl with the sugar and beat with a whisk. (Beat well if you want light-textured brownies, hardly at all if you want fudgy brownies.) Stir in the chocolate mixture. Add the flour, vanilla, and salt; mix just until blended. Fold in the nuts.

Pour the batter into the prepared pan. Bake for 20 minutes in the center of a 350° oven. Do not overbake. Spread with frosting while still warm.

Melt the chocolate and butter or margarine for the frosting over low heat in a heavy-bottomed saucepan or double boiler. Blend in the powdered sugar and water. Spread immediately over warm brownies. Let cool, then cut into 2¼-inch squares.

TO PREPARE IN ADVANCE: May be stored, wrapped in foil, at room temperature for up to three days or frozen for up to four months.

SPECIAL PACKAGING: Give the brownies on a doily on a small serving plate. Cover tightly with plastic wrap.

THE LABEL: May be stored, wrapped in foil, at room temperature for up to three days or frozen for up to four months.

Delectable Mincemeat Squares with Vanilla Glaze, Opus 1976

Since the age of three, Diana's best friend has been Alice Blair Simmons. They started their culinary interest and friendship at that time while one was eating a peanut butter sandwich and the other was working on a jelly. A bite here and a bite there and a lifelong relationship was sealed.

Their friendship extended to sharing. If one were to get a pair of skates for Christmas, you'd find them both skating down the block on Christmas morning, one skate apiece. Memory has it that they shared recipes as well. They passed by the Mud Souffle stage, zinged into the hard stuff like hamburger and Sure-Jell, distinguishing each creative endeavor with an opus number. Unofficially, they hold the block's record for the biggest pizza and perhaps the world's record for the largest cooky.

These days each has her own family with little girls, live within blocks of each other, and are still great friends. So great, in fact, that on running into a deadline crunch on this book, we could entrust Alice's extraordinary kitchen precision and technique to create a new recipe utilizing our Drunken Mincemeat. She made it into these delectable squares and handed us the recipe titled, Opus 1976.

This recipe makes three dozen bars, enough for three gifts of twelve bars each.

For Mincemeat Bars
Shortening for the pan
2½ cups Buttermilk Bisquick
1 cup sugar
1 large egg
3 tablespoons butter or margarine, at room temperature
¼ cup milk
1½ cups Drunken Mincemeat (page 114) (see Note)

For the Glaze
1 cup powdered sugar
1 to 2 tablespoons milk
½ teaspoon vanilla

Note: You may substitute other prepared mincemeat, though do jazz it up with a bit of booze (brandy, dark rum, Grand Marnier) and some grated orange or lemon rind.

Preheat oven to 375°. Grease 13-by-9-by-2-inch pan. Combine all ingredients for Mincemeat Bars except mincemeat and mix until dry ingredients are moistened. The dough will be soft and sticky. Spread half the dough in the bottom of the pan to within ½ inch of the sides of the pan (it will spread during baking). Spread the mincemeat to the edge of the dough. Spread out the other half of the dough on wax paper the same size. Turn over on mincemeat and pull off the wax paper carefully. Bake at 375° for 30 minutes. While the cookies bake, prepare the glaze.

To make the glaze, press the powdered sugar through a kitchen strainer into a small mixing bowl to remove any lumps. Add the milk and vanilla and stir until smooth. Spread the glaze over surface of warm pastry and cut, while still warm, into thirty-six bars.

TO PREPARE IN ADVANCE: May be stored in an airtight container at room temperature for up to three days, in the refrigerator for up to a week, or in the freezer for up to four months. For best flavor, serve at room temperature.

SPECIAL PACKAGING: Place these inside a napkin in a small basket. Wrap the whole thing in cellophane and tie with a ribbon.

THE LABEL: Enjoy these now or store them covered at room temperature for up to three days, in the refrigerator for up to a week, or in the freezer for up to four months. For best flavor, serve at room temperature.

Confections

You may have difficulty getting Aunt Mary to try Moroccan Couscous or Johnny to make some headway with his spinach, but you know you'd never have that predicament with candy. The whole world has a sweet tooth and approaches the candy dish with the same adventurous spirit and zeal of a Columbus.

Candy as we know it is a comparatively new invention that needed the development and distribution of refined sugar that finally came in the eighteenth century. Until then, the only available sweet was honey—never really an industry—since almost everyone raised his own bees. In the fourth century the soldiers of Alexander the Great brought back incredible stories of honey in a tube (sugar cane) they had seen in India. We now know it had been enjoyed there a thousand years before Christ (in Sanskrit it was called *sakara*). Alexander's armies spread the word far and wide about its delicious sweetness, but it wasn't until a thousand years later that Moslem armies brought the plants back to propagate throughout northern Africa and southern Europe.

The first giant step toward our present-day consumption of 100 pounds of sugar per year per man in America and the invention of the chocolate bar, gum-drops, licorice sticks, bonbons, and many others, was the decision of Christopher Columbus to bring the sugar cane plant back with him to the New World on his second voyage in 1493. As a cash crop, it was a winner from the start and quickly spread from Santo Domingo to Puerto Rico to Cuba to Central and South America. However, the decision may not have been entirely his own. His mother-in-law was in the "sugar business," and there were fortunes to be made.

Equally important to the confectioner's trade is chocolate, a roasted brown bean from the "cocao" tree, native to the tropical Amazon basin of South America. The enterprising and daring Spaniard, Cortez, discovered the bean used as money by the Aztecs in 1519 and sent stories back to the Spanish court about Montezuma drinking unsweetened "cocao" out of his golden cup each morning. This bit of court news so impressed his king that Cortez took courage, swiped the gold cup, the "cocao" bean, and everything else lying around. The powerful Spanish empire controlled the seas, and for 100 years forcibly maintained a monopoly on chocolate. The Spaniards added the first improvement, vanilla and sugar, and invented cocoa (reversing the last two vowels).

Honey is difficult to keep and cook with, but sugar will last indefinitely. It can be ground to superfineness, molded into cubes, heated and dissolved into a liquid, and mixed with practically anything. The whole world of candy lovers was wait-ing. All they needed was a lower price. And that came through the courtesy of Mr. Claus Spreckles, an American who developed a sugar refining process that took only eight hours instead of the usual three weeks.

If you try the following recipes, you will become a better candy cook and, best of all, perhaps discover how easy it is to work with sugar. From this point on, you'll never be at a loss for a hostess gift.

Dina's Rolled Baklava

Can you envision whole lambs, coal-roasted on spits, brushed with lemon herb marinade with brooms made out of mint leaves? Then know that this kind of cul-inary flair is what makes Dina Oldknow the vivacious hostess she has become. That occasion was the Greek lamb festival for Les Dames de Champagne of Los Angeles, an international hostess society.

The highlight of a lot of Dina's entertaining is baklava, perhaps the best known of Middle Eastern sweets in the Western hemisphere. Dina gives it a new twist. She rolls and slices it, making it easier to eat than the accustomed diamond-shaped ones. The recipe yields an enormous quantity. It could become a considerable chore to make for one person. Make it more manageable by inviting a friend to join you. You'll not only know the joy of mutual labor, but upon departure, both of you will have a tangible momento of your time together.

And if you run out of steam halfway through making the Baklava, simply use up the remaining filo by making the marvelous Spanakopita on page 76.

This recipe makes about 225 pieces, enough for ten gifts of 22 pieces each or fifteen gifts of 15 pieces each.

For the Pastry
12 ounces (about 3 cups) blanched almonds
12 ounces (about 3 cups) walnuts
6 ounces (about 1½ cups) pecans
1/3 cup sugar
2 tablespoons ground cinnamon
¾ teaspoon ground nutmeg
Scant ½ teaspoon ground cloves
2 pounds butter, clarified (see page 33)
1 (1-pound) package filo (phylo) or strudel pastry (see Note)

For the Syrup
4½ cups water
3¾ cups sugar
2 small cinnamon sticks
1½ teaspoons lemon juice
Grated rind (zest) of 1 lemon
1 tablespoon honey

Note: These tissue-thin layers of pastry are available in some supermarkets and at Greek, Middle Eastern, or Italian delicatessens.

Preheat the oven to 350°.

All the nuts must be finely ground. We use our Cuisinart food processor for this. A meat grinder or blender may be used instead, according to manufacturer's instructions. Mix the ground nuts with the sugar and spices in a large mixing bowl.

Choose a clean, smooth work surface where you can sit comfortably while working and arrange all your supplies.

Place the warm clarified butter with a pastry brush next to you. Open the plastic package inside the box of filo. Remove the sheets of pastry, unroll gently, and place them between two sheets of plastic or wax paper to keep them from drying out while you work. (We find a plastic wastebasket liner, slit open down the side, is a dandy thing to use for this.) Wet and thoroughly wring out a kitchen towel and lay it on top of the plastic-covered dough. (Take care that it doesn't touch the dough or you will have a soggy mess!)

To assemble, remove one sheet of filo from the stack and place it on your

166

work surface, making sure that the rest of the dough remains covered. Brush the sheet of dough all over with clarified butter. Spread about ½ cup of the nut-spice mixture evenly over the buttered surface. Roll the dough up tightly, handling it gently so it doesn't tear. Brush clarified butter across the end of the filo and seal edge.

Using a sharp knife, cut the roll in 1-inch lengths. Place them ½ inch apart on a buttered baking sheet that has a rim all the way around, such as a jelly-roll or roasting pan. (Dina says to place the odd-looking end pieces in a small separate pan to use as sample pieces for the family—they are not as pretty or symmetrical but taste just as good!)

Continue to form and slice the rolls in the same manner until all the nut mixture has been used.

Brush the top of each roll lightly with a little clarified butter. Bake the rolls at 350° for 20 minutes until they are golden. If you are baking more than one pan of rolls in the same oven, switch them around, top to bottom and vice versa, after 10 minutes so they will bake evenly. Let cool at room temperature in the baking pans.

To prepare the syrup, combine the water, sugar, cinnamon sticks, lemon juice, lemon peel, and honey in a heavy 3-quart saucepan. Bring the mixture to a boil, then lower the heat and let simmer for 10 minutes. Spoon the hot syrup over the cool rolls in the baking pans. Turn the rolls over and from side to side during the next few hours to help them absorb as much syrup as possible.

Serve at room temperature for best flavor.

TO PREPARE IN ADVANCE: Arrange the pieces, leaving space between them, on foil for wrapping. Add any remaining syrup and seal. May be stored in the refrigerator for up to two weeks or frozen for up to six months. Freezing does not harm baklava one bit, and it may even be refrozen. Thaw completely and serve at room temperature.

SPECIAL PACKAGING: Place the pieces in frilled paper candy cups, available at stores that sell gourmet supplies. Pack into candy tins or simply present them on a small serving plate.

THE LABEL: *Whether or not the baklava is frozen, the label should read:* Serve at room temperature. May be stored in the refrigerator for up to two weeks or frozen for up to six months. May be refrozen.

English Toffee

For some unknown reason, a great recipe for English Toffee is nearly impossible to find. But such odds only serve to spur the von Welanetz zeal and so we searched, tested and combined recipes, until we came up with this one that really dazzles us. Variations in weather and range temperature, length of time in stirring and boiling notwithstanding, you'll find this English Toffee every bit as good as may be found in the finest candy shops. It even mellows and improves with age. We've tested everything but the limit of its mellowness, a difficult task at best, since this is the kind of candy that you can't leave alone. It falls into the "take it and leave it" category. You can take and enjoy some yourself, but to avoid forsaking your diet forever, pack up the rest and leave it in the hands of an appreciative friend.

This recipe makes 1¾ pounds, or four cups, of toffee pieces, enough to fill four to six small candy tins.

Butter or margarine for the pan
3 sticks (¾ pound) butter
2 cups sugar
2 tablespoons water
⅛ teaspoon salt
6 ounces semi-sweet chocolate morsels
1 cup finely ground walnuts

Grease a 10-by-15-inch jelly-roll pan (or roasting pan in a pinch) with butter or margarine. Melt the butter in a heavy 3- to 4-quart saucepan over medium heat. Add the sugar, water, and salt. Stir over medium heat until the sugar is dissolved. Insert a candy thermometer (ours is a Taylor) and continue to cook, stirring often, until it registers 290°. Pour the mixture out into the prepared pan and spread evenly to the edges of the pan. Let it cool undisturbed at room temperature.

Melt the chocolate in a double boiler over hot water. Spread the melted chocolate over the toffee in the pan. Sprinkle with the ground walnuts and press them into the chocolate while it is still warm.

When the toffee has set, break it into pieces over wax paper. Store in airtight tins.

Both sides of the toffee may be coated with chocolate and nuts if you prefer. You will need twice the amount of chocolate morsels and nuts. When the toffee has hardened turn out, upside down, on a strip of wax paper. Coat the underside in the same manner.

TO PREPARE IN ADVANCE: The flavor and texture are enhanced if the toffee is made at least 48 hours before serving. It will keep for at least a month at room temperature in an airtight container.

SPECIAL PACKAGING: Candy tins are ideal gift containers because they are airtight and will keep the toffee fresh.

THE LABEL: May be stored in an airtight container at room temperature for up to a month. May be frozen.

Five Pounds of Easy, Fabulous Fudge

We're serious. It *is* easy. The comic or cynic might think the easy way is to beat a path down to the nearest candy shop and *buy* himself five easy pounds. Our way is better. True, our fudge is made with marshmallow creme, as are so many others, but we did a little experimenting by combining chocolates, and the result is lots of goodness for very little time and effort. Even Mimi, Diana's mother, is a convert, and alternates making this fudge with her own, which appears next.

This recipe makes 5 pounds of fudge, or 117 1-inch pieces. This amount is sufficient for six to eight gifts.

12 ounces Baker's German's sweet chocolate, broken into pieces
12 ounces semi-sweet chocolate morsels
1 (7-ounce) jar marsmallow creme
4½ cups sugar
1 (13-ounce) can evaporated milk
¼ stick (2 tablespoons) butter
⅛ teaspoon salt
1 tablespoon vanilla
2 cups broken walnuts

Place the chocolate bars, chocolate morsels, and marshmallow creme in the large bowl of an electric mixer.

Combine the sugar, milk, butter, and salt in a heavy 3- or 4-quart saucepan. Bring to a boil over high heat, stirring constantly. When the mixture comes to a boil, lower the heat to medium and set a timer for 6 minutes. Keep the mixture boiling steadily and stir constantly during this time to prevent scorching.

At the end of 6 minutes, pour the boiling syrup over the chocolate and marshmallow creme. Beat until the chocolate is melted and the ingredients are well blended. Beat in the vanilla and walnuts.

Pour into a lightly buttered 13-by-9-by-2-inch pan. Let the fudge cool at room temperature for 24 hours before cutting. Cut it into 1-inch square pieces and pack in airtight containers. Store in a cool place.

Do not chill the fudge in the refrigerator because it will lose its gloss.

TO PREPARE IN ADVANCE: The fudge may be stored in airtight containers at room temperature for up to two weeks. It may be frozen for up to six months, though it will lose its gloss.

SPECIAL PACKAGING: Small candy tins are ideal.

THE LABEL: May be stored in an airtight container for up to two weeks at room temperature. May be refrigerated or frozen, but the fudge will lose its gloss.

Mimi's Old-Fashioned Fudge

Before the advent of marshmallow creme, this was the fudge that everyone made. It holds fond memories for Diana, since it is a part of her Christmas childhood. Her mother, Mimi, made and stored it in the Bombe chest in their dining room and every time Diana passed the chest, she would filch a piece. It tasted better than anything in the world then, and still does. A bit tricky to make (you must fuss so much and no more), this fudge has exceptional flavor. Mimi is so adept that she can handle four times the recipe at one time. Before you attempt these proportions, we suggest you practice by making the recipe first, as it is. It's easier once you know the way.

This recipe yields 1 pound of candy. When cut into thirty-six or more pieces, it is sufficient for two to three gifts.

> 2 teaspoons butter or margarine for the pan
> ¾ cup milk
> 2 squares Baker's unsweetened chocolate
> 1 cup sugar
> 1 tablespoon light corn syrup
> ⅛ teaspoon salt
> ¼ stick (2 tablespoons) butter or margarine
> 1½ teaspoons vanilla
> ½ cup broken pecans

Grease an 8- or 9-inch square cake pan with butter or margarine.

Combine the milk and chocolate in a heavy 4-quart saucepan. Stir over low heat until the chocolate is melted. Add the sugar, corn syrup, and salt and stir constantly over medium-high heat until all grains of sugar are dissolved. As soon as the mixture comes to a boil, stop stirring. Use a wet paper towel to remove any grains of sugar that have adhered to the inside of the pan. Lower the heat, insert a candy thermometer, and boil gently without stirring until the thermometer registers 234° (soft ball).

Remove the pan from the heat and move it, without stirring, onto a rack. Gently place the butter and vanilla on top of the mixture and let the fudge cool undisturbed just until it registers 110°. Remove the thermometer, add chopped nuts, and begin beating. At the point when the fudge is just beginning to lose its gloss and thicken, quickly turn it out into the prepared pan. Use a spatula to spread the mixture quickly into the corners, then leave it alone — if you fuss with it too much, the fudge will not be creamy. Using a large knife dipped in hot water, score the fudge into thirty-six or more squares. Let cool completely, then cut again. Store in an airtight container. For best flavor and texture, store the fudge for 24 hours before serving.

TO PREPARE IN ADVANCE: This fudge will keep for up to three weeks at room temperature in airtight containers. It may be frozen for up to six months.

SPECIAL PACKAGING: Fudge will dry quickly if exposed to air, so airtight candy tins are your best bet. Any dish or container may be used if the fudge is to be eaten immediately.

THE LABEL: May be stored in an airtight container at room temperature for up to three weeks or frozen for up to six months.

Beautiful Buttermilk Fudge

This recipe from Mimi, the fudge freak (see page 170), takes a few liberties with the sugary confection, loaded with chocolate and calories, with which we're all familiar. The change lies in a few minor substitutions and in the substantial departure of exchanging buttermilk for chocolate. All in all, although the ingredients listed may not immediately captivate your interest in the reading, in truth, in the cooking they turn into a silky, brown sugar, penuche-tasting treat that's no trick to make and as beautiful as the name implies. Some things can't be changed, however. Those calories. There wasn't a thing Mimi could do about them.

The recipe yields forty to fifty pieces of candy, weighing about 1¾ pounds. This amount will be sufficient for three to four gifts.

1 cup buttermilk
1 teaspoon baking soda
2 cups white sugar
1½ sticks (¾ cup) butter
2 tablespoons light corn syrup
2 cups broken pecans
1½ teaspoons vanilla

Place the buttermilk and the soda in a heavy 4-quart saucepan. Stir to dissolve the soda. Add the sugar, butter, and corn syrup. Place the mixture over medium-high heat and stir constantly until it starts to boil. Stop stirring and use a wet paper towel to remove any grains of sugar that have adhered to the sides of the pan. Insert a candy thermometer, lower the heat, and boil gently until it registers 244°.

Remove the pan from the heat and beat in the pecans and the vanilla. The mixture will start to thicken almost immediately, so quickly begin dropping it by teaspoons on any oiled surface. The candy will harden as it cools.

TO PREPARE IN ADVANCE: May be stored in airtight containers at room temperature for up to a month, but is so irresistible that no one seems to keep it around for very long. It freezes perfectly for up to six months.

SPECIAL PACKAGING: Candy tins are the best airtight containers for keeping any kind of candy fresh. Other containers are suitable if the candy is to be eaten immediately.

THE LABEL: May be stored in an airtight container at room temperature for up to a month or frozen for up to six months.

Candied Orange Peel

If you've ever been disappointed on peeling a large, golden orange only to find mostly skin and pits and very little orange, turn it to your advantage. Make Candied Orange Peel. This particular recipe contains no preservatives; therefore, your peel will have a heightened flavor unmatched by any of the commercial varieties and be less expensive in the bargain. You can also successfully candy lemon, lime, and grapefruit peels in the same manner.

This recipe makes about 6 cups of candied peel in syrup, enough to fill six 8-ounce gift containers. Give it as is to be used in fruitcakes, etc., or make into a confection with the recipe for the following Gingered Orange Peel.

  10 large, thick-skinned oranges
  4 cups sugar
  2½ cups water

Place the oranges in a pot large enough to hold them with room to spare. cover with cold water. Bring the water to a boil over high heat and simmer for 30 to 40 minutes until the oranges are tender when pierced with a fork. Drain and let stand until cool enough to handle.

Cut each orange in half. Scoop out all the pulp and membrane from the insides with a spoon — it will come out easily. Using a sharp knife, cut the peel into narrow ¼-inch strips.

Combine the sugar and water in a heavy 4-quart saucepan. Bring to a boil, then lower the heat and let the syrup boil until it reaches 238° (the soft ball stage) on a candy thermometer. Stir in the orange strips. Simmer slowly for about 20 minutes until the strips look transparent. Do not overcook at this point, as the mixture can burn very easily toward the end of the cooking time. Remove the pan from the heat and let cool.

If you will be giving the peel in syrup as is, pack it into containers and store in the refrigerator. If you wish to make confections out of the peel, proceed as in the recipe for Gingered Orange Peel.

TO PREPARE IN ADVANCE: The peel in the syrup may be stored in a jar in the refrigerator for at least a year.

SPECIAL PACKAGING: Any kind of covered glass jar is appropriate.

THE LABEL: Use for fruitcakes, confections or baking. May be stored in the refrigerator for up to one year.

Gingered Orange Peel

This recipe is a cinch. All the work has been done for you in the previous recipe. Just take it one step further. Mix sugar with a liberal amount of the spice reminiscent of a Far East bazaar, and roll the fruit strips cooked in syrup in the mixture. Once dried, they may be one-ended into the chocolate coating on page 175. Work out another destiny for those tired after-dinner mints. Instead, serve this delicious confection with your coffee.

If you use one full recipe of Candied Orange Peel to make this, it will yield 6 cups of sugar-coated candy, enough for six 8-ounce gifts.

> 1 recipe of Candied Orange Peel (page 172), drained of syrup
> 1½ cups sugar
> 4 teaspoons ground ginger

Roll the strips of peel, a few at a time, in the combined sugar and ginger. Place on strips of wax paper and allow to dry for 3 or 4 hours at room temperature. Transfer to airtight containers.

TO PREPARE IN ADVANCE: Stored in airtight containers, the candy will keep for up to a month at room temperature. It may be frozen for up to a year.

SPECIAL PACKAGING: This candy looks especially appetizing in see-through containers; however, candy tins are ideal because they provide airtight storage.

THE LABEL: A confection to serve with after-dinner coffee. May be stored in an airtight container at room temperature for up to one month or frozen for up to a year.

Coco-Locos

Simplicity itself! Our daughter Lisa makes these at Christmastime for a small army of friends and teachers. If you supervise the last-minute boiling (that's a literal minute, sixty seconds), you can leave the kitchen without a hair out of place and let the children take over. Small teaspoonsful of batter, looking like haystacks in miniature, are then dropped onto wax paper to firm. Filled as it is with peanut butter, oats, and coconut, it's a fine candy to let the kids get bingey with.

This recipe makes about eighty pieces of candy, enough to fill four or five small candy tins. Do not double the recipe.

>2 cups sugar
>1 stick (¼ pound) butter or margarine
>½ cup milk
>2½ cups quick Quaker oats
>1 cup (3½-ounce can) flaked coconut
>2/3 cup (6-ounce jar) smooth peanut butter
>3 tablespoons cocoa
>1½ teaspoons vanilla

Measure and set out all the ingredients. Place the sugar, butter or margarine, and milk in a heavy 3-quart saucepan. Bring the mixture to a hard rolling boil and let boil for 1 minute. Remove from the heat and immediately stir in the remaining ingredients. Drop small teaspoons of the mixture on wax paper. Let cool for several hours at room temperature until firm. Transfer to airtight containers.

TO PREPARE IN ADVANCE: The candy may be stored in airtight containers at room temperature for up to a week, up to a month in the refrigerator, or up to six months in the freezer.

SPECIAL PACKAGING: Airtight candy tins are ideal to keep these candies fresh.

THE LABEL: May be stored in an airtight container for up to one week at room temperature or one month in the refrigerator, or may be frozen for up to six months.

Chocoholics

They say that Bernard Berenson, art historian and critic, stopped going to art galleries because his method of stepping close to paintings to study them caused people to study *him* instead of the paintings! Well, we're the Berensons of the food world. And no one studies with more intensity than Marge, Paul's mother. When we once served her a very thin wafer, coated with chocolate, purchased from a well-known pastry shop, she broke it in two and sat there and studied it, while everybody else was eating theirs and reaching for another. It really was very, very thin (our first clue), and you'd think there wouldn't be much to discover. But there was. And this is it.

We had recently been introduced to Norwegian flatbread, or we would never have been able to deduce that what was cloaked in chocolate was just such a wafer, easily purchased in any market. What posed the problem was finding the right coating of chocolate. Marge wrote to several chocolate companies and finally worked out the following formula. Paraffin is essential because it keeps the chocolate from melting at room temperature. It's great fun to paint the chocolate on both sides of the wafers using a wide paint brush. Get the kids to help you. It's that easy!

This recipe makes about forty chocolate-coated wafers, enough for two to three gifts. Double the recipe if desired.

⅛ bar (about 1 tablespoon) paraffin
1 (4-ounce) bar Baker's German's sweet chocolate
½ ounce (½ square) unsweetened chocolate
About 20 pieces Norwegian flatbread (see Note)

Note: Norwegian flatbread is available at most large markets. It is a wafer-thin bread that is marvelous with hors d'oeuvre spreads and for this confection.

Melt the paraffin in the top of a glass double boiler over hot, not boiling, water. Add the chocolate and stir just until melted. Remove from the heat.

Cut each wafer of flatbread in half crosswise to form squares. Hold a square of flatbread with tongs. Use a flat pastry brush or a new clean paint brush to coat both sides with the chocolate mixture and lay on wax paper to dry. Continue coating wafers until all the chocolate is used. Let the wafers dry at room temperature for at least 2 hours, then stack them to pack into containers.

TO PREPARE IN ADVANCE: Stored in airtight containers, Chocoholics will keep for three weeks in a cool, dry place. Do not refrigerate or freeze.

SPECIAL PACKAGING: Square candy tins are ideal.

THE LABEL: May be stored in an airtight container at room temperature for up to three weeks. Do not refrigerate or freeze.

Desserts

It was no accident that in the day of vaudeville the star was given the "next to closing" spot. It's the same with dessert. What concludes a meal can indeed be the show stopper. No matter how much your guests rave about the rest of your dinner, a smashing dessert brings thunderous applause, but only if it *is* a smashing dessert! The ones that follow can help make you a neighborhood legend in your own time.

The American cook has always been a great baker, possibly due to the abundance of the necessary raw materials, wheat, sugar, and dairy products. And our Yankee ingenuity has created a few all-time American greats such as apple pie, angel food cake, and chiffon cake.

We ourselves love county fairs and church bazaars where American baking can be sampled at its best, baked by the most unexpected cooks. We were once privileged to judge a pie contest, where the awarding of the ribbon was one of the most difficult culinary decisions we ever faced. We haggled for half an hour on every fine point. When we finally agreed which pie was the best, we were introduced to the new champ, a charming eight-year-old girl who had made a fantastic blue ribbon pie!

Speaking of greatness, the all-time world championship for pastry must go to Demel's of Vienna. They have been making pastries since 1786 and, in our opinion, far outdistance even the second runner-up, the distinguished Rumpelmayer's of Paris.

Vienna is the home of "La Grande Patisserie." It was here in Vienna in years past that a pastry cook once gently whipped the cream skimmed off the top of a bowl of milk and invented *Schlageobers,* or in short, *Schlage.* Nowhere in the history of mankind have so many talented artists created such sweet master-pieces. The exquisite baroque design of Vienna's Spanish wind torte is truly in-spired pastry magic. The whole city of Vienna is magic — and fattening! That's an unfortunate thought, so we won't pursue it.

This famous little city has over 1500 pastry shops displaying uncountable irresistible delights, each with its own history or legend. For example, the carni-val jelly doughnut, or Krapfen. Legend has it that if a lady were to break one in two, the gentleman receiving the other half is automatically engaged, a danger-ous place for a man with a sweet tooth! Then there is the pastrymaker's wife who, caught smiling at the visiting Indian tightrope walker, threw a handful of dough at her husband. He ducked, the dough landed in hot fat, cooked, was coated with chocolate, and became *Indianerkrapfen.* We may not believe these Viennese stories, but we certainly believe their pastries. Their enormous interest in this field is evidenced by a book we once read on Austrian cooking in which they devoted 96 pages to entrees and 111 pages to desserts.

A dessert is more than just a dessert. It's another chance to show off not on-ly your cooking skills, but your creativity and flair as well. We, in fact, could dine quite contentedly on corn flakes and hot water if we knew our hostess was serving a Red Velvet Cake with Coconut Icing for dessert.

Why not share one of the following good things with a friend? It's one beautiful way of doubling your pleasure.

Greek Walnut Torte
with Brandy Buttercream Icing

There are tortes, and there are cakes disguised as tortes. Here's an authentic Greek one. It contains no shortening or flour (that's what separates tortes from cakes), only eggs and walnuts. Becky Smith, an enthusiastic cooking buddy, brought this recipe back from a skiing trip at Vail, Colorado, which is probably why the buttercream icing is generously laced with brandy. Not only does it temper the effect of the cold night air but tempts discriminating diners into another piece. Never beware of Greeks bearing this gift. It makes a magnificent finale to any meal.

This recipe makes one 8-inch torte of three layers, enough for one elegant gift to serve ten to twelve.

Shortening for the pans
3 cups (about 12 ounces) finely ground walnuts (see Note)
½ cup fine dry bread crumbs
1 tablespoon grated orange rind
2 teaspoons grated lemon rind
2 teaspoons baking powder
1 teaspoon ground cinnamon
1 teaspoon ground cloves
½ teaspoon salt
9 large eggs, separated when they are still cold, at room temperature
1 cup sugar
1 teaspoon vanilla
½ cup cool water
¼ teaspoon cream of tartar or 1 teaspoon fresh lemon juice

For the Icing
1 stick (¼ pound) butter
1 (1-pound) box confectioner's sugar
⅛ teaspoon salt
1 egg
1 teaspoon vanilla
2 tablespoons (or more) brandy
Walnut halves or pieces

Note: The easiest methods for grinding nuts are an electric blender and Cuisinart food processor. To grind nuts in a blender, put only 1 cup of nuts at a time in the container, cover, and run the motor at medium for a few seconds. To grind the nuts in a food processor, place the full 12 ounces in the container and process with the steel blade until finely ground.

Preheat the oven to 350°. You will need three 8-inch round cake pans — foil ones are fine. Grease the pans well with shortening, then line them with wax paper (see illustration). Grease the wax paper or spray with a nonstick coating spray.

Combine the walnuts, bread crumbs, grated rinds, baking powder, spices, and salt in a very large mixing bowl. Beat the yolks with the sugar in the bowl of an electric mixer until thick. Beat the vanilla and water into the yolk-sugar mixture, then stir it into the nut-spice mixture in the mixing bowl.

Place the egg whites in a large clean mixing bowl with the cream of tartar or lemon juice. Beat just until the whites hold stiff peaks when the beater is lifted. Do not overbeat! Fold half of the whites thoroughly into the batter. Fold in the remaining whites just until combined — a few streaks of white will not matter. Divide the batter evenly among the three prepared pans.

Bake at the center rack position of a 350° oven for about 30 minutes until a toothpick inserted in the center comes out clean. Let cool in the pans. Turn out and carefully peel off the wax paper.

To make the buttercream icing, beat the butter in the bowl of an electric mixer until it is smooth and very creamy. Beat in the confectioner's sugar and salt followed by the egg, vanilla, and enough brandy to make a good spreading consistency. Spread the icing generously between the layers and over the top. Decorate the top of the torte as desired with walnut halves or pieces.

TO PREPARE IN ADVANCE: This is a moist cake which keeps beautifully. May be stored, covered, for up to three days at room temperature or in the refrigerator for up to a week. To freeze, wrap after solidly frozen to protect the icing. Freezing for up to four months does not harm the cake at all, and it may be cut into serving pieces while frozen.

SPECIAL PACKAGING: A footed cake plate or other serving dish would be ideal. Overwrap with cellophane and tie with a ribbon.

THE LABEL: *If the cake is freshly made, the label should read:* May be stored, covered, at room temperature for up to three days or in the refrigerator for up to a week, or may be frozen for up to four months. To freeze, wrap the cake *after* it is solidly frozen. *If the cake is frozen, the label should read:* May be kept frozen for up to four months. May be stored, covered, in the refrigerator for up to a week or at room temperature for up to three days after it has been thawed. May be refrozen.

Red Velvet Cake with Coconut Icing

If you skipped ahead and ran a practiced eye down the list of ingredients for this recipe, you may have stopped at the tenth ingredient and responded with a quick and emphatic, "No way!" We must admit there was a dubious quality to our own reaction when this cake was introduced to us by one of our loveliest students, Joan Phillips. She finally persuaded us to try it. We fell enough in love with its old-fashioned flavor to include it in our menus and in this volume. It's the cake Joan's family most opts for on birthdays. They're consistent in their request, but not with their choice of color, so given free rein, Joan usually makes it in red. It comes out a rich, dark, red velvet. And once in tribute of her husband's homecoming weekend at the University of Southern California, she colored one layer red and the other gold, the school's colors. It can also be baked into twenty-four cupcakes. Topped with fluffy white icing and coconut, it's fit to sit on anyone's table, ready to be enjoyed by man, woman or child.

The recipe makes a 9-inch two-layer cake. To make two gifts, the layers may be iced and given separately. Double the recipe if desired.

Shortening and flour for the pans
½ cup Crisco vegetable shortening
1½ cups sugar
2 large eggs
2 cups sifted all-purpose flour
1 tablespoon cocoa
½ teaspoon salt
1 cup buttermilk
½ teaspoon vanilla
¼ cup (2-ounce bottle) red food coloring (do not skimp on this!)
1 teaspoon baking soda
1 tablespoon white or cider vinegar

For the Icing
1 cup milk
¼ cup flour
Dash salt
½ cup Crisco vegetable shortening
1 stick (¼ pound) butter or margarine
1 cup sugar
1½ teaspoons vanilla
1 cup (3½-ounce can) flaked coconut

Preheat the oven to 350°. Grease two 9-inch round cake pans. Dust the insides of the pans with flour and shake out any excess.

In the large bowl of an electric mixer, cream the ½ cup shortening with the sugar. Add the eggs and beat until the mixture is very smooth and creamy. Sift together three times the flour, cocoa, and salt; add to the creamed mixture alternately with the buttermilk while beating. Add the vanilla and food coloring, beating until well combined and evenly colored.

Stir the soda into the vinegar and immediately blend it into the batter. Divide the batter evenly between the two prepared pans. Bake at the center rack position of a 350° oven for 30 to 35 minutes until a toothpick inserted in the center comes out clean. Turn the layers out onto a rack to cool completely before frosting.

To make the frosting, blend together the milk, flour, and salt (making sure no lumps remain) in a small, heavy saucepan. Cook over low heat, stirring constantly, until thick and puddinglike; remove from heat and cool. In the bowl of an electric mixer beat the ½ cup shortening, butter or margarine, and sugar until very light and creamy. Add the vanilla and the pudding mixture and beat at high speed until it is thick and spreadable. Frost the cake completely and sprinkle with coconut.

TO PREPARE IN ADVANCE: This cake is very moist and keeps beautifully. May be stored, covered, at room temperature for up to five days, in the refrigerator for up to two weeks, or in the freezer for up to four months. If the cake is to be frozen, place it in the freezer unwrapped. After the icing is solid, seal in a large plastic bag. This way, the icing will be less likely to be smudged. This cake may be refrozen.

SPECIAL PACKAGING: Any kind of serving plate would be ideal.

THE LABEL: The color is the surprise! *If the cake is freshly baked, the label should read:* May be kept, covered, at room temperature for up to five days, in the refrigerator for up to two weeks, or frozen for up to four months. May be refrozen. *If the cake is frozen, the label should read:* May be kept frozen for up to four months; may be stored in an airtight container for up to five days or in the refrigerator for up to two weeks after it has been thawed. May be refrozen.

Sour Cream Coffee Cake

Cooks who unfailingly produce cakes that stick to the roof of the mouth might like to alter the odds. This recipe, given to us by Audrey Mitchell, the owner of the Stockpot Restaurant in Stockbridge, Massachusetts, might help. The bath makes the difference. An equal amount of vanilla and water is poured over the cake before it is placed into the oven. The liquid drizzles down through the batter, dispensing moisture and a unique flavor which vanilla in this quantity imparts. It's best when sprinkling the nut mixture that you keep clear of the edge of the pan. Then the cake, with its rippled middle nut layers, won't break in two when turned out of the pan.

This recipe makes one 10-inch tube or bundt cake of at least twelve servings or two 9-by-5-by-3-inch loaves of at least six servings each.

Shortening or nonstick spray for the pan(s)
3 cups sifted all-purpose flour
1½ teaspoons baking powder
1½ teaspoons baking soda
¼ teaspoon salt
3 sticks (¾ pound) butter or margarine, at room temperature
1½ cups sugar
2½ teaspoons vanilla
3 large eggs
1½ cups commercial sour cream
2 tablespoons vanilla and 2 tablespoons water, combined

For the Nut Mixture
¾ cup chopped walnuts
¾ cup dark brown sugar
1½ teaspoons cinnamon

For Garnish
Confectioner's sugar to dust the top

Preheat the oven to 350°. Grease a 10-inch bundt or tube pan or two 9-by-5-by-3-inch loaf pans with either a heavy coating of shortening or a generous spray of nonstick coating.

Sift together the flour, baking powder, soda, and salt and set aside. In a large bowl of an electric mixer, cream the butter or margarine with the sugar until the mixture is light and very fluffy. Add the vanilla, then beat in the eggs, one at a time, beating well after each addition. Beat in the sour cream. Gradually add the sifted ingredients, beating until the batter is smooth and well combined. Combine the nut-mixture ingredients.

Spoon a third of the batter into the prepared pan(s). Sprinkle half the nut mixture over the surface, taking care not to sprinkle all the way to the edges of the pan — that could cause the cake to break when turned out. Repeat with the second third of the batter and the remaining nut mixture. Top with the remaining batter. Spoon the vanilla-water mixture evenly over the top of the batter.

Bake in the center of a 350° oven for 30 minutes, then lower the heat to 325° and continue baking for about 45 minutes longer until the cake feels quite firm. Remove from the oven and cool on a rack for 10 minutes before turning out of the pan(s). Loosen the cake(s) around the edges with a knife before turning out on a rack to cool completely.

Dust the top of the coffee cake with confectioner's sugar just before serving. Serve warm or at room temperature.

TO PREPARE IN ADVANCE: After the cake has cooled, wrap in aluminum foil. It may be stored for up to four days at room temperature or frozen for up to four months. To serve, thaw if frozen and heat, in its foil wrap, for 20 to 30 minutes at 325°. The coffee cake may be refrozen if desired.

SPECIAL PACKAGING: The coffee cake should be securely wrapped in aluminum foil to preserve freshness. Decorative wrappings, such as colored cellophane, may be placed over the foil and tied with ribbons.

THE LABEL: Heat, wrapped in foil, at 325° for 20 to 30 minutes. Dust with confectioner's sugar before serving. *If the coffee cake is freshly baked, the label should read:* May be stored in an airtight container at room temperature for up to four days or frozen for up to four months. Can be frozen. *If the coffee cake is frozen, the label should read:* May be kept frozen for up to four months or store at room temperature for up to four days after it has been thawed. Can be refrozen.

24-Karat Cake or Cupcakes

What lured adventurers to the New World were dreams of gold and spices. This cake will entice you for the same reason. It is pure gold, flecked with nuggets of grated carrots, spiced lightly with ground cinnamon. Bake it as a cake and top with the creamy icing, strewn with crunchy pecans. Or bake it in cupcakes if you want to spread the treasure around. This cake has a moist quality that lasts.

This recipe makes one 9-inch three-layer cake for one generous gift, serving ten to twelve, or twenty to twenty-four cupcakes for many gifts.

Shortening and flour for the pans or frilled paper liners for
    muffin tins
2 cups all-purpose flour
2 cups sugar
2½ teaspoons ground cinnamon
2 teaspoons baking soda
4 large eggs
1½ cups vegetable oil
3 cups grated carrots (about 1 pound whole)

For the Icing
1 stick (¼ pound) butter or margarine, at room temperature
1 (8-ounce) package cream cheese, at room temperature
1 (1-pound) box powdered sugar
2 teaspoons vanilla
1 cup (about 5 ounces) diced pecans
1 cup flaked coconut (optional)

Grease and flour three 9-inch round cake tins, shaking out excess flour. If making cupcakes, place 20 to 24 frilled paper liners in muffin tins.

Preheat the oven to 350°. Sift together the flour, sugar, cinnamon, and soda; set aside. Beat the oil, egg, and carrots in the large bowl of an electric mixer for 3 to 4 minutes. Add the sifted ingredients and beat for 1 minute. Divide the batter evenly among the prepared pans. Fill cupcake pans a little over half full. Bake at 350° 30 to 35 minutes for the layers, about 20 minutes for the cupcakes, until a toothpick inserted in the center comes out clean. Remove from the oven and let cool completely in the pans.

To make the icing, beat the butter or margarine with the cream cheese in the bowl of an electric mixer until very light and fluffy. Beat in the powdered sugar followed by vanilla, pecans and optional coconut. To frost the cake, spread a generous amount of filling between and over the top of the layers, leaving the sides of the cake unfrosted. Or use the icing to generously frost the top of the cupcakes.

TO PREPARE IN ADVANCE: This is a moist cake that keeps beautifully. May be stored, covered, at room temperature for up to five days, in the refrigerator for up to two weeks, or in the freezer for up to four months. To freeze, place the frosted cake or cupcakes unwrapped in the freezer. Transfer to a large plastic bag when solidly frozen to protect the icing.

SPECIAL PACKAGING: Some kind of serving plate would be suitable for either the cake or cupcakes.

THE LABEL: *If freshly baked, the label should read:* May be stored in an airtight container at room temperature for up to five days, in the refrigerator for up to two weeks, or frozen for up to four months. Wrap after solidly frozen. *If frozen, the label should read:* May be kept frozen for up to four months; may be stored in an airtight container at room temperature for up to five days or in the refrigerator for up to two weeks after it has been thawed.

Applesauce Spice Cake with Butterscotch Icing

No matter what size we make the first serving of this cake, we have found that a second one must surely follow. It's the dessert triumph of Frances Pelham, our favorite recipe-swapping pal. It will even improve in flavor over a week's time if you manage to keep it around that long.

This recipe makes two tall 9-inch-square cakes. Use singly or stack for a layer cake.

Shortening for the pans
2 sticks (½ pound) butter or margarine, at room temperature
2 cups sugar
2 large eggs
3 cups sifted all-purpose flour
1 tablespoon baking soda
½ teaspoon salt
1 tablespoon ground cinnamon
1½ teaspoons ground nutmeg
1 teaspoon ground cloves
2½ cups applesauce
2 tablespoons light corn syrup
1 cup seedless raisins
1 cup chopped pecans or walnuts

For the Icing
1 (1-pound) box dark brown sugar
1½ sticks (¾ cup) butter, at room temperature
¾ cup heavy cream (whipping cream)
1½ teaspoons vanilla
Pecan or walnut halves (optional)
Cream or milk to thin icing, if necessary

Preheat the oven to 325°. Generously grease two deep 9-inch-square baking pans. Do not use smaller pans or the batter will overflow during the baking. (You may, however, use three smaller pans in a pinch.)

Cream the butter and sugar thoroughly in the large bowl of an electric mixer until very light and fluffy. Add the eggs one at a time, beating well after each addition. Sift together the flour, soda, salt, and spices. Mix together the applesauce and corn syrup, and add, alternately with the dry ingredients, to the butter-sugar-egg mixture, while beating. Fold in the raisins and nuts.

Pour the batter into the prepared pans. Bake at 325° for 1 hour, 15 minutes, until a toothpick inserted in the center comes out clean and the cake feels firm when pressed. Let cool completely in the pans.

To make the icing, combine the brown sugar, butter, and cream in a heavy 3- or 4-quart saucepan. Cook over medium heat until the mixture registers 238° (soft-ball) on a candy thermometer. Remove from heat and stir in the vanilla. Beat until cool enough to spread without running and *immediately* frost the cake. If it becomes too thick, thin with cream or milk.

Frost both layers completely. Decorate, if desired, with perfect pecan halves.

TO PREPARE IN ADVANCE: This cake is infinitely better if allowed to sit for several days, iced or not, at room temperature. If not iced, wrap airtight in foil or plastic wrap. If iced, simply cover. Either way it will stay moist for a week. It freezes perfectly with or without icing for up to three months and may even be refrozen.

SPECIAL PACKAGING: Some kind of serving plate would be ideal.

THE LABEL: Serve at room temperature. *If the cake is freshly baked, the label should read:* May be stored in an airtight container at room temperature for up to a week, in the refrigerator for up to two weeks, or the freezer for up to three months. Wrap after solidly frozen. May be refrozen. *If the cake is frozen, the label should read:* May be kept frozen for up to three months; may be stored in an airtight container for up to a week or in the refrigerator for up to two weeks after it has been thawed. May be refrozen.

 **Mimi's Heirloom Fruitcake**

Now concerning Mimi's Heirloom Fruitcake. Check the ingredients. Did you sigh or exult? If you're back with us here, undaunted, we know you're among that happy band who are not intimidated by a long list of ingredients. You know what we know. This cake will make it worth your while, for it's the finest fruitcake imaginable: rich, dark, chockful of nuts, and candied fruit. It needn't age as long as most fruitcakes, ten days will do, and the size of the cake is up to you. Bake one enormous cake for a large number of small servings or a number of small cakes to cheer a multitude of holiday celebrants.

This recipe will make one 5-pound (10-inch tube) cake, two 9-by-5-inch loaves, three 8-by 4-inch loaves, or many small cakes baked in muffin tins or miniature bread pans.

1 pound golden raisins
½ pound seedless raisins
¼ pound dried black currants
½ cup dark Jamaican rum, Cognac, or brandy
Shortening and brown paper for the pans
1 pound candied pineapple
½ pound candied red cherries
¼ pound candied citron
⅛ pound candied lemon peel
⅛ pound candied orange peel
2 cups sifted all-purpose flour
½ teaspoon ground mace
½ teaspoon ground cinnamon
½ teaspoon baking soda
¼ pound (4 ounces) slivered almonds
¼ pound (4 ounces) diced pecans
1 stick (¼ pound) butter or margarine, at room temperature
1 cup sugar
1 cup dark brown sugar, firmly packed
5 large eggs
2 teaspoons vanilla
1 teaspoon almond extract

For Storing
Cheesecloth
Dark Jamaican rum, Cognac, or brandy

For Glazing and Decorating
1½ cups confectioner's sugar
3 to 4 tablespoons heavy cream or half and half
¼ teaspoon almond extract
Angelica or candied mint leaves
Candied red cherries

In a large mixing bowl, combine the two kinds of raisins and the currants. Add the rum, Cognac, or brandy and let it stand, covered, overnight.

The next day generously grease a 10-inch tube pan (not a bundt pan), or smaller pans as listed above, with shortening. Line the pan(s) with brown paper and grease the paper. (Sorry, this is a bit of a chore, but it's necessary for removing the cakes from the pan!)

Prepare the remaining fruits for the batter by cutting the pineapple in thick wedges, the cherries in half (except those used for the decoration), and the citron, lemon, and orange peels into very thin strips. Add the fruits, along with the almonds and pecans, to the raisins and currants and mix well. Add ½ cup of the flour and toss lightly.

Sift the remaining 1½ cups of flour with the spices and baking soda onto a sheet of waxed paper.

Preheat the oven to 275°. In an electric mixer, cream the butter until light. Gradually beat in both kinds of sugar until the mixture is light and fluffy. Beat in the eggs, vanilla, and almond extract until thoroughly combined. Add the flour mixture and beat at low speed just until combined. Spoon the batter over the fruits and nuts and mix well.

Spoon the batter into the prepared pans, pressing it down evenly all around. For a large tube cake, bake about 3 hours, until a skewer inserted in the center comes out dry. Small cakes will take anywhere from 45 minutes to 2 hours.

Remove cake(s) from the oven. Let cool on a wire rack for 30 minutes. Turn out of the pan(s) and carefully peel off the paper. Cool completely.

To store the cake(s), wrap in a double layer of cheesecloth which has been soaked in dark rum, Cognac, or brandy. Wrap the cloth-covered cakes airtight in several layers of aluminum foil. If you have made a tube cake, place a few pieces of raw apple in the center of the cake before wrapping to prevent it from drying out. Store the cake for at least ten days before glazing or serving.

Within 48 hours of serving, glaze and decorate. To prepare the glaze, beat the powdered sugar, cream and almond extract until smooth. Pour the glaze decoratively over the top as illustrated. Decorate with a floral design of thin leaf shapes of angelica or candied mint leaves and candied cherries in a floral design.

TO PREPARE IN ADVANCE: Fruitcake must be aged at least ten days before serving for excellence of flavor and texture. Store the tightly wrapped cake(s) in a cool place or in the refrigerator. Resoak the cheesecloth in rum, Cognac, or brandy every week or so for the first month. Once a month is often enough after that. If stored in the refrigerator, these fruitcakes will last indefinitely (forever, probably). They may also be frozen.

SPECIAL PACKAGING: Any kind of decorative wrapping can go over the foil wrapping.

THE LABEL: May be stored in the refrigerator indefinitely. Unwrap and resoak cheesecloth in rum, Cognac, or brandy once a month.

Our Favorite New York-Style Cheesecake

After shopping for ingredients and carefully following a recipe, nothing can give a creative cook greater satisfaction than watching, fearfully perhaps at first, the creation blossom into the perfection that was promised. If you, like us, have been looking for a moist, fluffy cheesecake that would rise like a souffle and threaten the top of your oven, then now is the time to butter up your spring-form pan. This cake is everything we promise, just the kind of airy, billowing Jewish-style cheesecake Paul remembers tasting when he was a kid in New York. It will serve up to twenty and makes a marvelous gift. In fact, it is almost too generous for one gift unless it is to be used for a party. We suggest you cut it in quarters and give it to four lucky people accompanied with fresh berries, grapes, or a container of homemade Sugar-Plum Jam.

This recipe makes one large cheesecake which will serve at least twelve or up to twenty. A whole cheesecake makes a very generous gift, or it may be divided into quarters to make four gifts of three to five servings each.

For the Crust
1 tablespoon butter or margarine to grease a 9-inch spring-form pan
1½ cups Zwieback crumbs made from a 6-ounce box Zwieback baby biscuits (crush with rolling pin, grind in blender, or food processor)
3 tablespoons sugar
½ cup (2 ounces) ground walnuts (grind in blender or food processor)
¼ teaspoon ground cinnamon
½ stick (¼ cup) butter or margarine, melted

For the Filling
3 (8-ounce) packages cream cheese, at room temperature
1¼ cups sugar
6 large eggs, separated and at room temperature
2 cups (1 pint) dairy sour cream
1/3 cup all-purpose flour
1 tablespoon fresh lemon juice
2 teaspoons vanilla
1 tablespoon grated lemon rind
1 tablespoon grated orange rind
¼ teaspoon cream of tartar or 1 teaspoon fresh lemon juice

Grease a 9-inch spring-form pan (3-inches deep) with the butter or margarine. (Do not use a smaller pan or the filling will overflow. The cake may be baked in a 10-inch pan if that is all you have, but it will be prettier if baked in a 9-inch pan.)

In a small mixing bowl combine the Zwieback crumbs, sugar, walnuts, cinnamon, butter, and stir until well blended. Press ¾ of the crumb mixture onto the sides. Reserve the remaining crumb mixture for the topping. Chill the crust while you make the filling.

Preheat the oven to 350°.

Beat the cream cheese in the large bowl of an electric mixer until it is very smooth and creamy. Gradually beat in the sugar until the mixture is fluffy. Stop the motor often to scrape the sides of the bowl with a rubber spatula. Add the yolks one at a time, beating well after each addition. Beat in the sour cream, flour, lemon juice, vanilla, and rinds until the mixture is very well blended.

In another large mixing bowl combine the egg whites with the cream of tartar or lemon juice. (In order for the whites to be beaten to their full volume, they should be at room temperature. If they are cold set the mixing bowl in a dish of warm water and stir the whites to bring them to room temperature before beating.) Beat until stiff peaks are formed when the beater is lifted and the whites do not slide when the bowl is tilted. Fold half of the beaten whites into the cheese mixture thoroughly. Carefully fold in the remaining half just until well combined and turn the mixture into the prepared crust.

Bake in the center of a 350° oven for 1 hour and 15 minutes. Turn off the oven and leave the cake in the oven for one more hour, then remove it to a rack and allow it to cool to room temperature. Sprinkle the remaining crumb mixture over the top and refrigerate for at least 12 hours before serving.

Serve chilled. If desired, accompany each serving with three fresh strawberries or a small bunch of grapes or top with a tablespoon of Sugar Plum Jam (page 108)—Yum!

TO PREPARE IN ADVANCE: Store, covered, in the refrigerator for up to a week. It may be frozen for up to three months, in which case let it thaw overnight in the refrigerator before serving.

SPECIAL PACKAGING: Few people own spring-form pans, so give the pan as part of the gift along with the whole cheesecake. If giving part of the cheesecake to several people, place each portion on a plate. Either way wrap in cellophane and tie with a bow. Include a jar of Sugar-Plum Jam (page 108) or fresh berries or grapes to garnish.

THE LABEL: Serve chilled. Store, covered, in the refrigerator for up to a week or in the freezer for up to three months. If frozen, thaw overnight in the refrigerator before serving. Garnish, if desired, with fresh berries, small bunches of grapes or spoonsful of Sugar-Plum Jam.

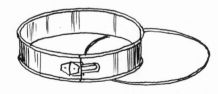

Puddings

Unbelievably Easy Chocolate Pots de Crème

We kid you not. This is an easy recipe. The only complexity lies in the fate of those two leftover egg whites. Everything else gets plunked into a blender, to which simmered cream is added. There's a fast whrrrrr, and the only decision left is what to pour it into. You could use miniature souffle dishes, but if you want to shed a bit of splendor all around, try the sets of little pots called petits pots that have become popular gift items in recent years. If you own a set or are planning to give one away as a gift, fill the tiny cups first with this easy chocolate mousse rather than the boiled or baked custard customarily served in them. Include the recipe. This one came from our friend, Margaret Skibitzke, who says her son, Paul, is addicted to it. Paul is only six years old, which accounts for the option given of using either brandy extract or the real thing.

This recipe will fill six petits pots with lids or six small souffle dishes two-thirds full. Do not double the recipe.

> 1 (6-ounce) package semisweet chocolate morsels
> 2 egg yolks
> 1 tablespoon brandy extract (see Note)
> 1¼ cups half and half

Note: Margaret prefers using brandy extract to the real thing. You may, if you prefer, substitute 1 tablespoon dark rum or 2 tablespoons brandy or Cognac.

Place the chocolate, egg yolks, and brandy extract in an electric blender. Bring the cream to a simmer in a small saucepan on top of the stove and pour it over the other ingredients. Immediately blend at high speed until the mixture is smooth. Pour into containers and chill for at least 3 hours. Serve cold.

TO PREPARE IN ADVANCE: Prepare this up to three days before needed and store, covered, in the refrigerator. Do not freeze.

SPECIAL PACKAGING: The petits pots usually come with a matching tray and right there you have a very special gift. Small souffle dishes are just as suitable. Be sure to include the recipe.

THE LABEL: Serve chilled. May be stored, covered, in the refrigerator for up to three days. Do not freeze.

New Orleans Bread Pudding
with Pecans and Whiskey Sauce

Of all the obvious charms of New Orleans, one must put food near the top of the list. Besides the oyster bars, daybreak beignets, and numerous restaurants, there's the New Orleans Food Festival which we attended one summer. In the guise of pure research (which it was, in part), we loosened our belts and settled down to serious work.

The huge crowd at the Rivergate Auditorium was a perfect testimony of the high regard people of New Orleans have for the better things in life. We swallowed antacid tablets, bought fifteen feet of tickets, blew kisses, and went our separate ways to search out the booths taken by restaurants and food chains who were selling bite-sized tastes of their house specialties in paper cups. We parted and met several times at prearranged standup tables to share our discoveries. Diana went back four times to taste and analyze the ingredients for this remarkable bread pudding. In experimenting, we added pecans to give it more texture and ended up with what may well be the best recipe in this book.

This recipe makes one large pudding for ten to twelve servings or two puddings of five to six servings. The sauce measures 2 cups.

12 ounces (¾ pound) crusty white French bread (about 12 cups) (see Note)
1 quart milk
3 large eggs
2 cups sugar
2 tablespoons vanilla
1 cup diced pecans
1/3 cup seedless raisins
Butter or margarine for baking dishes
Nonstick spray (optional)
2 tablespoons butter or margarine

For the Sauce
1½ cups sugar
1/3 cup water
1½ sticks butter or margarine, cut in about 12 pieces
½ cup bourbon
1 teaspoon cornstarch

Note: Use regular French bread for this, not sour dough. The bread need not be fresh; in fact, this is the best way we know to use up stale bread.

Preheat oven to 350°. Cut the bread into 1-inch cubes and, if the bread is fresh, let it dry at room temperature for about 30 minutes. Place the cubes in a large mixing bowl. Cover with milk and let stand about 15 minutes until milk is absorbed.

In a small mixing bowl, beat the eggs, sugar, and vanilla until thick and creamy. Add pecans and raisins, pour over the soaked bread cubes, and stir until mixed.

Grease a shallow baking-serving dish of about 3-quart capacity or two smaller dishes of 6-cup capacity with butter or margarine. (The large dish that we use measures 9 by 11 by 2 inches.) You may wish to spray a nonstick coating inside the dish as well for ease of serving. Spoon the pudding mixture into the baking dish(es) and dot the surface of the pudding evenly with 2 tablespoons butter or margarine.

The bread pudding must bake in a water-bath, so place a larger shallow pan in the center of a 350° oven. Set the dish(es) in it and pour boiling water into the outer pan to a depth of 1 inch. Bake for 55 to 65 minutes, until a knife inserted in the center of the pudding comes out clean. Let stand at room temperature for at least 10 minutes before serving.

To make the Whiskey Sauce, combine the sugar with the water in a heavy 2-quart saucepan. Bring to a boil without stirring. Insert a candy thermometer and let simmer until the mixture reaches 238°, about 4 to 5 minutes. Remove the thermometer. Lower the heat and add the pieces of butter all at once. Stir rapidly with a wire whisk until the butter has been absorbed and the mixture is creamy. Remove the pan from the heat. Blend the bourbon and cornstarch together until well combined and stir into the sauce. Beat with a whisk until smooth. Return the sauce to the heat and whisk for a minute or two, just until it reaches a hard boil and bubbles up in the pan. If the sauce remains hot for too long a time or is overcooked, it will eventually become grainy from the evaporation of the liquid. To remedy this, simply add a tablespoon or two of water and reheat, whisking constantly, to a hard boil. Remove from the heat. Serve over warm bread pudding.

TO PREPARE IN ADVANCE: The pudding is at its very best when freshly baked; however, it will reheat very nicely. It may be stored in the refrigerator for up to four days or in the freezer for up to four months. Bring to room temperature, then heat at 300° for about 20 minutes until it is warm through. The sauce may be made in advance and stored in the refrigerator for up to a month. To serve, bring it to a boil in a small heavy saucepan over medium heat, whisking constantly. If the sauce sugars, remedy it as above.

SPECIAL PACKAGING: The pudding dish and the sauce container should be part of the gift. Any kind of shallow ovenproof baking dish is appropriate for the pudding. The sauce might be given in a small saucepan or souffle dish or cruet that may be later used by the recipient for other purposes. You might tie on a whisk for mixing the Whiskey Sauce.

THE LABEL: Serve warm topped with hot Whiskey Sauce. Heat pudding at 300° for about 20 minutes. May be stored in the refrigerator for up to four days or in the freezer for up to four months. *If the pudding is frozen, the label should read:* May be kept frozen for up to four months or in the refrigerator for up to four days after it has been thawed. *The label for the sauce should read:* Just before serving, bring the sauce to a hard boil over medium heat, whisking constantly. Serve over warm pudding. If the sauce becomes sugary, stir in a bit of water and bring again to a boil while whisking.

Betsy Bloomingdale's Steamed Persimmon Pudding with Saint Cecelia Sauce

A little introduction seems to be in order. Saint Cecelia was patron saint of music and of the blind who inspired many a masterpiece in art and literature. Among those created by Raphael, Rubens, and Chaucer, you may add this one by Mrs. Alfred Bloomingdale. Mrs. Bloomingdale enjoys an enviable international reputation as a hostess and shares with us this old family recipe of her mother's. As Cervantes said, "The proof is in the pudding"—in this case the proof depends on the brandy used to serve this elegant dessert in the manner to which it has become accustomed, that is, in a fitting blaze of glory.

This recipe makes one 8-cup pudding with sauce to serve ten people.

> Butter or margarine to grease the mold
> 2 cups persimmon pulp from 6 to 8 ripe persimmons (see Note)
> 2 cups sifted all-purpose flour
> 4 teaspoons baking soda
> ½ teaspoon salt
> 2 cups sugar
> 1 cup chopped blanched almonds
> 1 cup seedless raisins, washed and drained
> 2 tablespoons butter or margarine, melted
> 1 cup milk
> 2 teaspoons vanilla
>
> *For Serving*
> Wedges of fresh persimmon, if desired
> ¼ cup brandy for flaming
>
> *For the Sauce*
> 2 cups heavy cream (whipping cream), whipped
> 4 egg yolks
> 2 cups powdered sugar
> 1/3 to ½ cup brandy

Note: Persimmons are in season from October to February. Choose soft ripe fruit—underipe persimmons have a bitter taste.

Generously grease an 8-cup steamed-pudding mold with butter or margarine. The mold should have a lid.

Remove the stems from washed persimmons and press through a sieve or food mill. Measure 2 cups pulp. Sift flour, baking soda, salt, sugar, and set aside. In a large bowl combine the almonds, raisins, and melted butter or margarine. Mix well. Stir in the milk and vanilla, followed by the dry ingredients. Beat until smooth and pour into the prepared mold. Cover the mold with buttered wax paper, a layer of aluminum foil, and the lid of the mold. Tie the lid tightly in place with string.

Place the mold on a rack such as a vegetable steamer in a large stockpot or other pot large enough to hold it. Pour in water to reach halfway up the side of the mold. Bring the water to a boil over high heat, then lower the heat to maintain a simmer and cover the pan. Steam the pudding for 3 hours, adding boiling water as necessary to keep the water at the same level.

If the pudding is to be given in the mold, there is no need to turn it out. Let the pudding cool uncovered at room temperature for 15 to 20 minutes, then turn it out of the mold onto a serving dish or sheet of foil. You may have to loosen it gently from the mold with a dull knife.

To make the sauce, whip the cream until it holds a shape. Beat the egg yolks in the bowl of an electric mixer until thick. Gradually add the powdered sugar and brandy, beating constantly. Fold in the whipped cream.

To serve, place the warm pudding on a round platter and garnish, if desired, with fresh persimmon. At the table warm about ¼ cup brandy in a ladle held over a candle, ignite with a match and pour it flaming over the pudding. When the flame goes out, cut into slices and serve with Saint Cecelia Sauce.

TO PREPARE IN ADVANCE: This pudding keeps beautifully. Wrap tightly in foil after it has cooled. May be stored in the refrigerator for up to one month or in the freezer indefinitely. Heat the pudding either in the mold or sealed in aluminum foil in a 300° oven for 45 minutes before serving. Saint Cecelia Sauce should be made within 3 hours of serving and kept chilled.

SPECIAL PACKAGING: It is especially nice to give the pudding right in the mold in which it was baked along with the recipe or simply wrap the pudding tightly in aluminum foil and overwrap decoratively with cellophane. Include the ingredients for making the Saint Cecelia Sauce and the brandy for flaming.

THE LABEL: Flame the pudding with ¼ cup warmed brandy at serving time. Cut into wedges and serve with Saint Cecelia Sauce (recipe and ingredients included). *If the mold is part of the present, the label should read:* Heat the pudding in the mold in a 300° oven for 45 minutes before serving. May be stored in the refrigerator for up to one month or frozen indefinitely. *If the pudding is wrapped in foil, the label should read:* May be stored in the refrigerator for up to a month or frozen indefinitely. Thaw and heat in foil wrapping in a 300° oven for 45 minutes before serving.

$\mathcal{P}ies$

Klayre's Super-Flaky Pie Crust

Too many have found that fooling around with flour and shortening can be frustratingly messy, and more to the point, decidedly unnerving when the honored guest's futile attack means pie plates returning to the kitchen with the crust still firmly in place. Indeed, why should a recipe with so few ingredients prove so troublesome that few bother to try again? Trouble your heart no more; there's a solution, and it's this recipe for Super-Flaky Pie Crust, named after Paul's sister, Klayre Kelly, a high school teacher in Buffalo, New York. When Klayre ventured into her school's cafeteria to help one year, she left—as all contact with educational institutions should leave us—with a heap of learning and this sensationally easy pie crust. It is "short," which means it contains a high percentage of shortening to flour, thus insuring the flakiness that's the ultimate goal of all pastrymakers. It's easy. It's fail-proof. And it will become your favorite, as it has with all our students.

This recipe makes four to five 9-inch pie shells, depending on how adept you are at rolling out the dough.

> 5 cups all-purpose flour
> 1½ teaspoons salt
> 1 (1-pound) can of Crisco
> 1 large egg
> 1 tablespoon white or cider vinegar
> Cold water

Sift the flour with the salt into a large mixing bowl. Add the Crisco and, using either a pastry cutter or two knives, cut the shortening into the flour until you have what looks like an even-textured meal.

Break the egg into a 1-cup measuring cup and beat it lightly with a fork. Add the vinegar, then fill the cup to the 1-cup level with cold water. Pour this liquid over the flour and shortening mixture and stir until the dry ingredients are moistened. The dough will be wet and a bit loose. Form the dough into four patties (or five if you are proficient at rolling out dough evenly without waste). Wrap each patty airtight in plastic wrap and refrigerate for at least an hour before rolling. If the dough becomes too firm to roll out, let it rest at room temperature for 15 minutes.

We like to use a pastry cloth and a stockinette cover over the rolling pin when rolling out dough because it makes cleaning up a snap, but any smooth floured surface will do. Roll a patty of dough into a 12-inch circle. To transfer the pastry to a 9-inch pie pan, roll it loosely around the rolling pin and then unroll it into position over the pie pan. Ease the pastry into the pan without stretching and press it firmly into the sides. Trim pastry ¾ inch from the rim of the pan. Moisten the overhang of dough and fold it into a neat ridge bordering the plate, then flute it or form scallops in the edging, or, even easier, press the edge decoratively with the tines of a fork.

Refrigerate or freeze in a plastic bag until ready to bake. For an airtight seal, draw out any air from the bag with a drinking straw.

For a prebaked crust, pierce sides and bottom every inch or so with a fork. Bake in a preheated 450° oven for 10 to 12 minutes.

TO PREPARE IN ADVANCE: The patties of dough will keep for a week if wrapped airtight in the refrigerator, or they may be frozen for up to four months. Take the patties out of the refrigerator or freezer and let them reach room temperature before rolling. The unbaked pastry may be frozen right in the pans and need not be thawed before baking.

Magnificent Mincemeat Pie with Lattice Crust

This is the pie to make with our Drunken Mincemeat. Mound the pie shell high with mincemeat which has been combined with an equal measure of chopped apples and walnuts. Finish it off with a lattice crust. If you are adept at weaving dough, twist the strips as you work to give a trellis effect. Either way, garnish the center with cut-out leaves of pastry and brush evenly with beaten egg to give the pie a rich, golden glaze. You'll come out with a triple treat that plays off the heartiness of mincemeat with the delicacy of the added fruit and nuts.

This recipe make one 9-inch pie of six to eight servings.

For the Crust
About 1/3 the recipe for Klayre's pie crust, page 196, or 2 commercial pie sticks, made according to package directions
1 egg, beaten

For the Filling
2 cups Drunken Mincemeat, page 114
1½ cups freshly grated peeled tart apple
½ cup broken walnuts

Preheat the oven to 425°. Combine the filling ingredients and set aside. Roll out a bit more than half of the dough on a floured surface into a 12-inch round, ⅛ inch thick. Fit the pastry into a 9-inch pie plate without stretching. Trim pastry 1 inch from edge of the plate. Brush the bottom of the crust with beaten egg to prevent sogginess. Save the remaining egg for glazing the top of the pie.

Pour the mincemeat filling into the shell, mounding the filling slightly in the center. Roll out the remaining dough into a ⅛ inch thick oval, 12 inches long and 6 inches wide. Using a knife or pastry wheel and a ruler, cut the oval dough into 10 long strips, ½ inch wide. Place 5 strips of pastry at even intervals across the top of the filling. Fold back the center strips and the two outside strips just beyond the middle of the pie, as illustrated. Place one of the 5 remaining pastry strips at a right angle to the others across the center of the pie.

Unfold the first 3 strips over it. Fold back the 2 strips on either side of the center strip and place another remaining strip across the pie. Repeat, folding back alternate sets of strips and placing the new ones to create a woven top as illustrated. If this all seems too complicated, just lay the strips on top of the pie without weaving.

Trim the strips to fit the edge of the bottom crust. Moisten the edge of the pastry shell and turn the excess dough over the ends of the strips to form an even edge and seal the edge of the dough with the tines of a fork. Brush beaten egg over all the surfaces of the dough.

Cut three 1½-inch leaves out of scraps of dough and place them on top of the lattice in the center of the pie. Brush with glaze.

Bake the pie at 425° for 45 minutes. Let stand at least one hour before cutting. Serve warm topped with sweetened whipped cream if desired.

TO PREPARE IN ADVANCE: The pie may be stored, covered, at room temperature for up to three days, or wrapped in foil and refrigerated for up to a week or frozen for up to four months. Thaw, if frozen, and reheat at 300° for about 20 minutes before serving.

SPECIAL PACKAGING: The pie plate should be part of the gift. Wrap the pie loosely in cellophane and tie with a ribbon.

THE LABEL: Heat unwrapped at 300° for about 20 minutes before serving. *If the pie is freshly baked, the label should read:* May be stored, covered, at room temperature for up to three days, or may be wrapped in foil and stored in the refrigerator for up to a week or frozen for up to four months. *If the pie is frozen, the label should read:* May be kept frozen in foil wrapping for up to four months. May be stored, covered, at room temperature for up to three days or in the refrigerator for up to a week after it has been thawed.

Apple Cream Pie

Well, how shall we break the news? In two parts, we think, by saying that on the plus side, this Apple Cream Pie has terrific combinations. It's crisp and crumbly, mellow and fruity, all at the same time. However, we must come, as all things must, to the minus side. It's not for the calorie-conscious among us. Mary Erpelding, a favorite friend who originally made this pie for us, compounded the pleasure by giving us the recipe. She says it's a popular old Southern dessert that's just perfect for apple pie lovers any point of the compass: North, South, East, or West.

This recipe makes one 9-inch pie loaded with calories! It will serve eight.

For the Crust
1 cup sifted all-purpose flour
1 stick (¼ pound) butter or margarine, at room temperature
2 tablespoons powdered sugar

For the Filling
¾ cup sugar
2 tablespoons all-purpose flour
1 cup commercial sour cream
1 large egg
1 teaspoon vanilla
¼ teaspoon salt
2 cups chopped, peeled tart apple (such as Pippins)

For the Topping
½ cup sugar
1 stick (¼ pound) butter or margarine, at room temperature
1/3 cup unsifted all-purpose flour

Preheat the oven to 350°. Combine the flour, butter or margarine, and powdered sugar in a small mixing bowl. Mix either by hand or with an electric mixer until well combined. Press the mixture evenly into a 9-inch pie pan. Bake at 350° for 7 minutes. Remove and set aside. Raise the oven temperature to 400°.

Meanwhile, prepare the filling. In a medium mixing bowl blend the sugar and flour to remove flour lumps. Add the sour cream, egg, vanilla, and salt and beat until smooth. Stir in the apples. Pour into the pie shell. Bake at 400° for 30 minutes.

Meanwhile, prepare the topping. In a small mixing bowl blend the sugar, butter, and flour until the mixture is crumbly. Spread evenly over the top of the hot pie and bake 10 minutes longer at 400°.

Let cool at least an hour before slicing. Serve warm or at room temperature for best flavor.

TO PREPARE IN ADVANCE: The pie may be made three days before serving. It may be stored, covered, at room temperature or in the refrigerator. Do not freeze.

SPECIAL PACKAGING: An earthenware or pottery pie plate would be a marvelous gift container.

THE LABEL: Serve at room temperature. May be stored, covered, at room temperature or in the refrigerator for up to three days. Do not freeze.

Pumpkin Chiffon Pie with Gingersnap Crust and Caramel Almonds

Can there be any among us who thinks that there is but one way to make a pumpkin pie? Behold, another! The gingersnap crust and caramel almond garnish make it a dessert of exceptional flavor and beauty. Pies aren't always the first things that pop into our heads when we think of gift-giving (as you can see, we've included just a few in this book), but this light-hearted one makes any holiday the occasion it deserves to be.

The recipe makes one 8-inch pie to be given for immediate use. Double the recipe for two pies.

For the Crust
½ stick (4 tablespoons) butter or margarine
1¼ cups fine gingersnap crumbs (30 gingersnaps)

For the Filling
2 egg yolks, beaten
½ cup firmly packed dark brown sugar
1 envelope unflavored gelatin
¼ teaspoon ground cinnamon
¼ teaspoon ground nutmeg
¼ teaspoon ground ginger
¼ teaspoon salt
¾ cup canned pumpkin
1/3 cup milk
3 egg whites, at room temperature
⅛ teaspoon cream of tartar or ½ teaspoon lemon juice
5 tablespoons sugar

For the Caramel Almonds (optional)
2 tablespoons sugar
½ cup sliced almonds

For Serving
Sweetened whipped cream

To make the crust, preheat the oven to 375°. Melt the butter or margarine in a medium saucepan and blend in the cumbs; press crumb mixture into the bottom and sides of an 8-inch pie pan. Bake for 7 minutes at 375°. Chill before filling.

To make the filling, beat egg yolks in a 1½- to 2-quart saucepan. Blend in the brown sugar, gelatin, spices, salt, pumpkin, and milk.

Place the pan over medium heat and cook, stirring constantly, just until the mixture comes to a boil. Set the saucepan in a bowl of ice water and stir until the mixture mounds slightly when dropped from a spoon. Remove from the ice water and transfer to a large mixing bowl.

Beat the egg whites with the cream of tartar or lemon juice until they do not slide when the bowl is tilted. Sprinkle in the sugar, 1 tablespoon at a time, while beating until you have a shiny smooth meringue that holds stiff peaks when the beater is lifted.

Fold half the meringue thoroughly into the pumpkin mixture to lighten the texture, then fold in the second half. Spoon the mixture into the cold gingersnap crust. Refrigerate at least 2 hours.

To make the caramel almonds, oil a 12-inch strip of aluminum foil. Place the sugar in a small, heavy skillet over low heat. Stir constantly until the sugar melts and turns a light golden brown. Stir in the almonds until coated and turn out immediately onto the foil. When cool, break into small pieces.

Serve the pie with large dollops of sweetened whipped cream and sprinkle with caramel almonds.

TO PREPARE IN ADVANCE: The pie may be made one day ahead and stored in the refrigerator. The caramel almonds will keep indefinitely if stored in an airtight container at room temperature. The sweetened whipped cream with which the pie is served should be prepared no longer than 3 hours ahead and kept chilled.

SPECIAL PACKAGING: Include the pie plate as part of the gift. Wrap the pie loosely in cellophane and include a container of caramel almonds and some whipping cream.

THE LABEL: Keep chilled, and serve within 24 hours. Top the pie with large dollops of sweetened whipped cream and caramel almonds.

Sauces

Phillip S. Brown's Version of Crème Frâiche

In France during the summer a thick, slightly nutty tasting cream is spooned over wild strawberries to make the simplest, most luscious dessert imaginable. Because American dairy products are so different from those in France, we must make a small change in our recipe to approximate the flavor. All you work with are just two ingredients. How can you miss? And, indeed, you won't, for this recipe comes from a great cook, a cook's cook, so to speak, Phillip Brown, whose cooking classes we've attended. His recipe, as far as we're concerned, is really La Creme de la Creme.

This recipe will make about 2 cups of cream, enough to fill two 8-ounce or four 4-ounce gift containers.

> 1 pint (2 cups) raw whipping cream or any other whipping cream (see Note)
> 1 tablespoon buttermilk

Note: Some dairies such as Altadena on the West Coast have raw whipping cream and raw unsalted butter. These taste like the cream and butter served in France.

Combine cream and buttermilk in a 2- to 3-cup container that may be used for refrigerator storage. Phillip uses a 1-pint Triomphe canning jar, which is practical for both serving and storage. Let stand, covered, at room temperature (60° to 80°) for about 24 hours until thickened. Stir and refrigerate.

Serve cold over fresh strawberries, raspberries, fruit tarts, or pies. It can, of course, be used in cooking and will not curdle as does sour cream.

TO PREPARE IN ADVANCE: May be stored, covered, in the refrigerator for up to three weeks. Do not freeze.

SPECIAL PACKAGING: Miniature cream jugs sealed with plastic wrap are especially suitable for giving. Insert in a basket of fresh berries.

THE LABEL: Serve over fresh berries, tarts or pies. May be stored, covered, in the refrigerator for up to three weeks. Do not freeze.

Easiest and Best Hot Fudge Sauce

Why only serve good hot fudge sauce when you can serve the very best? Here's the ultimate gift for that friend with the incurable sweet tooth. It's a thick, hot fudge sauce, easy to make, reminiscent of the kind served at the renowned C. C. Brown's ice-cream parlor near Mann's Chinese Theater in Hollywood, California. We've been sleuthing their recipe for years. When Mary Erpelding, our kind advisor and dearest of friends, served this to us, we whooped and hollered and sleuthed no more.

This recipe makes about 3 cups of sauce, enough for two or three gifts. Don't be stingy—no matter how much you eat, it always tastes like more!

>1 (6-ounce) package semisweet chocolate morsels
>1 (14-ounce) can sweetened condensed milk
>2/3 cup water
>1 teaspoon vanilla, or more to taste
>Dash of salt

Combine the ingredients in a heavy-bottomed, medium-size skillet. Stir over low heat just until the mixture is smooth and well blended. Serve hot over almost anything!

TO PREPARE IN ADVANCE: Transfer to containers, let cool, and cover. May be stored in the refrigerator for up to a week. Reheat in a double boiler over boiling water, stirring until the sauce is smooth and hot.

SPECIAL PACKAGING: If you are feeling generous, give a small container of this sauce inside a glass double boiler, an item we feel is indispensable in the kitchen. If the recipient already has one, he will welcome another.

THE LABEL: Serve hot over almost anything. Heat in a double boiler over boiling water, stirring until smooth and hot. May be stored, covered, in the refrigerator for up to a week.

Nonedibles

Not everything that comes out of the kitchen is eaten. In fact, some things meant to be eaten have proved quite inedible (maybe that's how Baker's Clay orginated). Here are five nonedible ornaments which you can give as gifts just as they are or tie right onto packages to add one stunning grace note. There is Baker's Clay, out of which you may make Black Forest Mushrooms, and three scented ornaments: Pomander Balls, Spicy Kitchen Potpourri Sachets, and Scented Strawberry Sachets.

Baker's Clay

Baker's Clay has emerged from a popular way of keeping children's little fingers busy on rainy afternoons to a rather creative art. It is simple, inexpensive, with necessary ingredients already on your pantry shelf. Use the dough to fashion ornamental cookies or experiment making a variety of dough sculptures. Morton's Salt Company puts out a fine booklet called *The Dough It Yourself Handbook,* packed with information on this fascinating craft. You may obtain the booklet by writing them at P.O. Box 8019, Chicago, Illinois 60687.

This proportion makes about three cups of dough, which you can fashion or cut into any desired shape. Yield, of course, will depend on size of the cut-outs.

    2 cups all-purpose flour
    1 cup salt
    1 cup water

Combine flour and salt in a mixing bowl and stir to blend. Add water a little at a time while mixing until a ball of dough is formed. (You may need a bit more water, depending on the humidity, but do not add too much because the dough will get sticky.) Knead the dough on a floured surface for about 10 minutes until it has a smooth, firm consistency. Store in a plastic bag and seal tightly to prevent it from drying out. If the dough does dry out, simply knead in a little more water. If this is too sticky, knead in a bit of flour. Then roll out and either cut with cooky cutters or sculpt your own free-form shapes.

TO PREPARE IN ADVANCE: The dough may be stored for a week in the refrigerator.

Black Forest Mushrooms Made From Baker's Clay

Our friend Susie Gross cooks and entertains superbly all year long, but Christmas food and decorations are her specialty. One year she decorated the family tree, the dining table centerpiece, and almost the entire house with tiny handpainted Black Forest Mushrooms, a traditional holiday ornament in Germany. She lettered her friends' names on tiny mushrooms and tied them on packages as gift tags. We have enjoyed using the ones she gave us as tree ornaments, so when we found mushroom-shaped cooky cutters in gourmet supply shops, we made our own. If the clay mushrooms are to last from year to year, however, they must be heavily coated with a spray acrylic varnish. Here is an actual-size outline of our mushroom cutter. (see illustration page 206)

We harvested a crop of ninety mushrooms the last time we made this recipe. Your own yield will depend entirely on the size of your cutter and how thick you roll the dough.

1 recipe Baker's Clay (page 205)
Mushroom-shaped cooky cutter
Flour
A screen or other surface for drying

To Decorate

Acrylic paints (see Note)
2 paint brushes
Spray acrylic varnish
A fine point pen for writing names
Gold thread for hanging

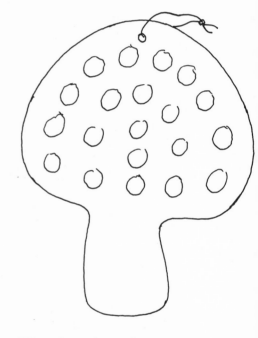

Note: The caps of the mushrooms are painted a solid color. When dry, dots are applied with white paint. Susie uses a dark red and a medium pink for the solid colors. We had success using all of the red tones.

Roll out a small portion of the dough on a floured surface to ¼-inch thickness. Do not roll it too thin or the dough will curl as it dries. Cut into mushroom shapes and, using a toothpick or skewer, make a ⅛-inch hole near the top of each (as illustrated) for hanging. Store in an airy place to dry for two days, turning occasionally. We use a screen from one of our windows so the air can circulate around and dry them evenly. If you use a solid sheet, turn occasionally to speed drying.

When the mushrooms are dry, paint the caps (as illustrated) in a solid color of acrylic paint. Dry. Paint white dots evenly over the cap. Write names, if desired, on the stems. When dry, take outdoors or to a well-ventilated area and spray both sides of the mushrooms with spray varnish. Let dry between coats. Put threads through the holes, as illustrated, for hanging.

TO PREPARE IN ADVANCE: Place the mushrooms in a box between layers of tissue paper and store in a dry place. They will keep indefinitely.

SPECIAL PACKAGING: Tie these as gift tags on packages or use as place cards (favors) at the table. The recipients can hang them as ornaments.

THE LABEL: Hang as an ornament. Store in a dry place indefinitely.

Pomander Balls

The fruits of your wares will infuse your (or some lucky recipient's) linen closets or lingerie drawers with the fragrance of cinnamon and cloves. It's so easy you can relax and enjoy a cup of coffee in your kitchen while you put together this trio of spicy spheres.

This recipe makes three pomanders: small, medium, and large.

> 1 each thick-skinned lime, lemon, and orange (or 3 small apples)
> 3 ounces whole cloves
> 1 tablespoon ground cinnamon
> 1 tablespoon orrisroot (see Note, page 208)

Wash the fruits and dry them. Use a skewer to make holes in the skin and insert whole cloves to cover the entire surface of the fruit. Mix the cinnamon and orrisroot together. Place 2 teaspoons of the mixture in a small plastic bag along with one of the clove-covered fruits. Shake the bag to coat the fruit completely. Repeat with the other fruits. Allow the fruits to dry at room temperature, turning them occasionally. They will be sufficiently dry for giving in about two weeks. If you are in a hurry, place them overnight in the oven at the lowest possible temperature to speed up drying. Tie with ribbons to form a loop for hanging at the top. Hang as tree ornaments or place in linen closets or lingerie drawers as sachets.

TO PREPARE IN ADVANCE: Allow to dry for two weeks without wrapping. These last indefinitely.

SPECIAL PACKAGING: The simplest way is to wrap in clear or colored cellophane tied at the top with a ribbon.

THE LABEL: Hang as an ornament or place in the linen closet or lingerie drawer as a sachet. The fragrance will last indefinitely.

Spicy Kitchen Potpourri Sachets

The custom of using sachets can be traced directly to the hideous Black Plague in fourteenth-century Italy where cloths soaked in a boiled mixture of cinnamon and cloves were placed beneath the noses of the sick. Spices and other aromatics, such as flower petals and pieces of vanilla bean, were used to "purify the air of malignant vapors." The tragedy of plagues has been forgotten, but spicy perfumed sachets linger on. Now they are used mainly to lend a fragrant freshness to stored linens and lingerie.

This recipe yields eighteen scented fabric bags. Not only are they lovely to look at, but they will add a delightful air to your closets as well as those of friends lucky enough to be given a few.

Filling for the Bags
90 large cosmetic-size cotton balls (5 per bag)
½ ounce *each* oil of cinnamon, oil of lemon, oil of orange, oil of lavender fleurs, and rose soluble (for making artificial rose water). Oils are available at well-stocked pharmacies.
2 ounces whole cloves
2 tablespoons orrisroot
1 tablespoon ground nutmeg

To make the Bags
½ yard of 36-inch wide tiny print cotton (a small patchwork pattern is ideal!)
9 yards ⅜-inch satin ribbon (or other ribbon of your choice)
Needle and thread

Note: Orrisroot is a mildly fragrant powder which is a fixative for other fragrances in sachets, pomanders, and other items. It is available at most pharmacies. It can be irritating to nasal tissues, so do not let it blow haphazardly around the room while you are working with it, or you could bring forth a sneeze or two from anyone present.

Divide the cotton balls into five groups of eighteen each. Moisten each cotton ball in one group with a few drops of oil of cinnamon. Repeat same procedure with remaining groups, using oil of orange, oil of lemon, oil of lavender fleurs, and the rose soluble which has been mixed with 1 tablespoon water. Keep the fragrances separate and allow to dry at room temperature while you make the bags for the sachets. In a container with a cover, mix together the cloves, orrisroot, and nutmeg. Cover and set aside.

To make the bags, cut the ½ yard of fabric into eighteen 6-inch squares (Figure 1). Take one square at a time (Figure 2) and fold in half right sides of the fabric together (Figure 3). Stitch ½-inch seams along two sides and trim the corners (Figure 3). Turn down one inch of the open side (Figure 4) and use a needle and thread to sew a 1-inch hem. This will be the top edge of the bag. Turn the bag right side out (Figure 5). Place scented cotton ball in the bottom and sprinkle with ½ teaspoon of the clove mixture. Poke in a ball of another scent and again sprinkle with the clove mixture. Continue in this manner until one cotton ball of each scent (five in all) is in the bag. Compact the filling and tie the bag closed with ½ yard of ribbon (Figure 6). Repeat with the remaining squares of fabric, cotton balls, and clove mixture.

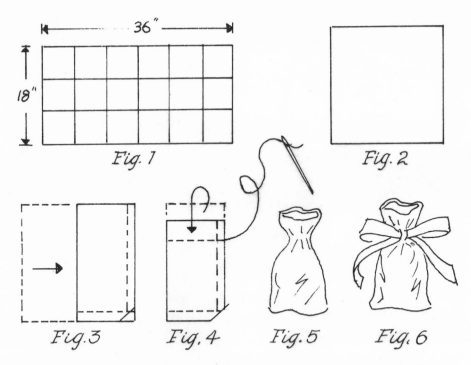

Fig. 1

Fig. 2

Fig. 3

Fig. 4

Fig. 5

Fig. 6

TO PREPARE IN ADVANCE: To help preserve the fragrance as long as possible, store bags between layers of wax paper or tissue paper in a closed box. When used as drawer sachets, the fragrance should last at least six months.

SPECIAL PACKAGING: Place several sachets in a small gift box or the berry basket described on page 215.

THE LABEL: Use as a sachet in linen closets, drawers, or anywhere else you would enjoy a spicy fragrance.

Scented Strawberry Sachets

Our all-time favorite package tie-on is a tiny fabric strawberry stuffed with scented cotton. These are so easy to make that even a five year old can do the job. They have such eye appeal they can be tossed into lingerie drawers as sachets, used as miniature pin cushions, or even hung on the Christmas tree as ornaments. One thing is certain: unlike the jar of preserves that is soon devoured, these little berries will long remain some place in the house as a continuing reminder of that extra personal touch from you.

The best way to give people the berries is to follow these directions, which will yield fifty-four scented fabric strawberries.

54 large, cosmetic-size cotton balls
Strawberry or other scent of your choice (see Note)
Powdered orrisroot, optional (see Note, page 208)
54 dime-size circles of green felt (a 6-inch square of felt will be ample)
1 foot (1/3 yard) 36" wide red cotton fabric with tiny white polka dots
A needle
Red and green thread for sewing

Note: We have experimented with many scents: strawberry air freshener (Wizard), strawberry extract (Wagner), bath oils, scented oils from the pharmacy. Use whatever appeals most to you. It needn't be a strawberry scent at all.

1. Dampen each cotton ball with whatever scent you are using, and let dry while you start making the strawberries. (The scent will linger longer if you dip the cotton ball in orrisroot.)

2. Cut the fabric into twenty-seven 4-inch squares (Figure 1). Each one of the squares will yield two sachets.

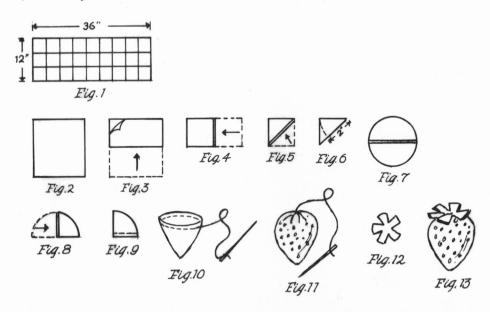

Fig. 1

Fig. 2   Fig. 3   Fig. 4   Fig. 5   Fig. 6   Fig. 7

Fig. 8   Fig. 9   Fig. 10   Fig. 11   Fig. 12   Fig. 13

3. Take one 4-inch square of fabric at a time (Figure 2). Fold in half (Figure 3). Fold in half again (Figure 4). Fold into a triangle (Figure 5). Cut the fabric along the dotted line (Figure 6) so that when the fabric is opened you will have a circle. Cut the circle in half (Figure 7). Fold one of the semicircles in half, right sides of fabric together (Figure 8). Using either a sewing machine or needle

and thread, sew a ¼-inch seam along the dotted line (Figure 9). Turn right side out. Take a needle and using red thread with a knot tied in the end, sew a line of stitching around the cut edges of the strawberry (Figure 10). Place one of the scented cotton balls inside and pull the thread to gather in the fabric to enclose the cotton ball completely (Figure 11). Secure the closing with a few stitches and fasten off.

4. To make the crown of the strawberry, cut notches in a circle of green felt (Figure 12). Sew in place with green thread over your previous stitching to give the appearance of a real strawberry with a leafy crown (Figure 13). Repeat with the other semicircle of fabric cut from the original square. Now, you have two strawberries from one 4-inch square.

Repeat Steps 3 and 4 until all the squares of fabric have been turned into strawberries.

TO PREPARE IN ADVANCE: The fabric strawberries can be used as sachets while their scent lasts depending on what type of scent you have used. They may be used as decorations indefinitely.

SPECIAL PACKAGING: These make a spectacular gift presented in a berry basket that has been woven with ribbon or lace (see page 215).

THE LABEL: Use in lingerie drawers as sachets or for decorations.

APPENDIX ONE

Cover it with glory

It's a joy to give, but even nicer to give with flair. A few materials, a little time, and the following suggestions can turn kitchen cookery into giveaways that dazzle.

If you happen to think about it, the egg is the perfect container for its purpose. Maybe you can find just as perfect a container from this list for that kitchenmade delicacy you want to transport. Most already sit on your shelf to be discarded when empty. Some are odd pieces too good to toss away. Now you can use them as carriers to fill one last meaningful purpose.

Containers: Some Just Waiting to Be Filled

AIRTIGHT TINS: The kind you see at Christmas, all shapes and sizes. *Use:* Candies, nuts, cupcakes, cookies, granola, Perino's Pumpernickel.

CANNING JARS: Confiture jars, old-fashioned canning jars, short and tall French jars (Triomphe) with rubber ring, modern vacuum-seal jars made by Ball or Kerr, jelly jars. *Use:* Jellies, jams, relish, chutney, nuts, liqueur, spiced tea, rum batter, spreads, granola, pickled eggs, mincemeat, salad dressings, Bouquet Garnis, Creme Fraiche, Saint Cecelia Sauce.

WINE GLASSES, CHAMPAGNE GLASSES. *Use:* Sangria jam, champagne jelly, other jams and jellies, champagne mustard, chutney, cranberry relish, pickles, salad dressings.

PLASTIC BERRY OR CHERRY TOMATO BASKETS: String with ribbon, lace, rickrack. *Use:* Nuts, candies, cookies, small crock of pate or cheese spread and crackers, fresh vegetables for dipping.

HOUSEHOLD JARS TO SAVE (can decorate lids): Baby food, olive, maraschino cherries, catsup, chile sauce, brandy flasks, wine bottles, instant coffee, peanut butter, pickles, mayonnaise, chutney.

SOUFFLE DISHES (all sizes, 4-ounce to 2-quart): *Use:* Pate, cheeses and spreads, mustard, dill sauce, vegetables and accompaniments, baked beans, chili, just about anything.

CROCKS (all sizes, with or without lids): Pottery crocks, custard cups, china and glass flower pots. *Use:* Whipped cream cheese, pate, mustards, spreads, jams, chutneys, lemon butter, nuts, herb blends, mincemeat, Bouquet Garnis.

REFRIGERATOR CONTAINERS: Pint and quart plastic with lids; margarine tubs. *Use:* Lemon butter, soups, stews, granola, rum batter, chili, spaghetti sauce, eggnog, mincemeat, herb blends, seasoned salts.

FOIL TINS WITH CARDBOARD LIDS: 4-, 6-, and 8-cup size, good for freezing; heat and serve. Write directions for serving on cardboard lid. Available in supermarkets. *Use:* Soups, chili, vegetables, spaghetti sauce, cookies, candies, cupcakes, muffins.

BOTTLES WITH CORKS: Wine bottles, Kitchen Chemistry by Corning, cruets. *Use:* Soups, sauces, chutney, tea, salad dressing, dill sauce, liqueurs, vinegars.

APOTHECARY JARS (all sizes): Can double as canisters or cookie jars. *Use:* Cookies, liqueur, mustard, candies, sauces, nuts, granola, mincemeat, herb blends, Bouquet Garnis.

WOOD OR PLASTIC BREAD BOARD OR CHOPPING BOARD: With knife and crackers or bread. *Use:* Breads, spreads and cheeses, pates, cakes.

SERVING BOWLS (all sizes): Lotus dishes (available at import stores), wooden salad bowls, old-fashioned mixing bowls. *Use:* Dips, cheese spreads, nuts, Tabooli, candies, cookies, muffins, cupcakes.

BAKING DISHES: 8-inch or 9-inch square dish, 9- or 10-inch pie plate, terrine, quiche dish, casserole dishes, oval baking dish, glass baking dish, bread pan, bundt pan, petits pots. *Use:* Casseroles, vegetables, pies, Sour Cream Coffee Cake, bread pudding, pots de creme, Artichoke or Vegie Squares, Mincemeat Squares, Lemon Pastries, Brownies. (Note: When giving a casserole, line baking dish with foil before filling and baking. After baking, freeze, then contents still in foil may be removed until ready to reheat. The dish will be sparkling clean, as if never used. Directions for reheating may be written directly on the foil with a felt pen.)

MOLDS: Small or 8-cup steamed pudding mold. *Use:* Pate en gelee, Boursin cheese, Persimmon Pudding.

PLASTIC CUBES, GLASS BOXES, SMALL BOXES: Plastic cubes are available from Williams-Sonoma, see page 236. *Use:* Herb blends, small candies.

LUNCH PAIL (lined and decorated with decoupage): Picnic for one or two people, can be used as a purse after the picnic. *Use:* Pate, crackers and wine, dip with crudites, sandwich fixings, soup and Tabooli pita sandwiches.

BASKETS WOVEN WITH RIBBON, RICKRACK, CORD: Planter size, picnic, nesting. *Use:* Pate, champagne and crackers, Pasta Picnic, soups and pumpernickel bread, dips with crudites, pies, jelly and jam jars, herbs.

TRAYS: Serving trays of all sizes. Can use alone or with baskets, flower pots, and other containers. *Use:* Spreads, breads, cakes and cupcakes, muffins, pots de creme. May line with napkins, embroidered kitchen towels, or bandanas for muffins, cupcakes, cookies, small loaves of bread.

ODDITIES (and their uses in parentheses): tureen (soups, muffins); two-piece glass soup bowls—icers (cheese spreads, cold soups); ginger jar (mustard, nuts, small candies); bean pot (chili, baked beans, muffins); glass double boiler (mustards, hot fudge sauce); sifter (cookies, candies, nuts); cheese fondue set (crab fondue, soup); petits pots (pots de creme, mustards, dill sauce); matching cordial bottles (cordials); honey pourers (sauces, salad dressings); nut mill (candies, nuts); measuring cups (jellies, jams, chutney, sauces); abalone shells (spreads, serving bowls for soups); condiment set (jams, jellies, mustard, dill sauce, chutney); large shells (cheese spreads, dips); planters (cookies, muffins); butter melter (candies, nuts); pickle or relish plates (pickles or chutney); pedestal cake stand (cakes and pies); flower pots painted, as described on page 216, or planters, line with napkins (candies, nuts, granola, cupcakes, muffins, Bouquet Garnis); cooky jar (cookies); antique tea cans (cookies, candies, nuts, herb blends, spiced tea. Bouquet Garnis); flour scoops (cookies, candies, nuts, herb blends); wire egg baskets (cookies, candies, muffins, cupcakes).

Containers: Four Handcrafted with Love

Little Red Riding Hood put her homemade goodies in a straw basket, covered them with a cloth napkin and started on her merry way to Grandmother's. We've often speculated about how that story might have ended if she had put all her food instead into a decoupage-decorated lunch pail, and hit the wolf smartly across the chops with it. The pail and these three other highly unusual gift containers will provide your homemade food and beverages with an added dash of splendor. With a little luck, you won't need to use any of them in self-defense.

Baskets Woven with Ribbons and Trims

Any lattice-type baskets can be used, from strawberry or cherry tomato baskets available at supermarkets to simpler wicker ones, with or without handles. This is an idea with a bonus. It's a great way to use up small pieces of trim and ribbon you may have tucked away in a sewing chest. Any and all measurements depend on the size of basket you choose, so we must leave exact specifications up to you. It is not necessary to do more than casual measuring unless you set out to buy ribbons, rickrack, or other trim especially for a particular basket. If this is your plan, measure the distance around the basket adding an extra inch or two so you may weave in any loose ends. Or, if you wish to tie a simple bow (see page 225), add an extra foot to your measurement. (One yard of ribbon is sufficient to go around a strawberry basket once and give you enough left over to tie a bow.) This is a container to have fun with. Let your imagination go wild and really create something one-of-a-kind.

One last hint. Large baskets may be further decorated by the addition of a fancy bow (page 225) and two or three tissue-paper roses (page 226).

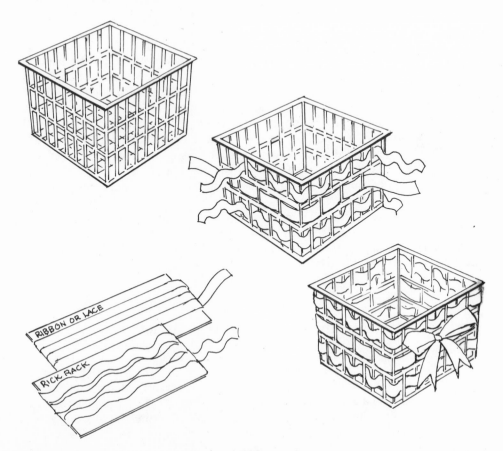

RIBBON OR LACE

RICK RACK

Personalized Flowerpots with Saucers

This is a dandy container for giving cookies, candy, granola, and can be used later by the recipient as a holder for a plant in a 5-inch plastic flowerpot. It is easy and quick to make, especially if you do several at a time.

Supplies Needed

1 or more red clay flowerpots and matching saucers, 5 inches in diameter
Flat spray paint in a light color
Enamel spray paint in the color of your choice
6 inches (1½ inches wide) flowered cotton ribbon per flowerpot
White household glue
Clear acrylic spray gloss

Spray the flowerpot(s) and saucer(s) with several coats of the flat paint and let dry between coats. This will seal the very porous surface and make application of the color much easier. Spray with several light coats of the colored enamel and let dry. Meanwhile, cut out of the ribbon any decorations you like: letters to write the recipient's name or a greeting, hearts, flowers, or whatever turns you on. To achieve the best picture positioning, first tape pictures lightly in place with a tiny piece of double-sided tape. Now take a look. Are you happy with their positioning? If not, it's a simple matter to lift off and rearrange. Now go ahead and spread glue lightly, but thoroughly, over the back of the cutouts and position in place on the pot. Press firmly and wipe away any excess glue with a tissue. Finish by spraying with a coat or two of clear acrylic gloss. Fill the flowerpot with edibles. Place it in its saucer in the center of a large square of cellophane (clear is best). Bring up the corners and tie a bow out of ribbon to match the one used on the pot.

Fabric Wine Bottle Carrier

When we had a reunion with Linda Bailey, one of our earliest students, she brought us a bottle of homemade liqueur in a charming wine bottle carrier she had made. It was so ingenious that we want to pass the directions for making it along to you. It helps to use a sewing machine, but even if you don't do much sewing, you will

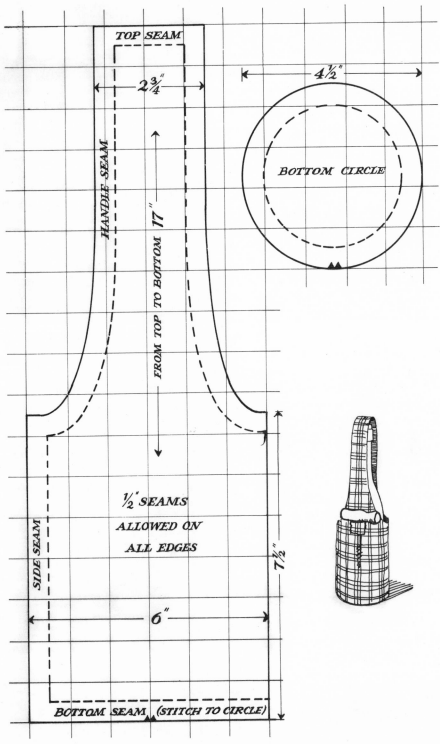

TOP SEAM

2¾"

4½"

BOTTOM CIRCLE

HANDLE SEAM

FROM TOP TO BOTTOM 17"

½" SEAMS
ALLOWED ON
ALL EDGES

SIDE SEAM

7½"

6"

BOTTOM SEAM (STITCH TO CIRCLE)

find this a cinch. Linda's carrier (pictured on the dust jacket of this book) is made of plaid taffeta. A very stiff fabric (such as taffeta or burlap) must be used, or the outside fabric must be underlined before stitching with a stiff interfacing such as Pellon. We often insert a tissue-paper rose (page 226) for extra pizzazz.

Fabric Requirements for Two Carriers

½ yard of 36- or 45-inch outer fabric *and* lining

Optional: 2/3 yard of 25 inches stiff interfacing (for underlining, if using a soft, outer fabric)

Optional: 3½-inch circle of cardboard for the bottom
one 59¢ corkscrew

Directions for One Carrier

Place the carrier pattern on a fold of the outside fabric and the lining (and interfacing if you are using it). Cut out bottom circles of each fabric as well. If using interfacing, baste it to the wrong side of the outside fabric (Figure 1) and use as one piece of fabric (referred to as the "outside" from this point on).

Stitch the side seams (Figure 2) of the outside and the lining separately, and press the seams open. Press to the inside ½ inch at each top of the handle. With right sides together, matching seams and notches, pin the outside and the lining together. Stitch handle seams to within ½ inch of top. Clip curves. Turn lining to outside, baste along handle edges and press. Remove basting (Figure 3).

Turn the carrier inside out. Place the right sides of the outside handle together and stitch along the top seam, taking care not to catch the lining in the seam. Press the outside seam open. Use a needle and thread to slip stitch the lining closed along the top seam (Figure 4). With the carrier still inside out, pin the outside bottom circle to both the outside and the lining (Figure 5). Stitch in place and press the seam to the center of the bottom. Baste under ½ inch of the lining circle edges and slip stitch to cover the previous stitching in the bottom of the carrier.

Turn the carrier right side out. Take a strip of material about 1 inch wide and 2 inches long. Fold in half. Stitch long end. Trim. Turn inside out. (Or you may simply use a 2-inch length of ribbon.) Turning ends under, stitch ends flat to base of carrier handle, making a handy loop in which to slip in a 59¢ corkscrew when presenting your gift. Insert cardboard circle in the bottom if desired. Tuck in a bottle of wine or liqueur and the gift is complete.

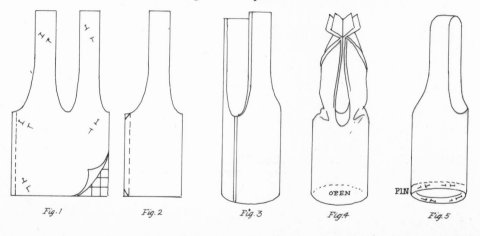

Fig. 1   Fig. 2   Fig. 3   Fig. 4   Fig. 5

Decoupage Lunch Pail Purse

After the feast, the recipient of this novel container may use it as a very personalized purse. You will probably love it so much you will want to keep it yourself, so why not make two at the same time? Pictures cut from magazines and pasted on the outside of the pail should reflect the interests of the owner. Diana's is covered with gorgeous color pictures of fruits, souffles, and names of favorite restaurants.

Supplies Needed for One Lunch Pail
A workman's lunch pail (Figure 1). Thermos not necessary (see
    Note)
Color pictures or sayings cut from magazines
Spray enamel paint
Felt to line the inside, approximate measurement 12 inches by
    30 inches
20-inch braid or other trim for the outside of the pail
60-inch braid or other trim for the inside of the pail
Rubber cement
White household glue
Clear acrylic spray gloss or other varnish to finish

Note: These lunch pails are available at every hardware store and most markets. They seem to be uniform in size, measuring 10 by 4¾ inches on the bottom. The thermos is unnecessary and should be removed along with its metal holder and used for another purpose. Use a screwdriver to bend out metal tabs that hold the clasps and handle (fittings) so they may be removed from the pail before painting (Figure 2). Spray inside and outside of pail with several coats of spray enamel, allowing each coat to dry separately.

Now you are ready to let your imagination go wild. Use rubber cement to affix cutout pictures and sayings (Figure 3) to the outside. (To achieve the best picture positioning, first tape pictures lightly in place with a tiny piece of double-sided tape. Reposition to get the best arrangement.) When the pail has been decorated to your satisfaction, use household glue to apply the 20 inches of trim: 10 inches to each side of the outer top as shown in Figure 3. Finish the outside by spraying with several coats of clear gloss or varnish. (Note: Reinsert metal fittings before lining pail.) Cover both the upper and lower inside sections with felt. (The upper section should not be lined all the way to the edge. Allow 1 inch all around the rim so the top will close over the lower section of the pail.) To make the pattern for the lining, place the lunch pail on a piece of paper and trace the outside ends for patterns. On the top end pattern, cut 1 inch off the straight end to allow the pail to close. Cut two pieces of felt from each pattern, one for each end of the pail (Figure 4). To cut the remaining pattern for top and bottom, cut two pieces of paper the width of the lunch pail and about 12 inches long. Insert one piece of paper in the bottom of the pail and cut ends to fit flush with the rim. Insert the other piece

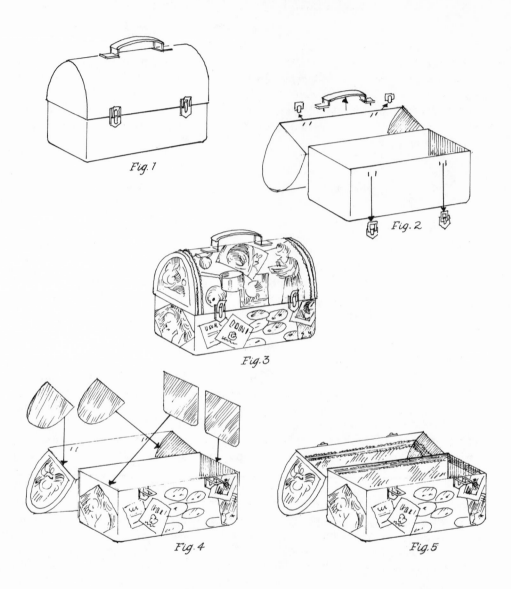

Fig. 1

Fig. 2

Fig. 3

Fig. 4

Fig. 5

of paper in the top of the pail and trim, leaving a 1-inch margin on both ends. Cut one piece of felt from each of these patterns. Use household glue to glue the felt lining into the pail. Use the 60 inches of braid or trim to make a decorative edge on the lining (Figure 5). Glue in place with household glue, secure with paper clips and let dry. Remove paper clips. When all is dry you are set to pack the pail with a personal picnic.

Labeling: Telling It Like It Is

Traditionally, well-written newspaper stories begin with six facts right in the first paragraph: Who, What, Where, When, How, and Why. A good food label provides you with five: From, Item, Date, Servings, Directions (use, storage, serving). Here are a few other tips.

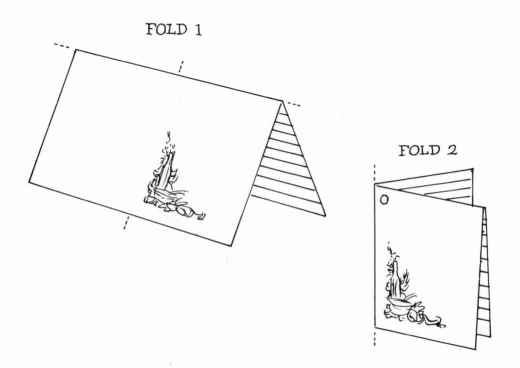

FOLD 1

FOLD 2

The following sample labels can be Xeroxed and then printed. Ample room is provided for writing information. They will fit into anyone's 3-by-5-inch recipe box if you would like to use them to write out the recipe for what you are giving. They may also be folded, punched with a hole and tied on, or simply inserted into a gift basket, as is.

OTHER LABEL IDEAS:
Greeting Labels: Cut the front off suitable greeting cards. Write the above five facts on the back and punch a hole in top corner. Thread with ribbon and tie on to your gift.
Self-Adhesive Party Badges: Available at stationery and gift stores. Are decorative and an ideal size for jellies and jams.
Personal Labels: Plain self-adhesive labels are available in many sizes at stationers. Use felt pens to draw a plain border or simple design.

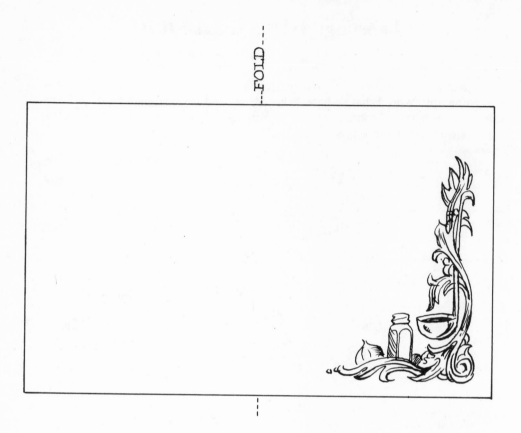

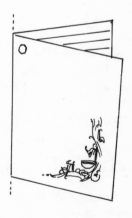

After you print this side, have the printer turn the printed sheets over and print the material from page 224 on the reverse side. (Tell him to back it up carefully.)

Directions for use

Date   *Servings*

Item

From

FOLD 1 - - -

FOLD 2 - -

A culinary secret from the private file of

RECIPE CARD LABEL

Gift Wrappings: In the Enclosing, an Added Artistry

Gifts of food look especially decorative when wrapped in clear or colored cellophane. Clear is best if the food itself is attractive. Colored cellophane, though beautiful to look at, obscures the contents. The easiest way to wrap is to place food in center of a square of cellophane. (Cellophane comes in two widths: 20-inch and 30-inch. Simply cut into squares.) Bring up corners on top of food and tie with a ribbon. We like the new cotton-printed ribbons that are on the market because they tie easily and are so fresh looking. The package might be further enhanced by tying on purchased or homemade tissue paper and strawflower roses (page 226), dried flowers, or other easily purchasable poseys.

The Bow

Rubber bands and string may be convenient but not very appealing. Seal your wrapping with tape or tie with ribbon. Then add a bow—simple or elaborate—for style.

The Tissue Paper, Strawflower Rose

A bouquet of these paper flowers will lift your gift packages into the Tiffany class. We tie them on baskets, insert them in fabric wine bottle carriers, and keep a large vase of them on our work desk to be used whenever we spot a place for them. Once you get the knack, you may wish to experiment with different sizes and shapes. Only God can make a tree, but there is no reason you can't make lovely strawflower roses.

Supplies Needed for Three Roses (Everything here is available at a hobby shop)
1 large (20-or 30-inch) sheet any color tissue paper
18 white "star" strawflowers
3 6-inch pieces florist's wire
3 artificial rose leaves
Green florist's tape
Wire cutters

Tissue paper is usually sold prefolded in plastic bags. If the paper you buy is not prefolded, fold it in half crosswise, then in half again, then in half again, forming a strip 20 inches long and 4 inches wide. After folding, cut the folded paper in 4-inch sections to form five square stacks of folded paper (Figure 1).

Cut each stack of squares into petals with scissors (Figure 2). You will have some single and some double petals connected at the bottom. For each rose petal you will use two thicknesses of tissue, so where you have single petals, put two together. Wrap one double petal around a *smooth* round object: plastic cigar holder, dowel, or what have you. Don't use an ordinary pencil because it has an octagonal shape. We use a pen that is ¾ inch in diameter (Figures 3 and 4). Push in the ends of the rolled petals to form wrinkles all along the paper (Figure 5). Slide the wrinkled tissue carefully off the round object. Continue rolling in the same manner until you have rolled and puckered six petals. Unroll each petal and stretch the center a bit to form a cup-shaped petal with the roll at the top curving outward (Figure 6).

Place 6 star flowers at the end of a length of florist's wire (Figure 7). Wrap one petal, curled edge pointing outward to form the center of a rose (Figure 8). Repeat with five more petals until a rose of six petals is formed. Wrap florist's tape tightly around the base of the petals to secure them tightly to the wire and stems of the star flowers. Insert an artificial rose leaf, if desired, and continue wrapping tape around the wire until you have the desired stem length. Cut with wire cutters. The finished rose (Figure 9) is a bit fragile so store it where it will not be crushed. Don't hoard, go ahead and give them away. It's easy to grow more.

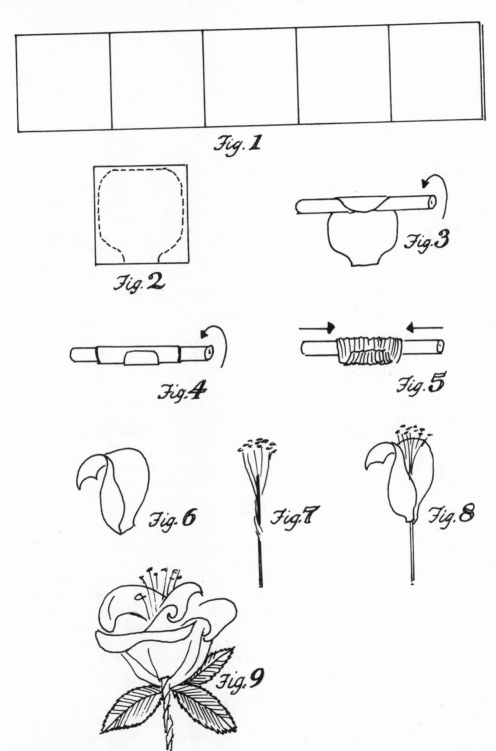

Fig. 1

Fig. 2

Fig. 3

Fig. 4

Fig. 5

Fig. 6

Fig. 7

Fig. 8

Fig. 9

The Tie-On

Once you've got your gift beautifully packaged, tie one on—something special for adults, something special for children.

TIE-ONS FOR ADULTS: Strawflowers or tissue paper roses (page 226); wire whisks; zester (great to include with Crisp Lemon Cookies); cinnamon sticks; bag of whole nutmegs and a grater; wooden spoon; wooden spaghetti lifter; garlic press; bag of herbs (Bouquet Garnis); baster; cookie cutters; tea caddy full of Herbs of Provence, Bouquet Garni; pizza cutter; meatball or melon baller; pastry blender; pastry brush.

TIE-ONS FOR KIDS: Sand pail, bicycle basket, cowboy hat, lunch pail, dump truck, fireman's hat, ambulance driver's hat, football helmet, children's watering cans, miniature cars, lollipops, or candy canes, doll house furniture, whistles, trading cards, a bag of marbles, bubblebath, any small toys.

Packing and Mailing:
Tender Loving Care Will Get It There

Take time to wrap packages for mailing with care. If you don't, recipients may not know how to thank you for that strange package with the crumby, red-jelly-covered interior. The following suggestions should steer you clear of most problems.

Food gifts may be mailed anywhere within the United States and its territories. Some foreign countries have laws governing food importation, so check with your postmaster on restrictions. Packages may be insured against breakage or loss, but not against spoilage.

Foods which are perishable should, of course, be mailed by the speediest and generally more expensive route (First Class). There is a new service offered by some post offices that is faster yet (overnight delivery guaranteed), called "Express Mail." Brochures on this service are available at post offices in large cities. Non-perishable foods, such as preserves and pickles, which are sealed in jars may be sent by the slower parcel post. For servicemen, use parcel post if the package weighs less than 2 pounds. Up to 5 pounds, use "Space Available Mail."

Pack food gifts in heavy corrugated cardboard boxes. Do a good job of padding all over. This means putting a thick (at least 1-inch) layer of newspaper or corrugated board on the top and bottom of your box. Seal with masking tape any lids that might leak. Wrap each item individually in foil or plastic bag (just in case there is breakage) to prevent leaking onto other items. Pack food inside tins or cans between layers of wax paper and cushion with tissue. Seal lids with masking tape.

Save all kinds of packing materials that come your way, such as styrofoam pellets, air-cushioned sheets of plastic, newspapers (which can be shredded or crumpled), or excelsior. Paul's mom used to mail him cookies in Korea packed in popcorn. An edible packing substance.

Pack containers several inches apart, with lots of cushioning material between and around them. Don't just *hope* for the best, *do* the best packing imaginable. Go overboard with the padding. There really can't ever be too much. It will prevent any sliding and crashing around and any potential heartbreak if King Kong tactics are employed along the way. Wrap package in heavy brown wrapping paper. Do not seal, but tie securely with twine. Print the *To* and *From* information legibly on the top of the package only. Mark *Perishable, Fragile, Handle with Care.*

APPENDIX TWO

Preserving

What Grandmother Never Told Us

The traditional methods of preserving food have not been passed down to most of us by our grandmothers for the simple reason that there has been no need to. Our generation, unlike theirs, finds it far more practical to run to the well-stocked corner market than to go to the well house or root cellar for a jar of beans, tomatoes, or preserves. So we often hear such questions today from the inexperienced, would-be canner as: How safe is it? What about food poisoning? What about botulism? These are important questions, so let's answer them right now.

First of all, put your mind at ease. If you follow the simple directions in each recipe, all your preserves will be supersafe. This is how we know it is safe. All foods can be easily classified according to content. For our purpose here we'll call them *high-acid content* and *low-acid content*. For your general information, high-acid foods are, specifically, all fruits, fruit juices, fruit purees, tomatoes, and pickles. Low-acid foods are poultry, meat, fish, and most vegetables. Scientists have learned over the centuries that high-acid content foods do not permit botulism to thrive and multiply. However, that deadly spore can exist and multiply in carelessly preserved low-acid foods.

There is an entirely different process for home preserving of the low-acid food group, but that is beyond the scope of this volume. There are many fine books available on the subject, if you are interested in pursuing it. As for the preparation of the recipes in this book, normal standards of kitchen cleanliness, care, and attention to the recipe will prevent food spoilage.

About Jars, Ring Bands, and Sealing

The preserving recipes in this book are only high-acid foods with a high sugar content, so there is no danger at all from botulism. Because of this, you can be more relaxed about sanitary procedures than if you were putting up vegetables or other foods in which no sugar is added.

Step-by-Step Instructions for Using Vacuum-Sealing Canning Jars with Ring Bands

This is by far the most efficient type of jar to use because it gives you a really tight seal. Preserves put up in these jars will keep at peak quality for at least six months when stored in a cool, dry place. They do not leak as jars or other containers sealed with paraffin are apt to do. The outer ring bands may be used again and again, but the lids should be used only once.

1. Before you begin, check the jars to see that there are no nicks or cracks. Do not use bands that are bent or rusted. For our recipes it is not necessary to boil the jars for 15 minutes as it is when putting up low-acid foods. (If you do a lot of canning and boil the jars as a habit, you may wish to do so anyway. Good habits should be preserved!) We simply put the jars through a cycle in our dishwasher or wash them in lots of soapy water and dry in a 225° oven until ready to use. Place the lids and the ring bands, along with kitchen tongs, in a saucepan of water and bring to a boil. Remove pan from heat. Leave items in the scalded water until ready to use.

2. It is good to wear a kitchen mitt on each hand. Pour the hot preserve into the hot jars to within ¼ inch to ⅛ inch from the top, depending on recipe used. Wipe rims with a clean paper towel dipped in the scalded water lids are in. Dry with a clean paper towel. Use the tongs to place the lids on the jars and screw ring bands on tightly.

3. Let jars cool undisturbed on a towel away from any draft. Lids will make popping sounds as they invert to form a seal. If any have not popped when cool, press down lightly with your fingers; if the lids stay down, they are sealed. (If there are any that have not sealed, store them in the refrigerator; they are still useable.)

4. When the jars are completely cool, you may remove the ring bands and wipe the outside of the jars to clean away any drips. The jars should sparkle; we use window cleaner on ours! Store the jars on the pantry shelf now without the ring bands. The lids will not come off unless you pry them off.

Step-by-Step Instructions for Sealing Jars or Other Containers with Paraffin

Paraffin can be an efficient seal for up to two months if the preserves are stored in a cool, dry place. Refrigerate the preserves after two months for longer storage. Paraffin is more difficult to work with than the self-sealing lids. It is a good idea to have a small metal pan or teapot just for melting paraffin. Place the paraffin in the pan and set the pan in boiling water. It takes longer to melt this way than it would over direct heat, but since paraffin is highly combustible, it is best to be safe. Be sure to wear oven mitts to protect your hands from hot wax.

1. Within an hour of sealing the preserves, set out the jars or other containers. (They should have been washed either by running through a cycle of the dishwasher or in lots of soapy water, drying them in a 225° oven until ready to use.)

2. Melt the paraffin by placing in a pan and setting pan in hot water until paraffin is melted.

3. Place a metal spoon in each container to prevent breakage. Pour the hot preserve into the hot containers to within ½ inch of the top. Wipe rims with a clean, dry towel.

4. Pour a small amount of paraffin on top of the preserve. Tilt and gently rotate the container so the paraffin runs around and adheres to edges of container. Pop any bubbles in paraffin with a small pin. Let the thin layer of paraffin harden completely. If not using whipped paraffin, repeat with a second layer of paraffin to form a ¼-inch to ½-inch seal.

Note: To seal bottles with corks, simply dip corks into melted paraffin before inserting cork.

TO MAKE A WHIPPED PARAFFIN TOPPING: This is very festive; it looks like snow. Do this after the first thin seal has hardened. Remelt the paraffin in the pan, if necessary; remove from hot water and let cool in pan for 5 to 10 minutes until it begins to solidify. With an egg beater or whisk, beat the paraffin until foamy. Immediately spoon the whipped paraffin on top of thin layer of paraffin. If paraffin in pan solidifies too much, remelt and begin again. Let containers stand undisturbed until paraffin hardens. Store in cool, dry place and use within two months or refrigerate for longer storage.

About Containers for Jellies, Jams, and Pickles

FRENCH CONFITURE JARS: Our favorite container for jellies, jams, chutneys, and even cheese spreads is the French confiture jar. They are about a dollar apiece and are available from some department stores and from Williams-Sonoma. You can write this company for their wonderful catalogue of cooking products at 576 Sutter Street, San Francisco, California 94102. We use confitures as coffee cups, highball glasses, drinking glasses, jelly or jam jars, pencil holders, and almost anything else.

Barbara Swain, our food editor on this book, had the idea of starting a preserve-of-the-month club and giving one per month throughout the year filled with something different each month that you've made. At the end of the year the recipient would have a whole set of twelve glasses.

The contents of the jar may be sealed with paraffin, or if it is to be hand-delivered, stretch plastic wrap across the top and secure with a rubber band. It can be topped with tiny-print fabric and tied with miniature rickrack, or you can wet cooking or stationery parchment paper and place it over the top of the glass and secure with a rubber band. When the parchment is dry, use a ribbon to hide the rubber band. The result is a tight, drum-like seal on which you can either write instructions for use or a special greeting.

VACUUM-SEALING JARS (see page 231): The most efficient and widely available canning jars of all are the vacuum-sealing type made by Kerr or Ball. They seal much more effectively than paraffin and eliminate the leakage that eventually occurs with paraffin. Any food sealed with paraffin should be left at room temperature for only two months and then refrigerated or used.

OTHER CONTAINERS: Old-fashioned glass jars with rubber sealing rings, glass jelly jars with lids (must be sealed with paraffin), condiment jars with spoons, regular household jars that have been used before, such as baby food, jams, peanut butter, (just put plastic wrap across the top of the jar before screwing on the lid), miscellaneous crocks, souffle dishes, and many other containers listed on pages 212 through 214.

CONTAINERS FOR MAILING: Use only vacuum-sealing jars. Seal lids tightly with masking tape to prevent any leakage. Pack carefully to prevent breakage. (See Packing and Mailing, page 229.)

APPENDIX THREE

Tools of the trade

Your kitchen is probably filled with more appliances and gadgets than any other room in the house. The trick is to decide what you definitely need and what would be nice to acquire from time to time to add to basic equipment. Cost also matters, since items can run from pennies to dollars.

We find these items indispensable in our kitchen because they help make cooking a pleasure.

Special Equipment: Some Are Basic, Some Are Not

ELECTRIC MIXER: The mixer we have owned for over a decade is a Kitchen Aid by Hobart, Model K5-A. To us it is the perfect mixer because it has a whisk attachment for whipping up beautiful egg whites and a dough hook for kneading bread. We prefer this to the slightly smaller K-45 since the motor is heavy-duty, the K5-A actually being intended for restaurant use. We have an extra stainless steel bowl because many recipes require the beating of two different mixtures. It has a meat grinder attachment as well as a grain mill attachment for bread-making enthusiasts. If you own a Cuisinart Food Processor, you won't need the vegetable cutter and slicing attachment. For information, write to Hobart Manufacturing Co., Inc., 4848 Fifth Street, Long Island City, New York 11101. A mixer is invaluable. Many other good models are also available on the market.

GLASS DOUBLE BOILER: We consider a glass double boiler (Pyrex) an essential piece of kitchen equipment. Whenever egg yolks are cooked as a thickening for a sauce or custard, it is important that the water in the lower part of a double boiler never reach a boil. How can you possibly see what the water is doing in a metal double boiler? The worst possible material is made from aluminum because it discolors egg yolks. We learned this to our dismay while whipping up some Sauce Bearnaise at a friend's house in her aluminum double boiler. The sauce came out an unappetizing gray! Glass double boilers are available at hardware stores and houseware sections of department stores all over the country. They make a wonderful gift!

OVEN THERMOMETER: Please buy an oven thermometer if you do not already own one. If you have two ovens, buy two. They are inexpensive and will save you much frustration because, as you know, if your oven temperature is not accurate, you cannot possibly have perfect baking results. Ours is made by Taylor and costs less than $5. It is worth its weight in gold.

CANDY THERMOMETER: Again, we recommend the Taylor product. Many of the recipes in this book require an accurate candy thermometer. Theirs is one of the best.

ZESTER (French Citrus Peeler): This dandy and inexpensive little gadget provides the only sensible method of obtaining grated citrus peel (zest) without the bitter white part underneath called the zist (not to mention needless waste and scraped knuckles called ouch). Hold zester at a 45-degree angle against thick-skinned oranges and lemons. Peel downward. The peel will come off in five long strips. Continue until all the zest has been removed from the fruit. Chop the strips with a knife when grated peel is called for. When using a zester to obtain zest, you would, no doubt, be referred to as the "zestee."

Nonessential, but Nice to Have

CUISINART FOOD PROCESSOR: The popularity of this amazing machine is sweeping the country. It is expensive, about $200, but it is a big help to people who do a lot of cooking. It grates, chops, grinds nuts, makes bread crumbs, minces parsley, shreds cheese, produces silky smooth pates and spreads, makes pie crusts and other doughs. (It does not make beds.) We could not happily live without it. For information on sources in your area, write to Cuisinarts, Inc., P.O. Box 353, Greenwich, Connecticut 06830. (The same company also manufactures the finest pots and pans that we've ever used. Expensive, yes, but worth every dollar!)

TIMER AND/OR STOP WATCH: The jam and jelly recipes in this book use either Certo or Sure-Jell fruit pectin. In most cases the mixture must boil for exactly one minute, so it is handy to have a watch or stop watch with a sweep second hand. An extra minute timer besides the one on your stove is also useful when cooking more than one recipe at a time.

NUTMEG GRATER AND/OR COFFEE MILL AND SPICE GRINDER: We enjoy using freshly grated nutmeg and other spices in our recipes. An inexpensive nutmeg grater is handy to keep next to the stove to use in making sauces, seasoning vegetables, and sprinkling spices over desserts. We use a coffee mill to grind other spices such as cinnamon sticks, cloves, cumin, mace, black pepper.

NINE-INCH SPRING-FORM PAN: This pan with removable bottom and sides springs free automatically when a clamp is released. It is a must for cheesecakes and other delicate cakes, allowing them to be removed from the pan without turning them out.

LARGE RUBBER SPATULA: Giant-size rubber spatulas are available at restaurant supply stores. They are wonderful anytime you are folding an ingredient, such as beaten egg whites or whipped cream, into a mixture. Usually only 50¢ to 60¢ apiece, they make wonderful gifts to include in a basket of homemade goodies.

A Shopping Guide: For Odds and Ends

Here are some handy addresses from East to West to help in your cooking adventures.

WILLIAMS-SONOMA, 576 Sutter Street, San Francisco, California 94102. Branches in Beverly Hills and Palo Alto, California. Confiture jars and all types of kitchen equipment, molds, etc. Send for catalogue.

CUISINARTS, INC., P.O. Box 352, Greenwich, Connecticutt 06830. Food processor, as well as the best (albeit expensive) pots and pans to be found anywhere. Write for list of stores nearest you.

GRANDMA WHEATON CANNING JARS, Wheaton Products, Millville, New Jersey 08332. Old-fashioned-style pressed glass canning jars, medicine bottles, apothecary jars, Triomphe canning and storage jars, much more. Write for list of stores nearest you.

DOUGH-IT-YOURSELF HANDBOOK, Morton Salt, P.O. Box 8019, Chicago, Illinois 60687. A fine booklet available for $1 on imaginative uses of Baker's Clay.

HALLMARK CANNING AND COOKERY LABELS. A brand new product that will be sold nationally in stationery and gift stores. Nine different designs, 75¢ for 12 labels.

CERTO FRUIT PECTIN, GIFT LABELS, P. O. Box 5029, Kankakee, Illinois 60901. For 60 canning labels, send name, address, and zip code plus 40¢ (no stamps) along with Certo label. For booklet entitled "Extra Special Jellies and Jams for Gift Giving," send name, address, and Zip Code along with 30¢ (no stamps) to P.O. Box 5067, Kankakee, Illinois 60901.

Index